T0127875

Get the eBook FREE!

(PDF, ePub, Kindle, and liveBook all included)

We believe that once you buy a book from us, you should be able to read it in any format we have available. To get electronic versions of this book at no additional cost to you, purchase and then register this book at the Manning website.

Go to https://www.manning.com/freebook and follow the instructions to complete your pBook registration.

That's it!
Thanks from Manning!

Full Stack GraphQL Applications

T0128004

Full Stack GraphQL Applications

WITH REACT, NODE.JS, AND NEO4J

WILLIAM LYON

MANNING

SHELTER ISLAND

For online information and ordering of this and other Manning books, please visit www.manning.com. The publisher offers discounts on this book when ordered in quantity. For more information, please contact

> Special Sales Department
> Manning Publications Co.
> 20 Baldwin Road
> PO Box 761
> Shelter Island, NY 11964
> Email: orders@manning.com

©2022 by Manning Publications Co. All rights reserved.

No part of this publication may be reproduced, stored in a retrieval system, or transmitted, in any form or by means electronic, mechanical, photocopying, or otherwise, without prior written permission of the publisher.

Many of the designations used by manufacturers and sellers to distinguish their products are claimed as trademarks. Where those designations appear in the book, and Manning Publications was aware of a trademark claim, the designations have been printed in initial caps or all caps.

♾ Recognizing the importance of preserving what has been written, it is Manning's policy to have the books we publish printed on acid-free paper, and we exert our best efforts to that end. Recognizing also our responsibility to conserve the resources of our planet, Manning books are printed on paper that is at least 15 percent recycled and processed without the use of elemental chlorine.

The author and publisher have made every effort to ensure that the information in this book was correct at press time. The author and publisher do not assume and hereby disclaim any liability to any party for any loss, damage, or disruption caused by errors or omissions, whether such errors or omissions result from negligence, accident, or any other cause, or from any usage of the information herein.

Manning Publications Co.	Development editor:	Karen Miller
20 Baldwin Road	Technical development editor:	Doug Warren
PO Box 761	Review editor:	Aleksandar Dragosavljević
Shelter Island, NY 11964	Production editor:	Andy Marinkovich
	Copy editor:	Christian Berk
	Proofreader:	Melody Dolab
	Technical proofreader:	Niek Palm
	Typesetter:	Gordan Salinovic
	Cover designer:	Marija Tudor

ISBN 9781617297038
Printed in the United States of America

brief contents

contents

preface

Thank you for reading *Full Stack GraphQL Applications*. The goal of this book is to demonstrate how GraphQL, React, Apollo, and Neo4j Database (the so-called GRANDstack) can be used together to build complex, data-intensive full stack applications. You may be wondering why we've chosen this specific combination of technologies. As you read through the book, I hope you will realize the developer productivity, performance, and intuitive benefits of using a graph data model throughout the stack—from the database to the API—and all the way through the frontend client data-fetching code.

This is the book that I wished existed when I was the first engineering hire at a small startup, tasked with building out our full stack web application. We spent months evaluating technologies for our stack and exploring how they fit together. Eventually, we figured it out and got to production with a combination of technologies we were happy with, but getting there required many iterations.

GraphQL is a technology that has fundamentally changed how developers approach web development over the last few years. This book is focused on GraphQL; however, understanding how to build GraphQL servers and write GraphQL operations is not enough to put a full stack application into production. We need to consider how to enable GraphQL data fetching and state management in our frontend application, how to secure our API, how to deploy our application, and myriad other considerations. That's why this book isn't about just GraphQL; instead, we explore using GraphQL holistically by showing how the pieces fit together. If you find yourself tasked with building a full stack application using GraphQL, then this book is for you!

acknowledgments

Writing a book is a long process that involves the help and support of many others. It's impossible to acknowledge everyone who helped this book come to fruition without missing some folks. Of course, this book wouldn't be possible without everyone involved in creating the amazing technologies we cover.

Thanks to Michael Stephens for approaching me with the idea of writing a book about GraphQL and helping to ideate on the idea of full stack GraphQL, to Karen Miller for all the great feedback on early versions of every chapter, and all the folks at Manning who were involved: Doug, Aleksandar, Andy, Christian, Melody, Niek, Gordan, and Marija. Thanks to my family for putting up with me while working on this book. Special thanks goes out to the graph community for helping to validate the ideas in this book as well as providing great feedback and contributions to the Neo4j GraphQL library as it has evolved.

To all the reviewers: Andres Sacco, Brandon Friar, Christopher Haupt, Damian Esteban, Danilo Zekovic, Deniz Vehbi, Ferit Topcu, Frans Oilinki, Gustavo Gomes, Harsh Raval, Ivo Sánchez Checa Crosato, Jose Antonio Hernandez Orozco, Jose San Leandro, Kevin Ready, Konstantinos Leimonis, Krzysztof Kamyczek, Michele Adduci, Miguel Isidoro, Richard Meinsen, Richard Vaughan, Rob Lacey, Ronald Borman, Ryan Huber, Satej Kumar Sahu, Simeon Leyzerzon, Stefan Turalski, Tanya Wilke, Theofanis Despoudis, and Vladimir Pasman, your suggestions helped make this a better book.

about this book

The goal of *Full Stack GraphQL Applications* is to show how the pieces of a full stack GraphQL application fit together and how full stack developers can leverage online services to enable development and deployment. This is done by introducing concepts and building upon each chapter as we build and deploy a full stack business review application.

Who should read this book?

This book is intended for full stack web developers interested in GraphQL who have at least a basic level of understanding of Node.js API applications and client JavaScript applications that connect to these APIs. The successful reader will have some basic familiarity with Node.js and a basic understanding of client-side JavaScript but, most importantly, they will have a motivation for understanding how to build GraphQL services and applications leveraging GraphQL.

How this book is organized: A roadmap

This book is composed of nine chapters, divided into three parts. Each chapter introduces new concepts and technologies in the context of building a full stack business review application.

In part 1, we introduce GraphQL, the Neo4j graph database, and the concept of thinking in graphs:

- Chapter 1 discusses the components of a full stack GraphQL application, including an introduction to each specific technology we'll be using in the book (GraphQL, React, Apollo, and Neo4j Database).
- Chapter 2 introduces GraphQL and the basics of building a GraphQL API (type definitions and resolver functions).
- Chapter 3 introduces the Neo4j graph database, the property graph data model, and the Cypher query language.
- Chapter 4 shows how to bring the power of GraphQL to the Neo4j graph database, using the Neo4j GraphQL library.

In part 2, we focus on developing our client application using React:

- Chapter 5 introduces the React framework and concepts that are important for working with React as we begin building our front-end application.
- Chapter 6 shows how to enable data fetching and client state management with React and GraphQL as we pull in data from the GraphQL API we built in previous chapters.

In part 3, we explore securing our application and deploying it using cloud services:

- Chapter 7 shows how we can secure our application, using GraphQL and Auth0.
- Chapter 8 introduces the cloud services we will use to deploy our database, GraphQL API, and React application.
- Chapter 9 closes the book with a look at how to leverage abstract types in GraphQL, cursor-based pagination, and handling relationship properties in GraphQL.

This book is designed to be read from beginning to end, as each chapter builds on work done in previous chapters, all working toward building a full stack business review application. Readers may choose to focus on individual chapters to dive into specific topics of interest, but be sure to refer to previous chapters for context on how and why other parts of the applications have been built.

About the code

This book contains many examples of source code both in numbered listings and in line with normal text. In both cases, source code is formatted in a `fixed-width font like this` to separate it from ordinary text. Sometimes code is also **in bold** to highlight code that has changed from previous steps in the chapter, such as when a new feature adds to an existing line of code.

In many cases, the original source code has been reformatted; we've added line breaks and reworked indentation to accommodate the available page space in the book. In rare cases, even this was not enough, and listings include line-continuation markers (➡). Additionally, comments in the source code have often been removed from the listings when the code is described in the text. Code annotations accompany many of the listings, highlighting important concepts.

You can get executable snippets of code from the liveBook (online) version of this book at https://livebook.manning.com/book/fullstack-graphql-applications. The complete code for the examples in the book is available for download from the Manning website at www.manning.com, and from GitHub at https://github.com/johnymontana/fullstack-graphql-book.

Software/hardware requirements

Readers will need to have installed a recent version of Node.js. I used the latest version, v16, so I recommend using the nvm tool for installing and managing Node.js versions. Installation and usage instructions for nvm can be found at https://github.com/nvm-sh/nvm.

We will also be using several (free) online services for deployment. Most of these can be accessed using a GitHub account, so be sure to create a GitHub account, if you don't currently have one, at https://github.com/.

liveBook discussion forum

Purchase of *Full Stack GraphQL Applications* includes free access to liveBook, Manning's online reading platform. Using liveBook's exclusive discussion features, you can attach comments to the book globally or to specific sections or paragraphs. It's a snap to make notes for yourself, ask and answer technical questions, and receive help from the author and other users. To access the forum, go to https://livebook.manning.com/book/fullstack-graphql-applications/discussion. You can also learn more about Manning's forums and the rules of conduct at https://livebook.manning.com/discussion.

Manning's commitment to our readers is to provide a venue where a meaningful dialogue between individual readers and between readers and the author can take place. It is not a commitment to any specific amount of participation on the part of the author, whose contribution to the forum remains voluntary (and unpaid). We suggest you try asking the author some challenging questions lest his interest stray! The forum and the archives of previous discussions will be accessible from the publisher's website as long as the book is in print.

Other online resources

Be sure to consult the documentation for the Neo4j GraphQL library at https://neo4j.com/docs/graphql-manual/current/. Other online resources that might be helpful include the free online courses available at GraphAcademy (https://graphacademy.neo4j.com/) and the Neo4j Community site (https://community.neo4j.com/).

about the author

 **William Lyon** is a Staff Developer Advocate at Neo4j, where he helps developers be successful building applications with graphs. Prior to joining Neo4j, he worked as a software engineer at startups working on systems for quantitative finance, mobile apps for the real estate industry, and predictive API services. He holds a master's degree in computer science from the University of Montana and publishes a blog at lyonwj.com.

about the cover illustration

The figure on the cover of *Full Stack GraphQL Applications* is captioned "Dame de l'Isle de Tinne," or "Lady of the Isle of Tinne," taken from a collection by Jacques Grasset de Saint-Sauveur, published in 1797. Each illustration is finely drawn and colored by hand.

In those days, it was easy to identify where people lived and what their trade or station in life was just by their dress. Manning celebrates the inventiveness and initiative of the computer business with book covers based on the rich diversity of regional culture centuries ago, brought back to life by pictures from collections such as this one.

Part 1

Getting started with full stack GraphQL

Before beginning our journey with full stack GraphQL, we will take a look at the technologies we will be using and introduce the powerful concept of thinking in graphs. This section of the book focuses on the backend of our full stack application, specifically the database and GraphQL API.

In chapter 1, we introduce the components of a full stack GraphQL application and take a look at the specific technologies we will use throughout the book: GraphQL, React, Apollo, and Neo4j Database. In chapter 2, we dive head first into GraphQL and the basics of building a GraphQL API application. In chapter 3, we explore the Neo4j graph database, the property graph data model, and the Cypher query language. Then, in chapter 4, we show how to leverage database integrations for GraphQL and, specifically, the Neo4j GraphQL library to build GraphQL APIs backed by a graph database. After completing this first part of the book, we will have our database and initial GraphQL API application up and running and will be ready to start building the frontend in part 2.

What is
full stack GraphQL?

This chapter covers

- Components that make up a typical full stack GraphQL application
- Technologies used throughout the book (GraphQL, React, Apollo, and Neo4j Database) and how each piece fits together in the context of a full stack application
- Requirements for the application we will build throughout the book

1.1 A look at full stack GraphQL

In this chapter, we take an introductory look at the technologies we will use throughout the book. Specifically, we'll look at the following:

- GraphQL—For building our API
- React—For building our user interface and JavaScript client web application
- Apollo—Tools for working with GraphQL, on both the server and client
- Neo4j Database—The database we will use for storing and manipulating our application data

Building a full stack GraphQL application involves working with a multitier architecture, commonly known as a *three-tier application*, which consists of a frontend application, the API layer, and a database. In figure 1.1 we see the individual components of a full stack GraphQL application and how they interact with each other.

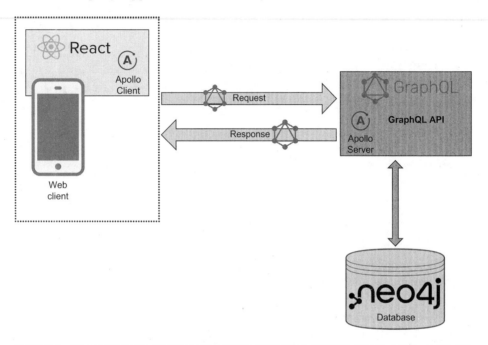

Figure 1.1   The components of a full stack GraphQL application: GraphQL, React, Apollo, and Neo4j Database

Throughout this book, we will use these technologies to build a simple business review application, working through each technology component as we implement it in the context of our application. In the last section of this chapter, we review the basic requirements of the application we will be building throughout the book.

The focus of this book is learning how to build applications with GraphQL, so as we cover GraphQL, we'll do so in the context of building a full stack application and using GraphQL with other technologies, including designing our schema, integrating with a database, building a web application that can query our GraphQL API, adding authentication to our application, and so on. As a result, this book assumes some basic knowledge of how web applications are typically built, but it does not necessarily require experience with each specific technology. To be successful, the reader should have a basic familiarity with JavaScript, both client side and Node.js, and concepts such as APIs and databases. You should have installed node and should be familiar with the basics of the npm command line tool (or yarn) and how to use it to create Node.js projects and install dependencies. We will use the latest LTS version of

Node.js as of this writing (16.14.2), which is available to download at https://nodejs.org/. You may wish to use a Node.js version manager such as nvm for managing Node versions. See https://github.com/nvm-sh/nvm for more information.

We include a brief introduction to each technology and suggest other resources for more in-depth coverage where needed by the reader. It is also important to note that we will cover specific technologies to be used alongside GraphQL and that at each phase, a similar technology could be substituted (e.g., we could build our frontend using Vue instead of React). Ultimately, the goal of this book is to show how these technologies fit together and provide the reader with a full stack framework for thinking about and building applications with GraphQL.

1.2 GraphQL

At its core, GraphQL is a specification for building APIs. The GraphQL specification describes an API query language and a way of fulfilling those requests. When building a GraphQL API, we describe the data available using a strict type system. These type definitions become the specification for the API, and the client is free to request the data it requires based on these type definitions, which also define the entry points for the API.

GraphQL is typically framed as an alternative to REST, which is the API paradigm you are mostly likely to be familiar with. This can be true in some cases; however, GraphQL can also wrap existing REST APIs or other data sources. This is due to the benefit of GraphQL being data-layer-agnostic, meaning we can use GraphQL with any data source.

> *GraphQL is a query language for APIs and a runtime for fulfilling those queries with your existing data. GraphQL provides a complete and understandable description of the data in your API, gives clients the power to ask for exactly what they need and nothing more, makes it easier to evolve APIs over time, and enables powerful developer tools.*
>
> —graphql.org

Let's dive into some more specific aspects of GraphQL.

1.2.1 GraphQL type definitions

Rather than being organized around endpoints that map to resources (as with REST), GraphQL APIs are centered around type definitions that define the data types, fields, and how they are connected in the API. These type definitions become the schema of the API, which is served from a single endpoint.

Since GraphQL services can be implemented in any language, a language-agnostic GraphQL Schema Definition Language (SDL) is used to define GraphQL types. Let's look at an example in figure 1.2, motivated by considering a simple movie application. Imagine you've been hired to create a website that allows users to search a movie catalog for movie details, such as title, actors, and description, as well as show recommendations for similar movies the user may find interesting.

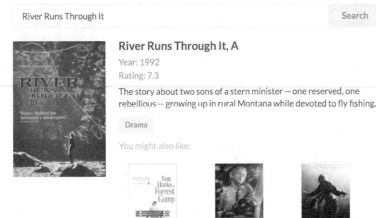

Figure 1.2   A simple movie web application

Let's start in the next listing by creating some simple GraphQL type definitions that will define the data domain of our application.

Listing 1.1   Simple GraphQL type definitions for a movie GraphQL API

```
type Movie {
  movieId: ID!
  title: String
  actors: [Actor]
}

type Actor {
  actorId: ID!
  name: String
  movies: [Movie]
}

type Query {
  allActors: [Actor]
  allMovies: [Movie]
  movieSearch(searchString: String!): [Movie]
  moviesByTitle(title: String!): [Movie]
}
```

Movie is a GraphQL object type, which means a type that contains one or more fields.

title is a field on the Movie type.

Fields can reference other types, such as a list of Actor objects in this case.

actorId is a required (or non-nullable) field on the Actor type, which is indicated by the ! character.

The Query type is a special type in GraphQL, which indicates the entry points for the API.

Fields can also have arguments; in this case, the movieSearch field takes a required string argument: searchString.

Our GraphQL type definitions declare the types used in the API, their fields, and how they are connected. When defining an object type (such as Movie), all fields available on the object and the type of each field are also specified (we can also add fields later, using the extend keyword). In this case, we define title to be a scalar String type—a type that resolves to a single value, as opposed to an object type, which can contain multiple fields and references to other types. Here actors is a field on the Movie type that resolves to an array of `Actor` objects, indicating that the actors and movies are connected (the foundation of the "graph" in GraphQL).

Fields can be either optional or required. The `actorId` field on the `Actor` object type is required (or non-nullable). This means that every `Actor` object must have a value for `actorId`. Fields that do not include a `!` are nullable, meaning values for those fields are optional.

The fields of the `Query` type become the entry points for queries into the GraphQL service. GraphQL schemas may also contain a `Mutation` type, which defines the entry points for write operations into the API. A third special entry-point-related type is the `Subscription` type, which defines events to which a client can subscribe.

> **NOTE** We're skipping over many important GraphQL concepts here, such as mutation operations, interface and union types, and so on, but don't worry; we're just getting started and will get to these soon enough!

At this point, you may be wondering where the *graph* is in GraphQL. It turns out that we've defined a graph using our GraphQL type definitions. A graph is a data structure composed of nodes (the entities or objects in our data model) and relationships that connect nodes, which is exactly the structure we've defined in our type definitions using SDL. The GraphQL type definitions previously shown have defined a simple graph with the following structure (see figure 1.3).

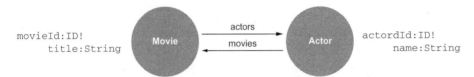

Figure 1.3 GraphQL type definitions for our movie web application expressed as a graph diagram

Graphs are all about describing connected data, and here we've defined how our movies and actors are connected in a graph. GraphQL allows us to model application data as a graph and traverse the data graph through GraphQL operations.

When a GraphQL service receives an operation (e.g., a GraphQL query), it is validated and executed against the GraphQL schema defined by these type definitions. Let's look at an example query that could be executed against a GraphQL service defined using the previously shown type definitions.

1.2.2 Querying with GraphQL

GraphQL queries define a traversal through the data graph defined by our type definitions and request a subset of fields to be returned by the query—this is known as the *selection set*. In this query, we start from the `allMovies` query field entry point and traverse the graph to find actors connected to each movie (see the next listing). Then, for each of these actors, we traverse to all the other movies they are connected to.

Listing 1.2 A GraphQL query to find movies and actors

```
query FetchSomeMovies {
    allMovies {
        title
        actors {
            name
            movies {
                title
            }
        }
    }
}
```

This is the optional naming of the operation. query is the default operation and can, therefore, be omitted. Naming the query—in this case, FetchSomeMovies—is also optional and can be omitted.

Here we specify the entry point, which is a field on either the Query or Mutation type. In this case, our entry point for the query is the allMovies query field.

The selection set defines the fields to be returned by the query.

In the case of object fields, a nested selection set is used to specify the fields to be returned.

A further nested selection is needed for the fields on movies to be returned.

Note that our query is nested and describes how to traverse the graph of related objects (in this case, movies and actors). We can represent this traversal through the data graph and the results visually (see figure 1.4).

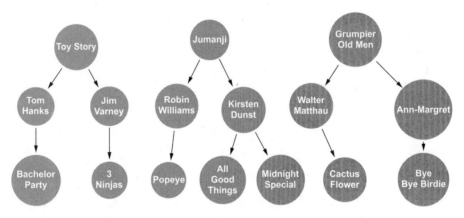

Figure 1.4 A GraphQL query traversal through the movies data graph

Although we can represent the traversal of the traversal of the data graph visually, the typical result of a GraphQL query is a JSON document, as shown in the next listing.

Listing 1.3 JSON query results

```
"data": {
  "allMovies": [
    {
      "title": "Toy Story",
      "actors": [
        {
          "name": "Tom Hanks",
          "movies": [
            {
              "title": "Bachelor Party"
            }
```

```
            ]
          },
          {
            "name": " Jim Varney",
            "movies": [
              {
                "title": "3 Ninjas: High Noon On Mega Mountain"
              }
            ]
          }
        ]
      },
      {
        "title": "Jumanji",
        "actors": [
          {
            "name": "Robin Williams",
            "movies": [
              {
                "title": "Popeye"
              }
            ]
          },
          {
            "name": "Kirsten Dunst",
            "movies": [
              {
                "title": "Midnight Special"
              },
              {
                "title": "All Good Things"
              }
            ]
          }
        ]
      },
      {
        "title": "Grumpier Old Men",
        "actors": [
          {
            "name": "Walter Matthau",
            "movies": [
              {
                "title": "Cactus Flower"
              }
            ]
          },
          {
            "name": " Ann-Margret",
            "movies": [
              {
                "title": "Bye Bye Birdie"
              }
            ]
          }
```

```
        ]
      }
    ]
}
```

As you can see from the results, the response matches the shape of the query's selection set—exactly the fields requested in the query are returned. But where does the data come from? The data-fetching logic for GraphQL APIs is defined in functions called *resolver functions*, which contain the logic for resolving the data for an arbitrary GraphQL request from the data layer. GraphQL is data-layer-agnostic, so the resolvers could query one or more databases or fetch data from another API—even a REST API. We will cover resolvers in depth in the next chapter.

1.2.3   Advantages of GraphQL

Now that we've seen our first GraphQL query, you may be thinking, "OK, that's nice, but I can fetch data about movies with REST, too. What's so great about GraphQL?" Let's review some of the benefits of GraphQL.

OVERFETCHING AND UNDERFETCHING

Overfetching refers to a pattern commonly associated with REST, in which unnecessary and unused data is sent over the network in response to an API request. Since REST is modeling resources, when we make a GET request for, say, /movie/tt0105265, we get back the representation of that movie—nothing more, nothing less.

> **Listing 1.4   REST API response for GET /movie/tt0105265**

```
{
    "title": "A River Runs Through It",
    "year": 1992,
    "rated": "PG",
    "runtime": "123 min",
    "plot": "The story about two sons of a stern minister -- one reserved,
      one rebellious -- growing up in rural Montana while devoted to
      fly fishing.",
    "movieId": "tt0105265",
    "actors": ["nm0001729", "nm0000093", "nm0000643", "nm0000950"],
    "language": "English",
    "country": "USA",
    "production": "Sony Pictures Home Entertainment",
    "directors": ["nm0000602"],
    "writers": ["nm0533805", "nm0295030"],
    "genre": "Drama",
    "averageReviews": 7.3
}
```

But what if the view of our application only needs to render the title and year of the movie? Then we've unnecessarily sent too much data over the network. Further, some of those movie fields may be expensive to compute. For example, if we need to calculate `averageReviews` by aggregating across all movie reviews for each request, but we're not even showing that in the application view, that's a lot of wasted compute time, which unnecessarily impacts the performance of our API. (Of course, in the real world, we may cache this, but that adds additional complexity as well.) Similarly, underfetching is a pattern associated with REST, in which insufficient data is returned by the request.

Let's say our application view needs to render the name of each actor in a movie. First, we make a `GET` request for `/movie/tt0105265`. As previously shown, we have an array of IDs for the actors connected to this movie. Now, to get the data required for our application, we need to iterate over this array of actor IDs to get the name of each actor by making another API request for each actor to be rendered in our view:

```
/actor/nm0001729
/actor/nm0000093
/actor/nm0000643
/actor/nm0000950
```

With GraphQL, since the client is in control of the data requested, we can accomplish this in a single request by specifying exactly the data needed by the application view in the selection set of the GraphQL query, solving both the overfetching and under-fetching problems. This results in improved performance on the server side, as we are spending less compute resources at the data layer, there is less overall data sent over the network, and latency is reduced by being able to render our application view with a single network request to the API service.

GRAPHQL SPECIFICATION

GraphQL is a specification for client-server communication that describes the features, functionality, and capability of the GraphQL API query language. Having this specification gives a clear guide of how to implement your GraphQL API and clearly defines what is and what is not GraphQL.

REST does not have a specification; instead, there are many different implementations, from what might be considered merely REST-ish to hypermedia as the engine of application state (HATEOAS). Having a specification as part of GraphQL simplifies debates over endpoints, status codes, and documentation. All of this comes built in with GraphQL, which leads to productivity wins for developers and API designers. The specification provides a clear path for API implementors.

WITH GRAPHQL, IT'S GRAPHS ALL THE WAY DOWN

REST models itself as a hierarchy of resources, yet most interactions with APIs are done in terms of relationships. For example, given our previous movie query—for this movie, show me all of the actors connected to it, and for each actor, show me all the other movies they've acted in—we're querying for relationships between actors and movies. This concept of relationships is even more prominent in real world applications, when we might be working with the relationships connecting customers and the products in their orders or users and their messages to other users in the context of a conversation.

GraphQL can also help unify data from disparate systems. Since GraphQL is data-layer-agnostic, we can build GraphQL APIs that integrate data from multiple services together and provide a clear way to integrate data from these different systems into a single unified GraphQL schema.

GraphQL can also be used to compartmentalize data fetching in the application in a component-based data interaction pattern. Since each GraphQL query can describe exactly the graph traversal and fields to be returned, encapsulating these queries with application components can help simplify application development and testing. We'll see how to apply this once we start building our React application in chapter 5.

INTROSPECTION

Introspection is a powerful feature of GraphQL that allows us to ask a GraphQL API for the types and queries it supports. Introspection becomes a way of self-documenting the API. Tools that make use of introspection can provide human-readable API documentation, as well as visualization tooling, and leverage code generation to create API clients.

1.2.4 *Disadvantages of GraphQL*

Of course, GraphQL is not a silver bullet, and we should not think of it as the solution to all of our API-related problems. One of the most notable challenges of adopting GraphQL is that some well-understood practices from REST don't apply when using GraphQL. For example, HTTP status codes are commonly used to convey success, failure, and other cases of a REST request; *200 OK* means our request was successful, and *404 Not Authorized* means we forgot an auth token or don't have the correct permissions for the resource requested. However, with GraphQL, each request returns 200 OK, regardless of whether the request was a complete success. This makes error handling a bit different in the GraphQL world. Instead of a single status code describing the result of our request, GraphQL errors are typically returned at the field level. This means we may have successfully retrieved part of our GraphQL query, while other fields returned errors and will need to be handled appropriately.

Caching is another well-understood area of REST that is handled a bit differently with GraphQL. With REST, caching the response for /movie/123 is possible because we can return the same exact result for each GET request. This isn't possible with GraphQL because each request could contain a different selection set, meaning we can't simply return a cached result for the whole request. This is mitigated by most GraphQL clients implementing client caches at the application level, and in practice, much of the time, our GraphQL requests are in an authenticated environment, where caching isn't applicable.

Another challenge is exposing arbitrary complexity to the client along with related performance considerations. If the client is free to compose queries as they wish, how can we ensure these queries don't become so complex as to impact performance significantly or overwhelm the computing resources of our backend infrastructure?

Fortunately, GraphQL tooling allows us to restrict the depth of the queries used and further restrict the queries that can be run to a whitelisted selection of queries (known as persisted queries). A related challenge is implementing rate limiting. With REST, we could simply restrict the number of requests that can be made in a certain time period; however, with GraphQL, this becomes more complicated, since the client could be requesting multiple objects in a single query. This results in bespoke query-costing implementations to address rate limiting.

Finally, the so-called $n + 1$ query problem is a common problem in GraphQL data fetching implementations that can result in multiple round trips to the data layer and can negatively impact performance. Consider the case in which we request information about a movie and all actors in the movie. In the database, we might store a list of actor IDs associated with each movie, which is returned with our request for the movie details. In a naive GraphQL implementation, we would then need to retrieve the actor details, and we would need to make a separate request to the database for each actor object, resulting in a total of n (i.e., the number of actors) $+ 1$ (i.e., the movie) queries to the database. To address the $n + 1$ query problem, tools like DataLoader allow us to batch and cache requests to the database, increasing performance. Another approach to addressing the $n + 1$ query problem is employing GraphQL database integrations, such as the Neo4j GraphQL library and PostGraphile, which allow us to generate a single database query from an arbitrary GraphQL request, ensuring only a single roundtrip to the database.

> **GraphQL limitations**
> While we're talking about databases, it is important to understand that GraphQL is an API query language and not a database query language. GraphQL lacks semantics for many complex operations required of database query languages, such as aggregations, projects, and variable length path traversals.

1.2.5 GraphQL tooling

In this section, we review some GraphQL-specific tooling that will help us build, test, and query our GraphQL API. These tools leverage GraphQL's introspection feature, allowing for extracting the schema of a deployed GraphQL endpoint to generate documentation, query validation, auto-completion, and other useful development functionality.

GRAPHIQL

GraphiQL is an in-browser tool for exploring and querying GraphQL APIs. With GraphiQL, we can execute GraphQL queries against a GraphQL API and view the results. Thanks to GraphQL's introspection feature, we can view the types, fields, and queries supported by the GraphQL API we've connected to. In addition, because of the GraphQL type system, we have immediate query validation as we construct our query. GraphiQL is an open source package now maintained by the GraphQL

Foundation. GraphiQL is packaged as either a stand-alone tool or a React component and, therefore, is often embedded in larger web applications (see figure 1.5).

```
GraphiQL  (▶)  Prettify

1 ▾ {
2 ▾   Person(name: "Kevin Bacon") {
3       name
4       born
5       movies {
6         title
7         released
8       }
9     }
10 }
11
```
```
▾ {
    "data": {
      "Person": [
        {
          "name": "Kevin Bacon",
          "born": 1958,
▾         "movies": [
            {
              "title": "Frost/Nixon",
              "released": 2008
            },
            {
              "title": "Apollo 13",
              "released": 1995
            },
            {
              "title": "A Few Good Men",
              "released": 1992
            }
          ]
        }
      ]
    },
    "extensions": {
      "type": "READ_ONLY"
    }
  }
}
```

```
QUERY VARIABLES

1  {}
```

Figure 1.5   GraphiQL screenshot

GRAPHQL PLAYGROUND

Like GraphiQL, GraphQL Playground is an in-browser tool for executing GraphQL queries, viewing the results, and exploring the GraphQL API's schema, powered by GraphQL's introspection feature (see figure 1.6). GraphQL Playground has a few additional features, such as viewing GraphQL type definitions, searching through the GraphQL schema, and easily adding request headers (e.g., those required for authentication). GraphQL Playground was once included by default in server implementations, such as Apollo Server; however, it has since been deprecated and is no longer actively maintained. We include GraphQL Playground here, since it is still deployed in many GraphQL endpoints, and you will likely come across it at some point.

APOLLO STUDIO

Apollo Studio is a cloud platform from Apollo that includes many features for building, validating, and securing GraphQL APIs (see figure 1.7). Apollo Studio is included in this section because the *Explorer* feature of Studio is similar to the GraphiQL and GraphQL Playground tools, mentioned previously, for creating and running GraphQL operations. Also, the Explorer in Apollo Studio is now used by default by Apollo Server (as of version 3 of Apollo Server), so we will be using Apollo Studio throughout this book to run GraphQL operations against our GraphQL API as we develop it.

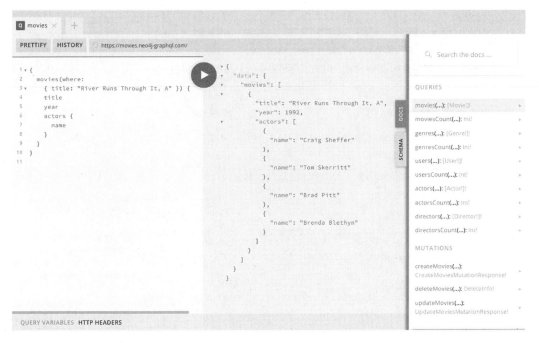

Figure 1.6   GraphQL Playground screenshot

Figure 1.7   Apollo Studio screenshot

1.3   React

React is a declarative, component-based library for building user interfaces using JavaScript. React uses a virtual DOM (a copy of the actual document object model) to efficiently calculate DOM updates required to render views as application state and data changes. This means users simply design views that map to application data and React handles rendering the DOM updates efficiently. Components encapsulate data handling and user interface rendering logic without exposing their internal structure, so they can easily be composed together to build more complex user interfaces and applications.

1.3.1   React components

Let's examine a simple React component in the next listing.

Listing 1.5   A simple React component

```
import React, { useState } from "react";          ◁──  We import React and the useState
                                                         hook for managing state variables.

function MovieTitleComponent(props) {         ◁──
  const [movieTitle, setMovieTitle] = useState( ◁──      Our component is a function that is
    "River Runs Through It, A"                             passed props or values from other
  );                                                       components higher in the React
                                                           component hierarchy.

▷  return <div>{movieTitle}</div>                         Using the useState hook, we create a
  }                                                        new state variable and the associated
                                                           function for updating this value.
  export default MovieTitleComponent;      ◁──
```

Here we access the movieTitle value from our component state and render that inside a div tag.

We export this component so it can be composed in other React components.

COMPONENT LIBRARIES

Since components encapsulate data handling and user interface rendering logic and are easily composable, it becomes practical to distribute libraries of components that can be used as dependencies of our project for quickly leveraging complex styling and user interface design. Using such component libraries is beyond the scope of this book; however, a good example is the Material UI component library, which allows us to import many popular, common user interface components, such as a grid layout, data table, navigation, and inputs.

1.3.2   JSX

React is typically used with a JavaScript language extension called JSX. JSX looks similar to XML and is a powerful way of building user interfaces in React and composing React components. It is possible to use React without JSX, but most users prefer the readability and maintainability that JSX offers. We will introduce JSX in chapter 5 as well as a number of other React concepts, such as unidirectional data flow, props and state, and data fetching with React.

1.3.3   React tooling

Next we'll review some useful tooling that will help us build, develop, and troubleshoot React applications. There is a healthy ecosystem of tooling for developing with React applications, so don't consider this a complete list.

CREATE REACT APP

Create React App is a command line tool that can be used to quickly create the scaffolding for a React application, taking care of configuring build settings, installing dependencies, and templating a simple React application to get started. We will use Create React App later in chapter 5 when we begin building the frontend of our application.

REACT CHROME DEVTOOLS

React DevTools is a browser extension that lets us inspect a React application and see the component hierarchy, props, and state of each component under the hood while our application is running, which enables debugging of our React applications. It can be very useful to see how our components are structured under different usage scenarios (see figure 1.8).

Figure 1.8   React Chrome DevTools

1.4   *Apollo*

Apollo is a collection of tools that make it easier to use GraphQL, including on the server, the client, and in the cloud. We will make use of Apollo Server, a Node.js library for building our GraphQL API, and Apollo Client, a client-side JavaScript library for querying our GraphQL API from our application, as well as Apollo Studio's Explorer for building and running queries, which was introduced previously.

1.4.1   *Apollo Server*

Apollo Server allows us to easily spin up a Node.js server serving a GraphQL endpoint by defining our type definitions and resolver functions. Apollo Server can be used with many different web frameworks; however, the default and most popular is Express.js. Apollo Server can also be used with serverless functions, such as Amazon Lambda and Google Cloud Functions. Apollo Server can be installed with npm: `npm install apollo-server`.

1.4.2   *Apollo Client*

Apollo Client is a JavaScript library for querying GraphQL APIs and has integrations with many frontend frameworks, including React and Vue.js, as well as native mobile versions for iOS and Android. We will make use of the React Apollo Client integration to implement data fetching via GraphQL in our React components. Apollo Client handles client data caching and can also be used to manage local state data. The React Apollo Client library can be installed with npm: `npm install @apollo/client`.

1.5   *Neo4j Database*

Neo4j is an open source native graph database. Unlike other databases that use tables or documents for the data model, the data model used with Neo4j is a graph, specifically known as the *property graph data model*, which allows us to model, store, and query our data as a graph. Graph databases like Neo4j are optimized for working with graph data and executing complex graph traversals, such as those defined by GraphQL queries.

One of the benefits of using a graph database with GraphQL is that we maintain the same graph data model throughout our application stack, working with graphs on both the frontend, backend, and database. Another benefit has to do with the performance optimizations graph databases make versus other database systems, such as relational databases. Many GraphQL queries end up being nested several levels deep—the equivalent of a `JOIN` operation in a relational database. Graph databases are optimized for performing these graph traversal operations very efficiently and, therefore, are a natural fit for the backend of a GraphQL API.

> **NOTE**   It's important to note that we aren't querying the database directly with GraphQL. While there are database integrations for GraphQL, the GraphQL API is a layer that sits between our application and the database.

1.5.1 Property graph data model

Like many graph databases, Neo4j uses a property graph model (see figure 1.9). The components of the property graph model are

- Nodes—The entities or objects in our data model
- Relationships—Connections between nodes
- Labels—A grouping semantic for nodes
- Properties—Key–value pair attributes, stored on nodes and relationships

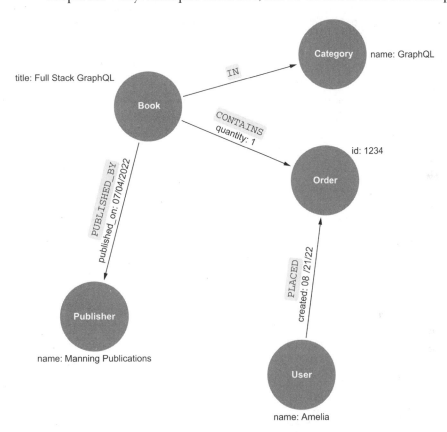

Figure 1.9 Property graph example of books, publisher, customers, and orders

The property graph data model allows us to express complex, connected data in a flexible way. This data model also has the additional benefit of closely mapping to the way we often think about data when dealing with a domain.

1.5.2 Cypher query language

Cypher is a declarative graph query language used by Neo4j and other graph databases and graph compute engines. You can think of Cypher as being similar to SQL, but instead of working with tables, Cypher is designed for graph data. A major feature of Cypher is *pattern matching*. With graph pattern matching in Cypher, we can define the graph pattern using an ASCII-art-like notation. In the next listing, let's look at a simple Cypher example: querying for movies and actors connected to these movies.

Listing 1.6   Simple Cypher query querying for movies and actors

```
MATCH (m:Movie)<-[r:ACTED_IN]-(a:Actor)
RETURN m,r,a
```

Describing a graph pattern
to find data in the database

We return the data matching
the graph pattern described.

In our Cypher query, `MATCH` is followed by a graph pattern described using an ASCII-art-like notation. In this pattern, nodes are defined within parentheses—for example, `(m:Movie)`. The `:Movie` indicates we should match nodes with the label `Movie`, and the `m` before the colon becomes a variable that is bound to any nodes that match the pattern. We can refer to `m` later throughout the query.

Relationships are defined by square brackets (e.g., `<-[r:ACTED_IN]-`) and follow a similar convention, in which `:ACTED_IN` declares the `ACTED_IN` relationship type, and `r` becomes a variable we can refer to later in the query to represent any relationships matching that pattern.

In the `RETURN` clause, we specify the data to be returned by the query. Here, we specify the variables `m`, `r`, and `a`, which are variables that were defined in the `MATCH` clause and are bound to nodes and relationships in the database that match elements of the graph pattern.

1.5.3   Neo4j tooling

We will make use of Neo4j Desktop for managing our Neo4j instances locally and on Neo4j Browser, a developer tool for querying and interacting with our Neo4j database. For querying Neo4j from our GraphQL API, we will use the JavaScript Neo4j client driver as well as the Neo4j GraphQL library, a Node.js GraphQL integration for Neo4j.

NEO4J DESKTOP
Neo4j Desktop is Neo4j's command center (see figure 1.10). From Neo4j Desktop we can manage Neo4j database instances, including editing configuration, installing plugins and graph apps (e.g., visualization tools), and accessing admin level features, such as dump/load database. Neo4j Desktop is the default download experience for Neo4j and can be downloaded at neo4j.com/download.

NEO4J AURADB
Neo4j AuraDB is Neo4j's fully managed cloud service that offers hosted Neo4j instances in the cloud. AuraDB includes a free tier, which makes it a great option for developing and deploying hobby projects. We will cover Neo4j AuraDB in more detail in chapter 8 when we explore deploying our full stack application making use of

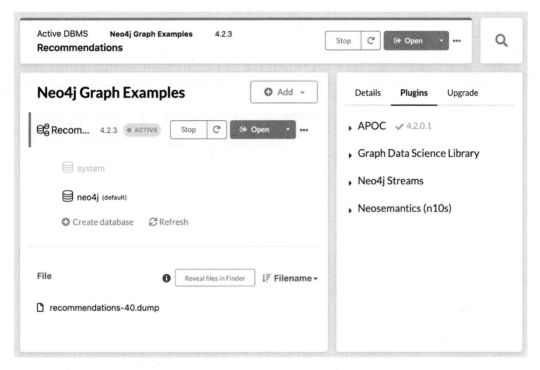

Figure 1.10   Neo4j Desktop

cloud services. You can get started with Neo4j AuraDB for free at dev.neo4j.com/neo4j-aura.

NEO4J BROWSER

Neo4j Browser is an in-browser query workbench for Neo4j and is one of the primary ways of interacting with Neo4j during development (see figure 1.11). With Neo4j Browser, we can query the database with Cypher and visualize the results, either as a graph visualization or with tabular results.

NEO4J CLIENT DRIVERS

Since our end goal is to build an application that talks to our Neo4j database, we will make use of the language drivers for Neo4j. Client drivers are available in many languages (Java, Python, .Net, JavaScript, Go, etc.), but we will use the Neo4j JavaScript driver.

> **NOTE** The Neo4j JavaScript driver has both a Node.js and browser version (allowing connections to the database directly from the browser); however, in this book, we will only use the Node.js version.

The Neo4j JavaScript driver is installed using npm:

```
npm install neo4j-driver
```

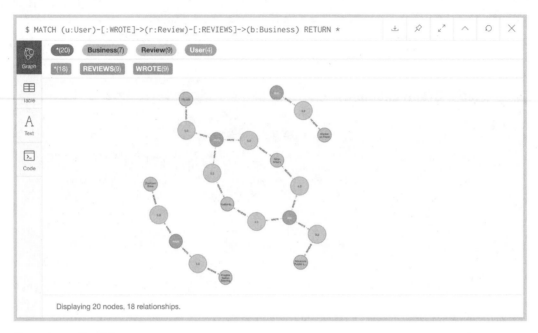

Figure 1.11   Neo4j Browser

In the following listing, let's look at an example: using the Neo4j JavaScript driver to execute a Cypher query and log the results.

Listing 1.7   Basic Neo4j JavaScript driver usage

```
const neo4j = require("neo4j-driver");
```
⟵ Importing the neo4j-driver module

⟶ Creating a driver instance and specifying the database connection string

```
const driver = neo4j.driver("neo4j://localhost:7687",
  neo4j.auth.basic("neo4j", "letmein"));
```
⟵ Specifying the database user and password

```
const session = driver.session();
```
⟵ Sessions are more lightweight and should be instantiated for a specific block of work.

The promise resolves to a result set. ⟶
```
session.run("MATCH (n) RETURN COUNT(n) AS num")
  .then(result => {
    const record = result.records[0];
    console.log(`Your database has ${record['num']} nodes`);
  })
  .catch(error => {
    console.log(error);
  })
  .finally( () => {
    session.close();
  )
```
Run the query in an auto-commit transaction; it returns a promise.

⟵ Be sure to close the session.

Accessing the records of the result set and selecting the first record

We will learn how to make use of the Neo4j JavaScript driver in our GraphQL resolver functions as one way to implement data fetching in our GraphQL API.

THE NEO4J GRAPHQL LIBRARY

The Neo4j GraphQL Library is a GraphQL-to-Cypher query execution layer for Neo4j. It works with any of the JavaScript GraphQL server implementations, such as Apollo Server. We will learn how to use this library for the following:

1 Using GraphQL type definitions to drive the Neo4j database schema
2 Generating a full CRUD GraphQL API from GraphQL type definitions
3 Generating a single Cypher database query for arbitrary GraphQL requests (solving the $n + 1$ query problem)
4 Adding custom logic to our GraphQL API using Cypher

While GraphQL is data-layer-agnostic—GraphQL APIs can be implemented using any data source or database—when used with a graph database, there are benefits, such as reducing mapping and translation of the data model and performance optimizations for addressing complex traversals defined with GraphQL. The Neo4j GraphQL library helps to build GraphQL APIs backed by the Neo4j graph database. Using the Neo4j GraphQL library is covered beginning in chapter 4, and you can read more about the library at dev.neo4j.com/graphql.

1.6   How it all fits together

Now that we've taken a look at each individual piece of our GraphQL stack, let's see how everything fits together in the context of a full stack application, using the movie search application as our example. Our imaginary movie application has three simple requirements:

1 Allow the user to search for a movie by title.
2 Display any matching results and details of those movies, such as rating or genre, to the user.
3 Show a list of similar movies that might be a good recommendation if the user liked the matching movie.

Figure 1.12 shows how the different components would fit together, following the flow of a request from the client application, searching for movies by title, to the GraphQL API, then resolving data from the Neo4j database, and back to the client, rendering the results in an updated user interface view.

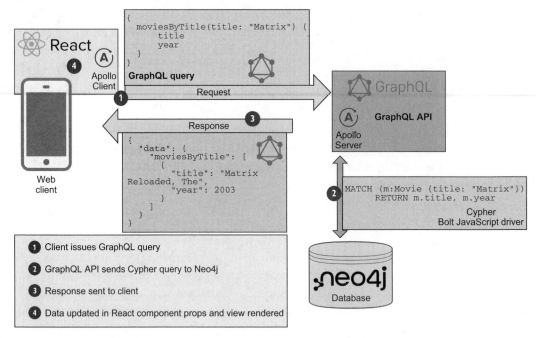

Figure 1.12 Following a movie search request through a full stack GraphQL application

1.6.1 *React and Apollo Client: Making the request*

The frontend of our application is built in React; specifically, we have a `MovieSearch` React component, which renders a text box that accepts user input (a movie search string to be provided by the user). This `MovieSearch` component also contains the logic for taking the user input, combining it with a GraphQL query, and sending this query to the GraphQL server to resolve the data using the Apollo Client React integration. The following listing shows what the GraphQL query sent to the API might look like if the user searched for "River Runs Through It."

Listing 1.8   GraphQL query searching for movies matching "River Runs Through It"

```
{
  moviesByTitle(title: "River Runs Through It") {
    title
    poster
    imdbRating
    genres {
      name
    }
    recommendedMovies {
      title
      poster
    }
  }
}
```

This data-fetching logic is enabled by Apollo Client, which we use in the `MovieSearch` component. Apollo Client implements a cache, so when the user enters their search query, Apollo Client first checks the cache to see if a GraphQL query has previously been handled for this search string. If not, then the query is sent to the GraphQL server as an HTTP POST request to `/graphql`.

1.6.2   *Apollo Server and GraphQL backend*

The backend for our movie application is a Node.js application that uses Apollo Server and the Express web server library to serve a `/graphql` endpoint over HTTP. A GraphQL server is composed of the network layer, which is responsible for processing HTTP requests, extracting the GraphQL operation, and returning HTTP responses, and the GraphQL schema, which defines the entry points and data structures for the API and is responsible for resolving the data from the data layer by executing resolver functions.

When Apollo Client makes its request, our GraphQL server handles the request by validating the query and then begins to resolve the request by first calling the root level resolver function, which, in this case, is `Query.moviesByTitle`. This resolver function is passed the `title` argument—the value the user typed into the search text box. Inside our resolver function, we have the logic for querying the database to find movies with titles matching the search query, retrieving the movie details, and finding a list of other recommended movies for each matching movie.

> ### Resolver implementation
>
> In this book, we will show two methods for implementing resolver functions:
>
> - The *naive* approach of defining database queries inside individual resolvers
> - Auto-generating resolvers using GraphQL *engine* libraries, such as the Neo4j GraphQL library
>
> This example covers only the first case.

Resolver functions are executed in a nested fashion (see figure 1.13)—in this case, starting with the `moviesByTitle` query field resolver, which is the root level resolver for this operation. The `moviesByTitle` resolver will return a list of movies, and then the resolver for each field requested in the query will be called and passed an item from the list of movies returned by `moviesByTitle`—essentially iterating over this list of movies.

Each resolver function contains logic for resolving data for a piece of the overall GraphQL schema. For example, the `recommendedMovies` resolver, when given a movie, has the logic to find similar movies that the viewer might also enjoy. In this case, this is done by querying the database, using a simple Cypher query to search for users who have viewed the movie, and traversing out to find other movies those users have viewed to provide a collaborative filtering recommendation, as shown in the

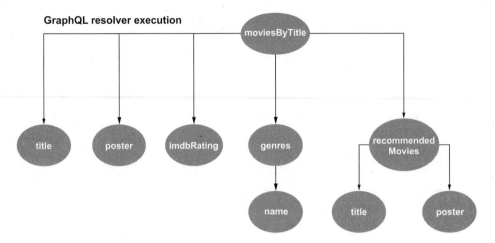

Figure 1.13 GraphQL resolver functions are called in a nested fashion.

following listing. This query is executed in Neo4j using the Node.js JavaScript Neo4j client driver.

Listing 1.9 A simple movie recommendation Cypher query

```
MATCH (m:Movie {movieId: $movieID})<-[:RATED]-(:User)-[:RATED]->(rec:Movie)
WITH rec, COUNT(*) AS score ORDER BY score DESC
RETURN rec LIMIT 3
```

n + 1 query problem

Here we have a perfect demonstration of the *n* + 1 query problem. Our root-level resolver returns a list of movies. Now, to resolve our GraphQL query, we need to call the `actors` resolver once for each movie. This results in multiple requests to the database, which can impact performance.

Ideally, we instead make a single request to the database, which fetches all data needed to resolve the GraphQL query in a single request. There are a few solutions to this problem:

- The DataLoader library allows us to batch our requests together.
- GraphQL engine libraries, like the Neo4j GraphQL library, can generate a single database query from an arbitrary GraphQL request, leveraging the graph nature of GraphQL without negative performance impacts from multiple database calls.

1.6.3 *React and Apollo Client: Handling the response*

Once our data fetching is complete and the data is sent back to Apollo Client, the cache is updated, so if this same search query is executed in the future, the data will be retrieved from the cache, instead of requesting the data from the GraphQL server.

Our `MovieSearch` React component passes the results of the GraphQL query to a `MovieList` component as props, which, in turn, renders a series of `Movie` components, updating the view to show the movie details for each matching movie—in this case, just one. And our user is presented with a list of movie search results (see figure 1.14)!

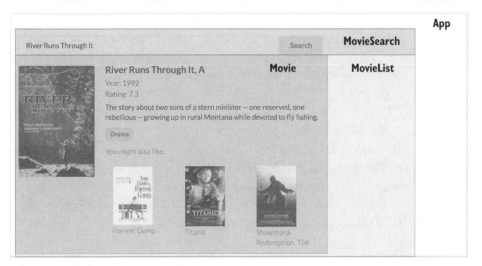

Figure 1.14   React components are composed together to build a complex user interface.

The goal of this example is to show how GraphQL, React, Apollo, and Neo4j Database are used together to build a simple full stack application. We've omitted many details, such as authentication, authorization, and optimizing performance, but don't worry, we will cover all this in detail throughout the book!

1.7   What we will build in this book

The simple movie search example we've used throughout the chapter was, hopefully, a decent introduction to the concepts we'll learn throughout this book. Instead of building a movie search application, let's start from scratch and build a new application, working through the requirements and GraphQL API design together as we build up our knowledge of GraphQL. To demonstrate the concepts covered in this book, we will build a web application that makes use of GraphQL, React, Apollo, and Neo4j. This web application will be a simple business review application. The requirements of the application are

- Listing businesses and business details
- Allowing users to write reviews of businesses
- Allowing users to search for businesses and showing personalized recommendations to the user

To implement this application, we will need to design and implement our GraphQL API, user interface, and database. We will need to handle issues such as authentication and authorization and deploy our application to the cloud.

1.8   Exercises

1   To familiarize yourself with GraphQL and writing GraphQL queries, explore the public movies GraphQL API at https://movies.neo4j-graphql.com. Open the URL in a web browser to access GraphQL Playground, and explore the DOCS and SCHEMA tabs to view the type definitions.

    Try writing queries to respond to the following prompts:

– Find the titles of the first 10 movies, ordered by title.
– Who acted in the movie *Jurassic Park*?
– What are the genres of *Jurassic Park*? What other movies are in those genres?
– What movie has the highest imdbRating?

2   Consider the business review application we described earlier in the chapter. See if you can create the GraphQL type definitions necessary for this application.

3   Download Neo4j, and familiarize yourself with Neo4j Desktop and Neo4j Browser. Work through a Neo4j Sandbox example dataset guide at neo4j.com/sandbox.

You can find solutions to the exercises as well as code samples from this book in the GitHub repository for this book: github.com/johnymontana/fullstack-graphql-book.

Summary

- GraphQL is an API query language and runtime for fulfilling requests. We can use GraphQL with any data layer. To build a GraphQL API, we first define the types, which include the fields available on each type and how they are connected, and describe the data graph.
- React is a JavaScript library for building user interfaces. We use JSX to construct components that encapsulate data and logic. These components can be composed together, allowing for building complex user interfaces.
- Apollo is a collection of tools for working with GraphQL, both on the client and the server. Apollo Server is a Node.js library for building GraphQL APIs. Apollo Client is a JavaScript GraphQL client that has integrations for many frontend frameworks, including React.
- Neo4j is an open source graph database that uses the property graph data model, which consists of nodes, relationships, labels, and properties. We use the Cypher query language for interacting with Neo4j.
- These technologies can be used together to build full stack GraphQL applications.

Graph thinking with GraphQL 2

This chapter covers

- Describing the requirements of our business review application
- Translating requirements into GraphQL type definitions
- Implementing resolver functions for data fetching for these type definitions, using a naive approach
- Using Apollo Server to combine our type definitions and resolvers and serve a GraphQL endpoint
- Querying our GraphQL endpoint with Apollo Studio

In this chapter, we will design a GraphQL API for a business review application. First, we will define the requirements of this application; then, we will describe a GraphQL API that addresses these requirements following a GraphQL-first development approach. We then explore how to implement the data fetching logic for this API. Finally, we explore how to combine our GraphQL type definitions and resolver functions to serve a GraphQL API using Apollo Server and to query it, using Apollo Studio. When building APIs, it is often useful to understand the data domain and the common access patterns—in other words, what are the problems to be solved by the API? The GraphQL-first development approach allows us to build APIs by first considering the data domain and defining a GraphQL schema describing that domain, which then serves as a blueprint for implementing the API.

> **GraphQL-first development**
>
> The GraphQL-first development paradigm is an approach for building applications that is driven by the GraphQL API design. The process begins by describing GraphQL type definitions synthesized from business requirements. These type definitions then become the basis for the API implementation, database data-fetching code, and client application code. GraphQL-first development is a powerful approach because it allows for parallel implementation of the backend and frontend systems once the GraphQL type definitions have been defined.

2.1 *Your application data is a graph*

A *graph* is a fundamental data structure that is composed of nodes (the entities or objects) and relationships that connect nodes. Graphs are an intuitive model that can be used to represent many different domains. Often, when we go through the exercise of producing a data model by examining the business requirements of a domain, we end up drawing a diagram of the objects and arrows showing how they are connected. This is a graph!

Let's go through this process for our business reviews application. The requirements for our application are

1 As a user, I want to search for a list of businesses by category, location, and name.
2 As a user, I want to view details for each business (name, description, address, photos, etc.).
3 As a user, I want to view reviews for each business, including a summary for each business, and rank my search by favorably reviewed businesses.
4 As a user, I want to create a review for a business.
5 As a user, I want to connect my friends and users who have tastes that I like, so I can follow my friends' reviews.
6 As a user, I want to receive personalized recommendations based on reviews I have previously written and my social network.

Now that we've identified the requirements for our application, let's think about the data requirements for this application and the data model that describes it.

First, what are the entities? These will become nodes in our graph. I can think of users, businesses, reviews, and photos as entities that we need to think about (see figure 2.1).

Figure 2.1   Entities become nodes.

Next, how are those entities connected? These connections are modeled as relationships between the entities, and what we've described is a graph (see figure 2.2). Let's add the following relationships:

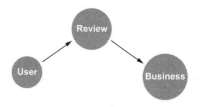

1 Users write reviews.
2 Reviews are connected to a business.
3 Users upload photos.
4 Photos are tagged to businesses.

Figure 2.2 Adding relationships to connect nodes

Now that we've described the data requirements of our application as a graph, we can start to think about how to build a GraphQL API to enable us to work with this data graph.

2.2 Graphs in GraphQL

GraphQL models our business domain as a graph. With GraphQL, we define this graph model by creating a GraphQL schema, which we do by writing GraphQL type definitions. In the schema, we define types of nodes, the fields available on each node, and how they are connected by relationships. The most common way of creating a GraphQL schema is by using the GraphQL schema definition language (SDL). In this section, we take the requirements of our application and create a GraphQL schema that models our business review domain in GraphQL using GraphQL type definitions.

2.2.1 API modeling with type definitions: GraphQL-first development

Having translated our business requirements into the graph data model necessary for our application, we can now formally write our GraphQL type definitions, using the GraphQL schema definition language. With the GraphQL SDL, we define the types, the fields on each type, and how they are connected. The GraphQL SDL representation of our data is just another representation of the graph data model we described in the previous section. Our GraphQL type definitions will become the specification for the API and guide the rest of our implementation. This process is known as *GraphQL-first development*.

Other ways of representing GraphQL types

The SDL is not the only way to create our type definitions. Each GraphQL implementation (e.g., graphql.js, the reference implementation used by most Node.js JavaScript GraphQL projects) also exposes a programmatic API to represent GraphQL type definitions. In fact, when the SDL is parsed, it is this object representation that is created internally for working with the GraphQL schema. This approach of constructing GraphQL types can be used by the API developer as well and is often the better option when programmatically generating GraphQL types, such as when generating types from existing classes.

ND 755 8671

Since GraphQL services can be implemented in any language, a programming-language-specific syntax is not relevant for all GraphQL implementations; therefore, the programming-language-agnostic GraphQL SDL is used to define GraphQL types. In chapter 1, we introduced the basic syntax of the GraphQL Schema Definition Language, using a simple movie and actor GraphQL schema. Using the syntax introduced in that example, let's create GraphQL type definitions for our business reviews application, based on the requirements we created in the previous section of this chapter, as shown in the following listing.

Listing 2.1   GraphQL type definitions for our business review application

```
type Business {
  businessId: ID!          Each type of object or entity in our
  name: String             graph becomes a GraphQL type.
  address: String
  avgStars: Float
  photos: [Photo!]!
  reviews: [Review!]!
}

type User {             Each type should have some field
  userId: ID!           that uniquely identifies that object.
  name: String
  photos: [Photo!]!
  reviews: [Review!]!      Fields can be references to other types—
}                          in this case, a one-to-many relationship.

type Photo {
  business: Business!
  user: User!
  photoId: ID!
  url: String
}

type Review {
  reviewId: ID!
  stars: Float
  text: String        Connection references can also
  user: User!         represent one-to-one relationships.
  business: Business!
}
```

Note that the entities we identified become GraphQL types, the properties of the entities become fields on the types, and the connections or relationships connecting the types are defined as fields that reference other types. Each type contains fields, which can be scalar types, objects, or lists.

Each type should have some field that uniquely identifies that object. ID is a special GraphQL scalar used to represent this unique field. Internally, we treat ID fields as strings. The exclamation ! indicates this field is required; we cannot have a User object in our GraphQL API without a value for the userId field. The brackets [] here indicate this is a one-to-many relationship; one `User` can create zero or more reviews and a `Review` can be written by only one `User`. To represent one-to-one relationships, we simply leave off the brackets, indicating this is not an array field.

Built-in GraphQL types

The following built-in types are supported by the GraphQL schema language:

- `String`
- `Int`
- `Float`
- `Boolean`
- `ID`

By default, every type is nullable, meaning `null` is a valid value for the field. Use an exclamation point `!` to indicate a type is non-nullable. For example, `Int!` is a non-nullable integer.

To indicate a list type, use square brackets `[]`. For example, `[Int]` is a list of integers.

Brackets and exclamations can be combined. For example, `[String!]` is a list of non-nullable strings: every item in the list must have a `String` value, but the list itself can be `null`, while `[String]!` is a non-nullable list of nullable strings.

Now that we have our type definitions, we need to define the entry points for our API. The entry points for read operations are defined in a special type called the `Query` type. Entry points for write operations are defined in a special type called the `Mutation` type. In this chapter, we focus only on queries. Mutations will be covered in chapter 4, where we will update data in a database. In addition to the `Query` and `Mutation` types, there is a third special GraphQL type that defines entry points, called `Subscription`.Subscriptions are GraphQL's event-publishing functionality and are beyond the scope of this book.

The entry points for our API should map to the client requirements of our application. In other words, ask yourself, "What operations does the client need to complete?" These needs should guide what `Query` and `Mutation` fields we define. Let's first focus on read-only requirements in the next listing.

Listing 2.2   `Query` fields as API entry points

```
type Query {
  allBusinesses: [Business!]!
  businessBySearchTerm(search: String!): [Business!]!
  userById(id: ID!): User
}
```

Now that we've created our GraphQL type definitions, we can construct some GraphQL queries that might be used by our application. Consider the query that our application might need to issue to populate a search results page, based on a user-provided search string, as shown in the following listing.

Listing 2.3 GraphQL query to search for businesses and reviews

```
{
  businessBySearchTerm(search: "Library") {
    name
    avgStars
    reviews {
      stars
      text
      user {
        name
      }
    }
  }
}
```

With this query, we can search for "Library" businesses, view the businesses that are a match, and see the business details necessary for the search results, as well as all the reviews for the business and the user who wrote them.

This is great, but there are a few issues with this query. What happens if we have many matches for "Library" businesses? What if a given business has thousands of reviews? Our client application will be overwhelmed with data to render. Also, we probably don't want to show business results in just any order; we should allow the search results to be ordered by name, in either ascending or descending order.

ADDING PAGINATION AND ORDERING TO OUR API

GraphQL does not have semantics for filtering, pagination, or ordering out of the box; instead, it is up to the API designer to add these to the GraphQL schema as they deem necessary and relevant for the requirements of the application.

For pagination, we will add a `first` (think limit) argument to our API to allow the client to specify the number of objects to be returned. We do this both at the root `Query` field and for any relationship fields—those describing a one-to-many relationship. In addition, an `offset` argument (think skip), which specifies the number of records to skip before returning results, allows the client to implement pagination.

> **Arguments vs. fields**
>
> It is important to understand the distinction between arguments and fields. For example, `first` and `offset` are arguments, whereas `name` and `address` are fields. Arguments appear inside parentheses after a field name and are passed to resolver functions. Fields appear inside braces after an object name and represent attributes of an object. Fields can be thought of as holding values, while arguments are used more as selectors and are passed in GraphQL operations.

Listing 2.4   Updated query and business type definitions with first and offset arguments

```
type Business {
    businessId: ID!
    name: String
    address: String
    avgStars: Float
    photos(first: Int = 3, offset: Int = 0): [Photo!]!
    reviews(first: Int = 3, offset: Int = 0): [Review!]! ⟵
}
```

Here we add first and offset arguments to the reviews field on the Business type. This means we can control pagination on the nested connected Review objects for each business returned in our query.

```
type Query {
    allBusinesses(first: Int = 10, offset: Int = 0): [Business!]!    ⟵
    businessBySearchTerm(
        search: String
        first: Int = 10
        offset: Int = 0
    ): [Business]
    userById(id: ID!): User
}
```

Here we add the first and offset arguments to the allBusinesses field, allowing the client to specify skip and limit values for the query, controlling the number and offset of the businesses returned. Note that we assign default values, and if not specified, the value of 10 and offset of 0 will be assigned first, ensuring we receive the first 10 results.

There is no need to add first and offset arguments to the userById field because it is guaranteed to return at most one result.

Pagination options

There are several patterns for implementing pagination in GraphQL. Here we focus on a fairly simple first/offset pattern. Other options include numbered pages and cursor-based pagination, such as Relay Cursor Connections. Cursor-based pagination using the Relay Cursor Connection specification is covered in chapter 9.

That solves pagination for us, but what about ordering? This is needed when showing search results—we want to present the user with the businesses in an order that makes sense. To accomplish this, we will add an ordering enum that will enumerate the options for ordering fields of type [Business] in our GraphQL API.

Listing 2.5   Business ordering enum

```
enum BusinessOrdering {  ⟵
    name_asc  ⟵
    name_desc
}
```

enum is a built-in GraphQL type that is restricted to a set of allowed values.

We add two enum options for each field on which we want to support ordering: one field for ascending ordering, ending in _asc, and another field for descending ordering, ending in _desc.

Typically, the convention is to set enums in uppercase (e.g., NAME_ASC); however, since in this case our enum values describe field names, we make an exception and keep the naming of the enums consistent with our field names. Now, we need to add this field as an optional argument to our Query field for searching for businesses, as shown in the next listing.

Listing 2.6   Adding ordering for business search results

```
type Query {
  allBusinesses(first: Int = 10, offset: Int = 0): [Business!]!
  businessBySearchTerm(
    search: String!
    first: Int = 10
    offset: Int = 0
    orderBy: BusinessOrdering = name_asc
  ): [Business!]!
  userById(id: ID!): User
}
```

> Here we've added the orderBy argument to the businessBySearchTerm field, which is of type BusinessOrdering.

Now, we are ready to use our new pagination and ordering arguments. In the next listing, let's update our earlier query, in which we were searching for businesses with "Library" in the name to return only the top five rated businesses and two reviews for each business.

Listing 2.7   GraphQL query to search for businesses and reviews

```
{
  businessBySearchTerm(search: "Library", first: 5, orderBy: name_desc) {
    name
    avgStars
    reviews(first: 2) {
      stars
      text
      user {
        name
      }
    }
  }
}
```

Typically, when using argument values in our application queries, we want to use variables with values that can be substituted at query time, so we don't end up constructing query strings in our application. Instead, we want to pass our parameterized GraphQL query string and an object with the variable values. We can do this in GraphQL by first declaring the variables we plan to use as well as their type, and then including them in the query, prefixed by the $ character. The following listing shows how our query would look using GraphQL variables.

Listing 2.8   GraphQL query to search for businesses and reviews using pagination

```
query businessSearch(
  $searchTerm: String!
  $businessLimit: Int
  $businessSkip: Int
  $businessOrder: BusinessOrdering
  $reviewLimit: Int
) {
```

```
businessBySearchTerm(
  search: $searchTerm
  first: $businessLimit
  offset: $businessSkip
  orderBy: $businessOrder
) {
  name
  avgStars
  reviews(first: $reviewLimit) {
    stars
    text
    user {
      name
    }
  }
}
}
```

Note that this query now includes some additional information, along with our GraphQL variable declaration. We are explicitly specifying the GraphQL *operation type* and *operation name.* The operation type is query, mutation, or subscription. Previously, we used a shorthand that excluded the operation type and treated query as the default operation type. We'll cover mutation types later in the book. The operation type is not required, unless specifying an operation name or variable definitions, or using a type other than query.

The other additional piece of information here is the operation name—in this case, businessSearch. The operation name is an explicit name for the operation that can be helpful for debugging and logging. It can be much easier to find queries using the operation name while looking through logs when there is a problem or when troubleshooting. Along with the GraphQL query, we would also pass an object that contains the variable values:

```
{
  searchTerm: "Library",
  businessLimit: 5,
  businessOrder: "name_desc",
  reviewLimit: 2
}
```

Of course, we don't have a way to query our nonexistent API at this point, so let's fix that by implementing some resolvers for data fetching!

2.2.2   *Resolving data with resolvers*

Following our GraphQL-first development approach, the next step we need to complete is implementing the code to actually fetch this data from the data layer. We do this by writing functions called *resolvers*, which contain logic for how to resolve data from the data layer. Resolvers are standalone functions with the purpose of fetching data for a single field of a GraphQL type, and they can be thought of as the primary unit of execution in a GraphQL service. Resolvers are called in a nested fashion, starting with the root-level resolver (a field on the query, mutation, or subscription types) in a depth-first execution, until all requested fields have been resolved. Data resolved in a previous resolver is passed on to nested resolvers via the obj parameter.

You can think of resolvers as functions that go alongside the GraphQL type definitions defined in SDL and, effectively, make the GraphQL schema executable. A GraphQL schema must have resolver functions for all fields (a default resolver is used for any resolver functions not explicitly defined), so a collection of resolver functions corresponds to the type definitions and is known as a resolver map.

THE RESOLVER FUNCTION SIGNATURE

Each resolver function receives four arguments:

- obj—The previously resolved object. Not used for a root query field resolver.
- args—The arguments for the field used in the GraphQL query.
- context—An object that can hold contextual data, such as authorization information or a database connection.
- info—The GraphQLResolveInfo object contains a version of the GraphQL query as well as the full GraphQL schema and other metadata about the query and schema.

Valid results returned by resolver functions include the following, depending on the GraphQL type definition of the field being resolved:

- A scalar or object value
- An array
- A promise
- undefined or null

DEFAULT RESOLVERS

If a resolver is not provided for a field requested in a GraphQL query, then a default resolver will be called, passing in the data resolved so far (the obj mentioned previously). This default resolver will return a property from the obj parameter with the field name. For example, a default resolver for the name field on the Business type would look something like the following code:

```
Business: {
  name: (obj, args, context, info) => {
    return obj.name
  }
}
```

2.2.3   *Our first resolver*

Let's implement resolvers for the type definitions we've created (see listing 2.9). The first thing we need is some data to return, so let's create some static data that will represent our data layer. We'll simply create some object literals and store these in an object called db, which we can think of as a mock for a database that we would query in our resolver functions. We will inject this db object with our fake data into the context object, ensuring it is available in each resolver.

Listing 2.9 **Sample data for businesses, reviews, and users representing our data layer**

```
const businesses = [
  {
    businessId: "b1",
    name: "Missoula Public Library",
    address: "301 E Main St, Missoula, MT 59802",
    reviewIds: ["r1", "r2"],
  },
  {
    businessId: "b2",
    name: "San Mateo Public Library",
    address: "55 W 3rd Ave, San Mateo, CA 94402",
    reviewIds: ["r3"],
  },
];

const reviews = [
  {
    reviewId: "r1",
    stars: 3,
    text: "Friendly staff. Interlibrary loan is super fast",
    businessId: "b1",
    userId: "u1",
  },
  {
    reviewId: "r2",
    stars: 4,
    text: "Easy downtown access, lots of free parking",
    businessId: "b1",
    userId: "u2",
  },
  {
    reviewId: "r3",
    stars: 5,
    text: "Lots of glass and sunlight for reading.",
    businessId: "b1",
    userId: "u1",
  },
];

const users = [
  {
    userId: "u1",
    name: "Will",
    reviewIds: ["r1", "r2"],
  },
  {
    userId: "u2",
    name: "Bob",
```

```
      reviewIds: ["r3"],
  },
];
```

```
const db = { businesses, reviews, users };
```

We'll assume these objects are passed to the resolvers in the context object like we would pass a database connection object.

Mocking GraphQL data

Rather than creating a static object to use as an example, we could use the mocking functionality of Apollo Server to create resolvers that return mocked data. This mocking functionality is useful for testing UI and frontend code and enabling frontend and backend teams to work concurrently. We can be sure this data is relevant because it uses schema introspection and the GraphQL type system to ensure the mocked data is the same form as we've defined in our GraphQL type definitions. Learn more about data mocking with Apollo Server in the documentation: http://mng.bz/Pnlw.

Based on our GraphQL type definitions, our initial resolver map would look like the following listing.

Listing 2.10   Resolver map skeleton

```
const resolvers = {
  Query: {
    allBusinesses: (obj, args, context, info) => {
      // TODO: return all businesses
    },
    businessBySearchTerm: (obj, args, context, info) => {
      // TODO: search businesses for matching search term
    }
  },
  Business: {
    reviews: (obj, args, context, info) => {
      // TODO: find reviews for a particular business
    },
    avgStars: (obj, args, context, info) => {
      // TODO: calculate average stars aggregation
    }
  },
  Review: {
    user: (obj, args, context, info) => {
      // TODO: find the user who wrote this review
    },
    business: (obj, args, context, info) => {
      // TODO: find the business for this  review
    }
  },
  User: {
```

```
    reviews: (obj, args, context, info) => {
     // TODO: find all reviews written by a user
    }
  }
};
```

Note that we don't need to bother implementing trivial resolvers that will be handled by the default resolver, such as `Business.name`. Let's start by implementing the `all-Businesses` resolver (see listing 2.11). This resolver simply fetches all businesses from our data layer and returns them, without worrying about pagination or ordering. Remember that for this example, our data layer consists of a nested object exposed via the context object in each resolver. (We'll cover how to actually inject this object in the next section.)

> **Listing 2.11   Root-level resolver: `allBusinesses`**

```
Query: {                                              ◁──────      We are resolving a field on the
    allBusinesses: (obj, args, context, info) => {                Query type, so this resolver is a
      return context.db.businesses;          ◁─────               function under the Query key in
    }                                                             our resolver map.
}
```

Here we see the standard signature for resolver functions. obj will be empty here, since this is the root level resolver—no data has been resolved yet. args will also be an empty object, since this field does not accept any arguments. context, however, will contain our static data object.

We return the businesses array on the db object, accessed via the context object.

Now that we have our first resolver function implemented, let's see how we can combine our GraphQL type definitions and resolvers to serve a GraphQL API, using Apollo Server.

2.3   Combining type definitions and resolvers with Apollo Server

We've created our GraphQL type definitions and our first resolver function to query our data layer, so now it's time to put them together and spin up a GraphQL server with Apollo Server. Apollo Server is available as an npm package, so let's install that with npm:

```
npm install apollo-server graphql
```

2.3.1   Using Apollo Server

In the next listing, we create index.js, which will use the type definitions and resolvers we previously defined as well as Apollo Server to serve a GraphQL API based on these type definitions.

Listing 2.12   index.js GraphQL server created with Apollo Server

```
const ApolloServer = require('apollo-server');

const server = new ApolloServer({
    typeDefs,
    resolvers,
    context: { db }
});

server.listen().then(({ url }) => {
    console.log(`Server ready at ${url}`);
});
```

Create a server instance.

Our resolvers were defined previously.

Import ApolloServer from the package we just installed.

We pass in our type definitions that we defined above.

db is our mock data object and is injected into the context. This object will be available in each resolver.

Here we start the server and begin listening for incoming GraphQL requests.

2.3.2   Apollo Studio

By default, Apollo Server will serve the GraphQL endpoint for POST requests, but for a GET request from a web browser at the same URL (http://localhost:4000, in our case), Apollo Server will redirect to the Apollo Studio in-browser tool (see figure 2.3).

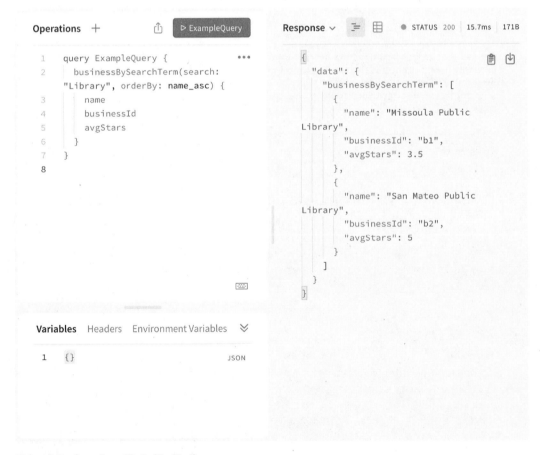

Figure 2.3   Querying with Apollo Studio

Apollo Studio can be used to view the type definitions and schema of the GraphQL API as well as execute queries and mutations and view the results. So far, the only Query field resolver we've implemented is `allBusinesses`. Let's test that by running the following query in Apollo Studio:

```
{
  allBusinesses {
    name
  }
}
```

This will result in a call to the Query field resolver `allBusinesses`, which will return the `businesses` object from our mocked database. Then, since we are requesting just the `name` field on the Business type, the default resolver for `name` will be used to return the name of each business (see figure 2.4).

Figure 2.4   A simple query, using Apollo Studio

If you experiment by adjusting the query in Apollo Studio, you can see pretty quickly that we need to implement the rest of our resolvers. Let's return to our resolver map skeleton and complete the resolvers.

2.3.3   Implementing resolvers

We've created some fake data to work with and have written our first resolver, `all-Businesses`, which simply returns all the businesses in our mock database. Now, it's time to implement more complex resolvers, such as `businessBySearchTerm`, which will allow us to filter results based on a user's search term, and array resolvers, such as `Business.reviews`, that will be responsible for resolving connections between businesses and reviews.

ROOT-LEVEL RESOLVER: BUSINESSBYSEARCHTERM

Root-level resolvers are those that map to the entry points for our API. Looking back at our GraphQL type definitions, we have the following entry points, as defined in the Query type:

```
type Query {
  allBusinesses: [Business!]!
  businessBySearchTerm(
    search: String!
    first: Int = 10
    offset: Int = 0
    orderBy: BusinessOrdering = name_asc
  ): [Business!]!
  userById(id: ID!): User
}

enum BusinessOrdering {
  name_asc
  name_desc
}
```

We already implemented the `allBusinesses` root-level resolver in the previous section. That example was fairly simple, since we didn't have to deal with any arguments. Now let's implement the `businessesBySearchTerm` resolver, which takes a search string, ordering, and pagination arguments, as shown in the next listing.

Listing 2.13   Root-level resolver: `businessBySearchTerm`

Since this is a root-level resolver, the obj parameter will be empty, but we will make use of the args object, which will contain the GraphQL query arguments—in this case, orderBy, search, first, and offset. Since our type definitions made use of default values for orderBy, first, and offset, and search is a required field, we can be sure these values will be defined.

```
businessBySearchTerm: (obj, args, context, info) => {
    const compare = (a, b) => {
      const [orderField, order] = args.orderBy.split("_");
      const left = a[orderField],
        right = b[orderField];

      if (left < right) {
        return order === "asc" ? -1 : 1;
      } else if (left > right) {
        return order === "desc" ? -1 : 1;
      } else {
        return 0;
      }
    };
    return context.db.businesses
      .filter(v => {
        return v["name"].indexOf(args.search) !== -1;
      })
```

Here we define a comparator function to use for ordering, making use of our BusinessOrdering enum. We split the orderBy value on underscore to identify the field name and direction of ordering (e.g., name_asc means we will order by the name field in ascending order).

Here we filter for businesses, where the name property contains the search term passed in the GraphQL query.

```
          .slice(args.offset, args.first)
          .sort(compare);
    }
```

We make use of the slice function to implement first/offset pagination.

Here we apply our compare function to order the results according to the value specified in the orderBy argument. If no orderBy argument is specified, then name_asc will be used, since it is specified as the default value in the GraphQL type definitions.

ARRAY RESOLVER: BUSINESS.REVIEWS

Our previous root-level resolvers returned arrays of objects, but we can also return arrays of objects from resolvers for non-root-level resolvers if the field is a list field (e.g., Business.reviews, which is of type [Review], or a list of Review objects). With non-root level resolvers, the obj parameter will include any previously resolved data. For example, if we first execute the Query.businessBySearchTerm resolver to fetch businesses, the results of that resolver will be passed to the Business.reviews resolver. Let's make use of that data to implement the Business.reviews resolver in the next listing.

Listing 2.14   Root-level resolver

```
Business: {
  reviews: (obj, args, context, info) => {
    return obj.reviewIds.map(v => {
      return context.db.reviews.find(review => {
        return review.reviewId === v;
      });
    });
  },
}
```

SCALAR RESOLVER: BUSINESS.AVGSTARS

We talked about default resolvers that simply return an object property with the same name as the field from the obj parameter, but there are cases when we need to implement resolvers that return scalar values and the default resolver is not used. Aggregations are a good example of that. The Business.avgStars field is an aggregation field, and we need to find all reviews for a particular business and then calculate the average of the stars for these reviews, returning a single scalar value.

Listing 2.15   Scalar field resolver

```
avgStars: (obj, args, context, info) => {
  const reviews = obj.reviewIds.map(v => {
    return context.db.reviews.find(review => {
      return review.reviewId === v;
    });
  });

  return (
    reviews.reduce((acc, review) => {
      return acc + review.stars;
```

```
        }, 0) / reviews.length
    );
}
```

OBJECT RESOLVER: REVIEW.USER

So far, we've seen resolvers that return scalar values and arrays; now, let's implement a resolver that returns a single object, as the next listing shows. In our type definitions, a Review is connected to a single User, which means that Review.user is an object field, not a list field.

Listing 2.16   Object field resolver resolver

```
Review: {
  user: (obj, args, context, info) => {
    return context.db.users.find(user => {
      return user.userId === obj.userId;
    });
  }
}
```

And with that last resolver implementation, we can now return to querying our GraphQL API using Apollo Studio.

2.3.4   *Querying using Apollo Studio*

Now that we've implemented the rest of our resolver functions, let's return to Apollo Studio by opening http://localhost:4000/ in a web browser. First, let's search for businesses using the search term "Library" (see figure 2.5).

```
{
businessBySearchTerm(search: "Library") {
  businessId
  name
  address
  avgStars
}
}
```

```
{
"data": {
  "businessBySearchTerm": [
    {
      "businessId": "b1",
      "name": "Missoula Public Library",
      "address": "301 E Main St, Missoula, MT 59802",
      "avgStars": 3.5
    },
    {
      "businessId": "b2",
      "name": "San Mateo Public Library",
      "address": "55 W 3rd Ave, San Mateo, CA 94402",
      "avgStars": 5
    }
  ]
}
}
```

Figure 2.5   Querying for businesses by search term

And now let's retrieve reviews for each business matching our search results (see figure 2.6).

```
{                                   •••      {                                                                    📋
  businessBySearchTerm(search: "Library") {     "data": {
    businessId                                     "businessBySearchTerm": [
    name                                             {
    address                                            "businessId": "b1",
    avgStars                                           "name": "Missoula Public Library",
    reviews {                                          "address": "301 E Main St, Missoula, MT 59802",
      stars                                            "avgStars": 3.5,
      text                                             "reviews": [
    }                                                    {
  }                                                        "stars": 3,
}                                                          "text": "Friendly staff. Interlibrary loan is super fast"
                                                         },
                                                         {
                                                           "stars": 4,
                                                           "text": "Easy downtown access, lots of free parking"
                                                         }
                                                       ]
                                                     },
                                                     {
                                                       "businessId": "b2",
                                                       "name": "San Mateo Public Library",
                                                       "address": "55 W 3rd Ave, San Mateo, CA 94402",
                                                       "avgStars": 5,
                                  ⌨                     "reviews": [
                                                         {
```

Figure 2.6   Adding business reviews to the query

You can find the code for the completed example GraphQL API in this book's GitHub repository: http://mng.bz/J2jo. In the next chapter, we will introduce the Neo4j graph database and learn how to model, store, and query data using the Cypher query language.

2.4   Exercises

1   Consider some of the other requirements of our business reviews application that we didn't implement. Can you write GraphQL queries to address these requirements? What are the results?

2   What other fields should make use of pagination and ordering in our API? Update the type definitions to include the appropriate ordering and pagination fields and update the resolvers to handle these pagination arguments.

3   Implement the root-level resolver for usersById.

4   Our example GraphQL API conspicuously lacks business categories. Update the sample data, GraphQL type definitions, and resolvers to take advantage of business categories. Consider how you would model categories in the API, given that searching by category was specifically identified as a business requirement.

You can find solutions to the exercises as well as code samples in the GitHub repository for this book: github.com/johnymontana/fullstack-graphql-book.

Summary

- API data modeling can be approached using the business requirements of the application. When done this way—mapping out the mental model of the data—a graph is created, nodes are the entities, and relationships connect them.
- GraphQL type definitions are used to define the data, relationships, and entry points of a GraphQL API. Type definitions can be defined using the Schema Definition Language (SDL), a language-agnostic notation for specifying GraphQL types. In addition to the built-in GraphQL types (`ID`, `String`, `Int`, `Float`, `Bool`, etc.), custom user-defined scalars and types can be defined as well.
- Resolvers are functions that contain the data-fetching logic for a GraphQL API. Resolvers are called in a nested fashion, depending on what fields have been requested in the GraphQL query. Each resolver is passed a context object, which can contain database connections or other helper objects for accessing data.
- Apollo Server is used to combine GraphQL type definitions and resolvers into an executable GraphQL schema and serve the GraphQL API.
- Apollo Studio can be used for viewing the schema of a GraphQL API as well as for executing queries and viewing the results.

Graphs in the database 3

This chapter covers
- An introduction to graph databases with a focus on Neo4j
- The property graph data model
- Using the Cypher query language to create and query data in Neo4j
- Using client drivers for Neo4j, specifically the JavaScript Node.js driver

Fundamentally, a graph database is a software tool that allows the user to model, store, and query data as a graph. Working with a graph at the database level is often more intuitive for modeling complex connected data and can be more performant when working with complex queries that require traversing many connected entities.

In this chapter, we begin the process of creating a property graph data model using the business requirements from the previous chapter and compare it to the GraphQL schema created in the previous chapter. We then explore the Cypher query language, focusing on how to write Cypher queries to address the requirements of our application. Along the way, we show how to install Neo4j, use Neo4j Desktop to create new Neo4j projects locally, and use Neo4j Browser to query

TQ 132 0376

Neo4j and visualize the results. Finally, we show how to use the Neo4j JavaScript client driver to create a simple Node.js application that queries Neo4j.

3.1   *Neo4j overview*

Neo4j is a native graph database that uses the property graph model for modeling data and the Cypher query language for interacting with the database. Neo4j is a transactional database with full ACID guarantees necessary for operational workloads and can also be used for graph analytics. Graph databases like Neo4j are optimized for working with highly connected data and queries that traverse the graph (think of the equivalent of multiple JOINs in a relational database) and, therefore, are the perfect backend for GraphQL APIs, which describe connected data and often result in complex, nested queries. Neo4j is open source and can be downloaded from neo4j.com/download.

We will make use of Neo4j Desktop and Neo4j Browser in this chapter as we learn how to create and query data in Neo4j, but first, let's dig into the property graph model used by Neo4j and see how it relates to the model used to describe GraphQL APIs that we reviewed in the previous chapter.

3.2   *Graph data modeling with Neo4j*

Unlike other databases that use tables or documents to model data, graph databases like Neo4j model, store, and allow the user to query data as a graph. In a graph, nodes are the entities, and relationships connect them. In a relational database, we represent relationships with foreign keys and join tables. In a document database, we reference other entities using IDs or even denormalizing and embedding other entities in a single document (see figure 3.1).

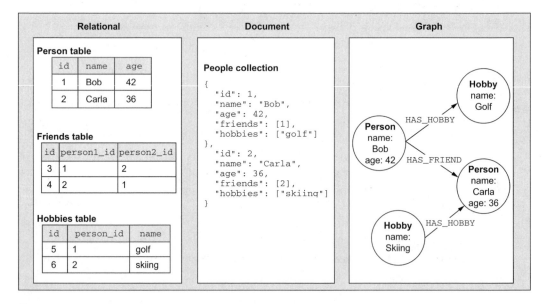

Figure 3.1   Comparing relational, document, and graph data models

The first step when working with a database is to determine the data model that will be used. In our case, our data model will be driven from the business requirements we defined in the previous chapter—working with businesses, users, and reviews. Review the requirements listed in the first section of the previous chapter for a refresher. Let's take those requirements and our knowledge of the domain to create a whiteboard model.

Whiteboard model

We will use the term *whiteboard model* to refer to the diagram typically created when first reasoning about a domain, which is often a graph of entities and how they relate, drawn on a whiteboard (see the following figure).

Building the property graph
model: whiteboard model

How do we translate this mental model from the whiteboard model to the physical data model used by the database? In other systems, this might involve creating an entity-relationship (ER) diagram or defining the schema of the database. Neo4j is said to be *schema optional.* While we can create database constraints to enforce constraints, such as property uniqueness, we can also use Neo4j without these constraints or a schema. But the first step is to define a model using the property graph data model, which is the model used by Neo4j and other graph databases. Let's convert our simple whiteboard model, shown previously, into a property graph model we can use in the database.

3.2.1   The property graph model

We gave a brief overview of the property graph data model in chapter 1. Next, we will go through the process of taking our whiteboard model and converting it to a property graph model used by the database.

The property graph data model

The property graph model is composed of

- Node labels—Nodes are the entities or objects in our data model. Nodes can have one or more labels that describe how nodes are grouped (think type of entity).
- Relationships—Relationships connect two nodes and have a single type and direction.
- Properties—These are arbitrary key-value pair attributes that are stored on either nodes or relationships.

NODE LABELS

Nodes represent the objects in our whiteboard model. Each node can have one or more labels, which is a way of grouping nodes. Adding node labels to a whiteboard model is usually a simple process, since some grouping will already have been defined during the whiteboard process. Here we formalize the descriptors used to refer to our nodes into node labels (later, we will add node aliases and multiple labels, so we use a colon as a separator to indicate the label; see figure 3.2).

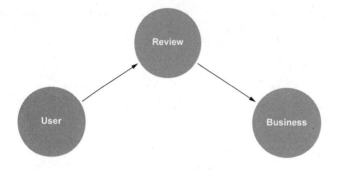

Figure 3.2   Building the property graph model: node labels

Graph data model diagramming tools

There are many tools available for diagramming graph data models. Throughout this book, we use the Arrows tool, a simple web-based application that allows for creating graph data models. Arrows is available online at https://arrows.app.

The Arrows user interface is minimal and is designed around creating property graph data models:

- Create new nodes with the (+ Node) button or by dragging out from an existing node.
- Drag relationships out of the halo of a node, either to an empty space for a new node or centered over an existing one to connect them.
- Double-click nodes and relationships to edit them, set names, and set properties (in a key: value syntax).
- You can export to PNG, SVG, and other formats (including GraphQL type definitions).

The convention used for casing node labels is PascalCase. See the Cypher style guide for more examples of naming conventions at neo4j.com/developer/cypher/style-guide/. Nodes can have multiple labels and allow us to represent type hierarchies, roles in different contexts, or even multitenancy.

RELATIONSHIPS

Once we've identified our nodes labels, the next step is to identify the relationships in our data model. Relationships have a single type and direction but can be queried in either direction (see the figure in the following sidebar).

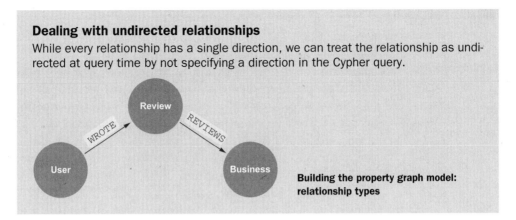

Dealing with undirected relationships
While every relationship has a single direction, we can treat the relationship as undirected at query time by not specifying a direction in the Cypher query.

Building the property graph model: relationship types

A good guideline for naming relationships is that the traversal from a node along a relationship to another node should read as a somewhat comprehensible sentence (e.g., "User wrote review" or "Review reviews business"). You can read more about best practices for naming and conventions in the *Cypher Style Guide*: neo4j.com/developer/cypher-style-guide.

PROPERTIES

Properties are arbitrary key-value pairs stored on nodes and relationships. These are the attributes or fields of entities in our data model. Here we store userId and name as string properties on the User node, as well as other relevant properties on the Review and Business nodes.

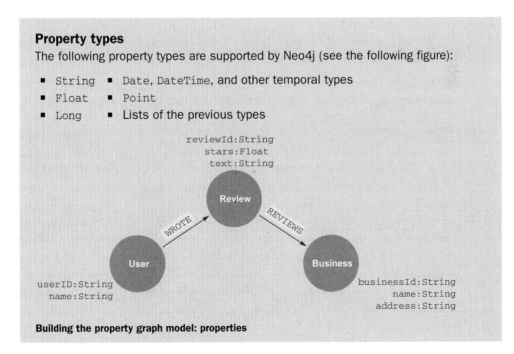

Property types
The following property types are supported by Neo4j (see the following figure):

- String
- Float
- Long
- Date, DateTime, and other temporal types
- Point
- Lists of the previous types

reviewId:String
stars:Float
text:String

userID:String
name:String

businessId:String
name:String
address:String

Building the property graph model: properties

3.2.2   *Database constraints and indexes*

Now that we've defined our data model, how do we make use of it in the database? As mentioned earlier, unlike other databases that require us to define a complete schema before inserting data, Neo4j is said to be schema optional and does not require the use of a pre-defined schema. Instead, we can define database constraints that ensure the data adheres to the rules of the domain. We can create uniqueness constraints that ensure property values are unique across a node label (e.g., guaranteeing that no two users have a duplicate ID property value), property existence constraints (e.g., ensuring that a set of properties exist when a node or relationship is created or modified), and node key constraints, which are similar to a composite key and create a constraint using multiple properties.

Database constraints are backed by indexes, which can be created separately as well. In a graph database, indexes are used to find the starting point for a traversal, not to traverse the graph. We will cover database constraints and indexes in more detail in the following section, which introduces Cypher.

3.3   *Data modeling considerations*

Graph data modeling can be an iterative process. In general, this is the process followed:

1 What are the entities? How are they grouped? These become nodes and node labels.
2 How are these entities connected? These become relationships.
3 What are the attributes of the nodes and relationships? These become properties.
4 Can you identify the graph traversal that answers your questions? These become Cypher queries. If not, iterate on the graph model.

However, there are often some nuances not covered by this general approach. We address some common graph data modeling questions in the following section.

3.3.1   *Node vs. property*

Sometimes, it can be difficult to determine whether a value should be modeled as a node or a property on the node. A good guideline to follow here is to ask yourself the question, "Could I discover something useful by traversing through this value if it was a node?" If the answer is yes, then it should be modeled as a node; if not, then treat it as a property. For example, consider if we were to add the category of business to our model. Finding businesses with overlapping categories is potentially useful and easier to discover if the category is modeled as a node. On the other hand, consider a business address. If we modeled the address as a node instead of a property, would it be useful to traverse through the address node? Most likely, that is not useful, and we should model the address as a property.

3.3.2 Node vs. relationship

In the case where we have a piece of data that seemingly connects two nodes (e.g., a review of a business, written by a user), should we model this data as a node or as a relationship? At first glance, it seems like we might want to just create a `REVIEWS` relationship connecting the user and business, storing the review information, such as `stars` and `text`, as relationship properties. However, we might want to extract data from the review, such as keywords mentioned, through some natural language processing technique, and connect that extracted data to the review. Or perhaps we want to use the review nodes as the starting point for a traversal query. These are two examples of why we may want to choose to model this data as an intermediate node instead of as a relationship.

3.3.3 Indexes

Indexes are used in graph databases to find the starting point of a traversal, not during the actual traversal. This is an important performance characteristic of graph databases like Neo4j, known as *index-free adjacency*. Only create indexes for properties that will be used to find the starting point of a traversal, such as a user name or business ID.

3.3.4 Specificity of relationship types

Relationship types are a way of grouping relationships and should convey just enough information to make it clear how two nodes are connected without being overly specific. For example, `REVIEWS` is a good relationship type connecting `Review` and `Business` nodes. `REVIEW_WRITTEN_BY_BOB_FOR_PIZZA` is an overly specific relationship type; the name of the user and restaurant are stored elsewhere and do not need to be duplicated in the relationship type.

3.3.5 Choosing a relationship direction

All relationships in the property graph model have a single direction but can be queried in either direction or queried without consideration of direction. There is no need to create duplicate relationships to model bidirectionality. In general, you should choose relationship directions that allow for a consistent reading of the data model.

3.4 Tooling: Neo4j desktop

Now that we understand the property graph data model and have defined a simple version of the model we will use for our business reviews application, let's create a Neo4j database and start executing some Cypher queries. To do this, we will make use of Neo4j Desktop, which is the mission control center for Neo4j (see figure 3.3). In Neo4j Desktop, we can create projects and instances of Neo4j. We can start, stop, and

Controls for the selected DBMS (including starting and stopping) are shown here.

Projects are shown here. Each project can contain multiple Neo4j DBMSs.

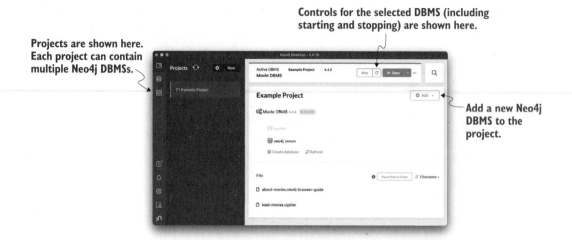

Add a new Neo4j DBMS to the project.

Figure 3.3   Neo4j Desktop: Mission control for Neo4j

configure Neo4j database instances in Neo4j Desktop, as well as install optional database plugins, such as Graph Data Science and APOC (a standard library of database procedures for Neo4j). Neo4j Desktop also includes functionality for installing *graph apps*, which are applications that run in Neo4j Desktop and connect to the active Neo4j instance. Neo4j Browser, installed by default, is an example of one of these graph apps. See install.graphapp.io for examples of other graph apps.

   If you haven't yet downloaded Neo4j Desktop, do so now at neo4j.com/download. Neo4j Desktop is available to download for Mac, Windows, and Linux systems.

   Once you have downloaded and installed Neo4j, create a new local Neo4j instance by selecting *Add Graph*. You'll be prompted to enter a database name and password. The password can be anything you want; just be sure to remember it for later. Once you've created the graph, click the *Start* button to activate it; then we'll use Neo4j Browser to start querying the database we just created.

3.5   *Tooling: Neo4j Browser*

Neo4j Browser is a query workbench for Neo4j that allows developers to interact with the database by writing Cypher queries and visualizing the results (see figure 3.4). Start Neo4j Browser by selecting its application icon in the *Application* section of Neo4j Desktop.

   Neo4j Browser allows us to run Cypher queries against Neo4j and work with the results. Before digging into Neo4j Browser, let's review the Cypher query language.

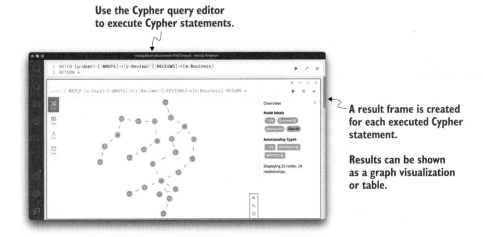

Figure 3.4   Neo4j Browser: a query workbench for Cypher and Neo4j

3.6 *Cypher*

Cypher is a declarative graph query language with some features that may be familiar from SQL. In fact, a good way to think of Cypher is as *SQL for graphs*. Cypher makes use of pattern matching, using an ASCII-art-like notation for describing graph patterns. In this section, we will take a look at some basic Cypher functionality for creating and querying data, including making use of predicates and aggregations. We will only cover a small part of the Cypher language; see the Cypher refcard r.neo4j.com/refcard for a through reference, or consult the documentation at neo4j.com/docs/cypher-manual/current/.

3.6.1 *Pattern matching*

As a declarative graph query language, pattern matching is a fundamental tool used in Cypher, both for creating and querying data. Instead of telling the database the exact operations we want it to take (an imperative approach), with Cypher, we describe the pattern we are looking for or want to create, and the database is responsible for determining the series of operations that satisfies the statement in the most efficient way possible. Describing graph patterns using an ASCII-art-like notation (also called motifs) is at the heart of this declarative functionality.

NODES

Nodes are defined within parentheses (). Optionally, we can specify node label(s), using a colon as a separator—for example, (:User).

RELATIONSHIPS

Relationships are defined within square brackets []. Optionally, we can specify type and direction: `(:Review)-[:REVIEWS]->(:Business)`.

3.6.2 *Properties*

Properties are specified as comma-separated `name: value` pairs within braces '{}', like the name of a business or user.

ALIASES

Graph elements can be bound to aliases or variables that can be referred to later on in the query. For example, given this pattern `(r:Review)-[a:REVIEWS]->(b:Business)`, the alias `r` becomes a variable bound to the review node matched in the graph, `a` is bound to the `REVIEWS` relationship, and `b` is bound to the business node. These variables are only in scope for the Cypher query in which they are used. Follow along by running the following Cypher queries in the Neo4j browser as we introduce Cypher commands for creating and querying data that matches the data model we've built throughout this chapter.

3.6.3 *CREATE*

The first thing we need to do is create some data in our database using the `CREATE` command. First, to create a single `Business` node in the graph, we start with the `CREATE` command followed by a graph pattern that describes the data to be created:

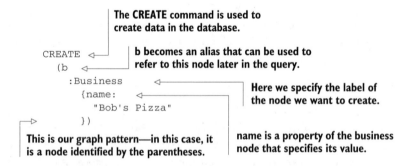

The result of running in Neo4j Browser shows the following:

```
Added 1 label, created 1 node, set 1 property, completed after 4 ms.
```

This means we've created one node with a new label in the database and set one node property value—in this case, the `name` property on a node with the label `Business`. Alternatively, we can use the `SET` command. The following is equivalent:

```
CREATE (b:Business)
SET b.name = "Bob's Pizza"
```

To visualize the data being created, we can add a `RETURN` clause to the Cypher statement, which will be rendered in Neo4j Browser as a graph visualization. Running

```
CREATE (b:Business)
SET b.name = "Bob's Pizza"
RETURN b
```

gives the visualization in Neo4j Browser shown in figure 3.5.

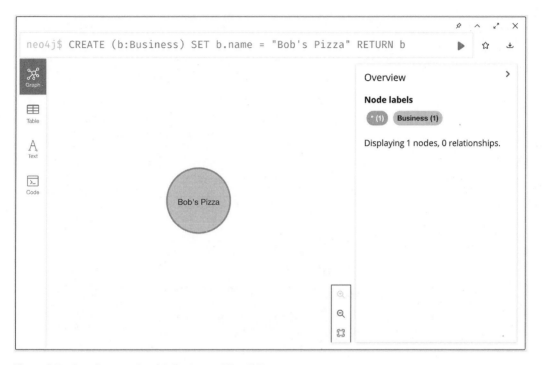

Figure 3.5   Creating a node with Cypher and Neo4j Browser

We can specify more complex patterns in the `CREATE` statement, such as relationships.
Note the ASCII-art notation of defining a relationship using square brackets `<-[]-`,
including the direction of the relationship (see figure 3.6):

```
CREATE (b:Business)<-[:REVIEWS]-(r:Review)
SET b.name = "Bob's Pizza",
    r.stars = 4,
    r.text = "Great pizza"
RETURN b, r
```

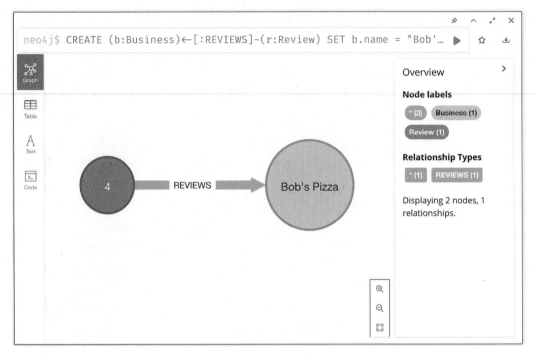

Figure 3.6   Creating two nodes and a relationship

We can create arbitrarily complex graph patterns with Cypher. Here we also specify the user connected to the review in the CREATE statement (see figure 3.7):

```
CREATE p=(b:Business)<-[:REVIEWS]-(r:Review)<-[:WROTE]-(u:User)
SET b.name  = "Bob's Pizza",
    r.stars = 4,
    r.text  = "Great pizza",
    u.name  = "Willie"
RETURN p
```

Note that in this Cypher query we bind the entire graph pattern to a variable p and return that variable. In this case, p takes on the value of the entire path (a combination of nodes and relationships) being created.

So far, we've only returned the data we've created in each Cypher statement. How do we query and visualize the rest of the data in the database? To do this, we use the MATCH keyword. Let's match on all nodes in the database and return them:

```
MATCH (a) RETURN a
```

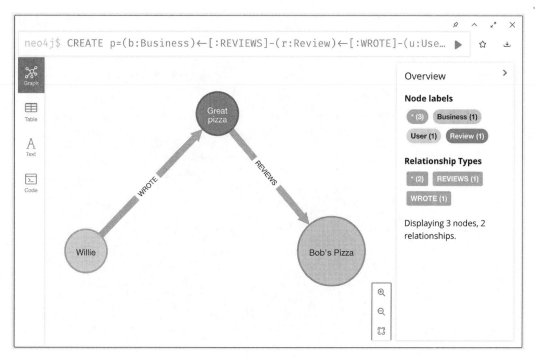

Figure 3.7 Creating a subgraph

We should see a graph that looks something like figure 3.8.

Right away we can see that something is wrong; we've created lots of duplicate nodes in our graph! Let's delete all data in the database:

```
MATCH (a) DETACH DELETE a
```

This will match on all nodes and delete both the nodes and any relationships. We should see output that tells us what we've deleted:

```
Deleted 11 nodes, deleted 4 relationships, completed after 23 ms.
```

Now, let's start over and see how to create data in the database without creating duplicates.

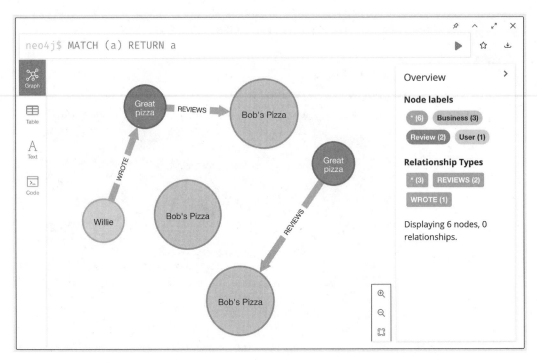

Figure 3.8   Duplicate nodes were created

3.6.4   *MERGE*

To avoid creating duplicates, we can use the MERGE command. MERGE acts as an upsert, only creating data specified in the pattern if it does not already exist in the database. When using MERGE, it is best to create a uniqueness constraint on the property that identifies uniqueness—often an ID field. By creating a uniqueness constraint, this will also create an index in the database. See the next section for an example of creating uniqueness constraints. For simple examples, it is fine to use MERGE without these constraints, so let's revisit our Cypher statement that created a business, review, and user, but this time we will use MERGE:

```
MERGE (b:Business {name: "Bob's Pizza"})
MERGE (r:Review {stars: 4, text: "Great pizza!"})
MERGE (u:User {name: "Willie"})
MERGE (b)<-[:REVIEWS]-(r)<-[:WROTE]-(u)
RETURN *
```

Figure 3.9 shows the resulting graph visualization with the data we've created.

The results of this Cypher statement look identical to the previous version using CREATE; however, there is an important difference: this query is now *idempotent*. No matter how many times we run the query, we will not create duplicate nodes because

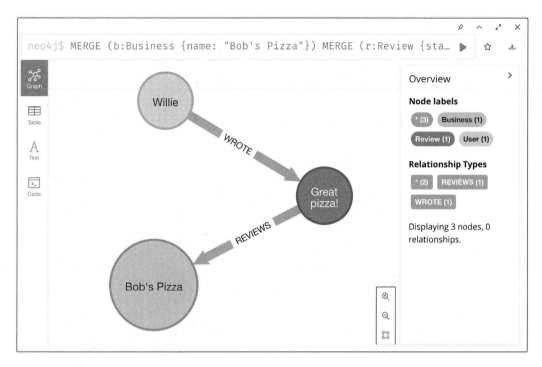

Figure 3.9 Using MERGE to create data

we are using MERGE instead of CREATE. We will revisit MERGE again in the next chapter when we show how to create data in the database via our GraphQL API.

Indexes in Neo4j

It's important to understand how indexes are used in a graph database like Neo4j. We said earlier that Neo4j has a property called index-free adjacency, which means that traversing from a node to any other connected node does not require an index lookup. So how are indexes used in Neo4j? Indexes are used to find the starting point for a traversal only, unlike relational databases, which use an index to compute set (table) overlap, graph databases are simply computing offsets in the filestore, essentially chasing pointers, which we know computers are very good at doing quickly.

3.6.5 *Defining database constraints with cypher*

We mentioned database constraints and how they relate to (optionally) defining a schema in Neo4j earlier in the chapter as we built up our data model. Next, we'll look at the Cypher syntax for creating database constraints relevant to our data model.

UNIQUENESS CONSTRAINT

```
CREATE CONSTRAINT ON (b:Business) ASSERT b.businessId IS UNIQUE;
```

PROPERTY EXISTENCE CONSTRAINT

```
CREATE CONSTRAINT ON (b:Business) ASSERT b.businessId IS NOT NULL
```

NODE KEY CONSTRAINT

```
CREATE CONSTRAINT ON (p:Person) ASSERT (p.firstName, p.lastName) IS NODE KEY;
```

Note that if you still have duplicate data in the database that conflicts with any of these constraints, then you will receive an error message saying the constraint cannot be created. In that case, you may want to delete all data in the database, and then try creating the constraint again.

3.6.6 *MATCH*

Now that we've created our data in the graph, we can start to write queries to address some of the business requirements of our application. The MATCH clause is similar to CREATE in that it takes a graph pattern; however, we can also use a WHERE clause for specifying predicates to be applied in the pattern. A MATCH statement is used to find data in the database that matches a specified graph pattern. For example, here we search for all user nodes in the database:

```
MATCH (u:User)
RETURN u
```

We can, of course, use more complex graph patterns in a MATCH clause:

```
MATCH (u:User)-[:WROTE]->(r:Review)-[:REVIEWS]->(b:Business)
RETURN u, r, b
```

This query matches on all users who have written a review of any business. What if, instead, we only want to query for reviews of a certain business? In that case, we need to introduce predicates into our query, using a WHERE clause.

WHERE

The WHERE clause can be used to add predicates to a MATCH statement. To search for a business named Bob's Pizza, we could write the following Cypher statement:

```
MATCH (b:Business)
WHERE b.name = "Bob's Pizza"
RETURN b
```

For equality comparisons, an equivalent shorthand notation is available:

```
MATCH (b:Business {name: "Bob's Pizza"})
RETURN b
```

3.6.7 Aggregations

Often, we want to compute an aggregation across a set of results. For example, we may want to calculate the average rating of all the reviews of Bob's Pizza. To do this, we make use of the `avg` aggregation function:

```
MATCH (b:Business {name: "Bob's Pizza"})<-[:REVIEWS]-(r:Review)
RETURN avg(r.stars)
```

Now, in Neo4j Browser, we are presented with a table showing the results of our query instead of a graph visualization because we are not returning graph data, but rather tabular data:

What if we wanted to calculate the average rating of *each* business? In SQL, we might use a `GROUP BY` operator to group the reviews by business name and calculate the aggregation across each group, but there is no `GROUP BY` operator in Cypher. Instead, with Cypher there is an *implicit group by* operation applied when returning the results of an aggregation function along with non-aggregated results. For example, we do the following to compute the average rating of each business using Cypher:

```
MATCH (b:Business)<-[:REVIEWS]-(r:Review)
RETURN b.name, avg(r.stars)
```

The results table is as follows:

"b.name"	"avg(r.stars)"
"Bob's Pizza"	4.0

Of course, this isn't very exciting because we only have one business and one review. In the exercise section of this chapter, we will work with a larger dataset.

3.7 Using the Neo4j client drivers

So far, we have been using Neo4j Browser to execute our Cypher queries, which is useful for ad-hoc analysis or prototyping; however, typically, we want to create an application that interacts with the database programmatically. To do this, we make use of the Neo4j client drivers. These client drivers are available in many languages, such as JavaScript, Java, Python, .NET, and Go, and they allow the developer to execute Cypher queries against a Neo4j instance with a consistent API that is idiomatic to the programming language being used. In chapter 1, we saw an example of using the

Neo4j JavaScript driver to execute a Cypher query and work with the results. Refer to the driver and language guides for more information on Neo4j client drivers: neo4j .com/developer/language-guides/.

In the next chapter, we will combine the concepts and tools we have discussed so far (GraphQL and Neo4j) by building a GraphQL API that uses Neo4j as the data layer. To do this, we will use the Neo4j GraphQL Library, which simplifies and accelerates the process of building GraphQL APIs backed by Neo4j.

3.8 Exercises

To complete the following exercises, first run the following command in Neo4j Browser to load a browser guide with embedded Cypher queries: :play grandstack. This browser guide will walk you through the process of loading a larger, more complete sample dataset of businesses and reviews. After running the query to load the data in Neo4j, proceed to the following exercises:

1 Run the command CALL db.schema.visualization() to inspect the data model. What are the node labels used? What are the relationship types?
2 Write a Cypher query to find all the users in the database. How many users are there? What are their names?
3 Find all the reviews written by the user named Will. What is the average rating given by this user?
4 Find all the businesses reviewed by the user named Will. What is the most common category?
5 Write a query to recommend businesses to the user named Will that he has not previously reviewed.

You can find solutions to the exercises as well as code samples in the GitHub repository for this book: github.com/johnymontana/fullstack-graphql-book.

Summary

- A graph database allows the user to model, store, and query data as a graph.
- The property graph data model is used by graph databases and consists of node labels, relationships, and properties.
- The Cypher query language is a declarative graph query language focused around pattern matching and is used for querying graph databases, including Neo4j.
- Client drivers are used for building applications that interact with Neo4j. These drivers enable applications to send Cypher queries to the database and work with the results.

The Neo4j GraphQL Library

This chapter covers

- Reviewing common issues that arise when building GraphQL API applications
- Introducing database integrations for GraphQL that aim to address these common problems, including the Neo4j GraphQL library
- Building a GraphQL endpoint backed by Neo4j, taking advantage of the features of the Neo4j GraphQL library, such as generated query and mutation types, filtering, and temporal and spatial data types
- Extending the functionality of our autogenerated GraphQL API with custom logic
- Introspecting a GraphQL schema from an existing Neo4j database

GraphQL backend implementations commonly run into a set of issues that negatively impact performance and developer productivity. We've identified some of these problems previously (e.g., the $n + 1$ query problem), and in this chapter, we take a deeper look at these common issues and discuss how they can be mitigated, using database integrations for GraphQL that make it easier to build efficient GraphQL APIs backed by databases.

Specifically, we look at using the Neo4j GraphQL library, a Node.js library designed to work with JavaScript GraphQL implementations, such as Apollo Server for building GraphQL APIs backed by Neo4j. The Neo4j GraphQL library allows us to generate a fully functional GraphQL API from GraphQL type definitions, driving the database data model from GraphQL and autogenerating resolvers for data fetching and mutations, including complex filtering, ordering, and pagination. The Neo4j GraphQL library also enables adding custom logic beyond the generated create, read, update, and delete operations.

In this chapter, we look at using the Neo4j GraphQL library to integrate our business review GraphQL API with Neo4j, adding a persistence layer to our API. In this initial look at the Neo4j GraphQL library, we focus on querying existing data using the sample dataset in Neo4j used in the previous chapter. We will explore creating and updating data (GraphQL mutations) as well as more complex GraphQL querying semantics, such as interfaces and fragments, in future chapters, introducing these concepts in the context of building out our user interface. Figure 4.1 shows how the Neo4j GraphQL library fits into the larger architecture of our application. The goal of the Neo4j GraphQL library is to make it easy to build an API backed by Neo4j, not to the database directly with GraphQL.

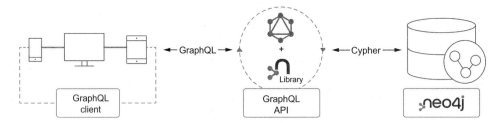

Figure 4.1   The Neo4j GraphQL library helps build the API layer between the client and database.

4.1   Common GraphQL problems

When building GraphQL APIs, there are two types of problems that developers typically face: poor performance and writing lots of boilerplate code, which can impact developer productivity.

4.1.1   Poor performance and the n + 1 query problem

We previously discussed the $n + 1$ query problem, which can arise when multiple requests are sent to the data layer to resolve a single GraphQL request. Because of the nested way GraphQL resolver functions are called, multiple database requests are often required to resolve a GraphQL query from the data layer. For example, imagine a query searching for businesses by name as well as all reviews for each business. A naive implementation would first query the database for all businesses matching the search phrase. Then, for each matching business, it would send an additional query to the database to find any reviews for the business. Each query to the database would incur network and query latency, which can significantly impact performance.

A common solution for this is to use a caching and batching pattern known as DataLoader. This can alleviate some performance issues; however, it can still require multiple database requests and cannot be used in all cases, such as when the ID of an object is not known.

4.1.2 Boilerplate and developer productivity

The term *boilerplate* is used to describe repetitive code that is written to accomplish a common task. In the case of implementing GraphQL APIs, writing boilerplate code to implement data-fetching logic in resolvers is often required. This can negatively impact developer productivity, slowing down development, as the developer is required to write simple data-fetching logic for each type and field instead of focusing on the key components of their application. In the context of our business review application, this would mean manually writing the logic for finding businesses by name in the database, finding reviews associated with each business and each user connected to each review, and so on, until we've manually defined the logic for fetching all fields of our GraphQL schema.

4.2 Introducing GraphQL database integrations

GraphQL integrations for databases are a class of tools that enable building GraphQL APIs that interact with databases. There are a handful of these tools with different feature sets and levels of integration—in this book, we focus on the Neo4j GraphQL library. However, in general, the goal of these GraphQL engines is to address the common GraphQL problems previously identified in a consistent way by reducing boilerplate and addressing data-fetching performance issues.

Throughout the rest of this chapter, we focus on using the Neo4j GraphQL library to build a GraphQL API backed by Neo4j. It is important to note that our GraphQL API serves as a layer between the client and the database—we do not want to directly query our database from the client. The API layer serves an important function, allowing us to implement features, such as authorization and custom logic, that we don't want to expose to the client. Also, since GraphQL is an API query language (not a database query language), it lacks many semantics (e.g., projections) that we would expect in a database query language.

4.3 The Neo4j GraphQL Library

The Neo4j GraphQL library is a Node.js library that works with any JavaScript GraphQL implementation, such as GraphQL.js and Apollo Server, and is designed to make it as easy as possible to build GraphQL APIs backed by a Neo4j database. The two main functions of the Neo4j GraphQL library are *GraphQL schema generation* and *GraphQL to Cypher translation*. You may wish to refer to the project's documentation at http://mng.bz/woNO.

GraphQL to Cypher translation enables the following:

- Generating a single database query at runtime from arbitrary GraphQL requests
- Handling custom logic defined in the GraphQL schema as subqueries in the generated database queries

The GraphQL schema generation process takes GraphQL type definitions and generates a GraphQL API with create, read, update, delete (CRUD) operations for the types defined. In GraphQL semantics, this includes adding a `Query` and `Mutation` type to the schema and generating resolvers for these queries and mutations. The generated API includes support for filtering, ordering, pagination, and native database types, such as spatial and temporal types, without having to define these manually in the type definitions. The result of this process is a GraphQL executable schema object, which can then be passed to a GraphQL server implementation, such as Apollo Server, to serve the API and handle networking and GraphQL execution processes. The schema generation process eliminates the need to write boilerplate code for data fetching and mapping the GraphQL and database schemas.

The GraphQL translation process happens at query time. When a GraphQL request is received, a single Cypher query is generated, which can resolve the request and is sent to the database. Generating a single database query for any arbitrary GraphQL operation solves the $n + 1$ query problem, assuring only one round trip to the database per GraphQL request. You can find the documentation and other resources for the Neo4j GraphQL library at dev.neo4j.com/graphql.

4.3.1   Project setup

Throughout the rest of the chapter, we will explore the features of the Neo4j GraphQL library by creating a new GraphQL API for Neo4j, using the sample dataset of businesses and reviews from the *Exercise* section of the previous chapter. We will first create a new Node.js project that makes use of the Neo4j GraphQL library and the Neo4j JavaScript driver to fetch data from Neo4j. Then, we will explore the various features of the Neo4j GraphQL library, adding additional code to our GraphQL API application as we move along.

NEO4J

First, make sure a Neo4j instance is running (you can use Neo4j Desktop, Neo4j Sandbox, or Neo4j Aura, but we will assume you are using Neo4j Desktop for the purposes of this chapter). If using Neo4j Desktop, you will need to install the APOC standard library plugin. Don't worry about this step if you're using Neo4j Sandbox or Neo4j Aura; APOC is included by default in those services. To install APOC in Neo4j Desktop, click the *Plugins* tab in your project, and then look for APOC in the list of available plugins, and click *Install*. Next, make sure your Neo4j database is empty by running the Cypher statement (see listing 4.1).

WARNING   This statement will delete all data in your Neo4j database, so make sure this is the instance you want to use, not a database you don't want to delete.

Listing 4.1   Clearing out our Neo4j database

```
MATCH (a) DETACH DELETE a;
```

Now, we're ready to load our sample dataset, which you may have done already if you completed the exercise section in the previous chapter. Run the following command in Neo4j Browser (see figure 4.2):

```
:play grandstack
```

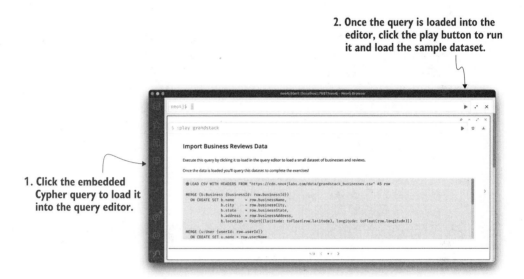

2. Once the query is loaded into the editor, click the play button to run it and load the sample dataset.

1. Click the embedded Cypher query to load it into the query editor.

Figure 4.2   Loading the sample dataset into Neo4j

This will load a sample dataset into Neo4j that we will use as the basis for our GraphQL API. In the next listing, we can explore the data a bit by running a command, which will give us a visual overview of the data included in the sample dataset (see figure 4.3).

Listing 4.2   Visualizing the graph schema in Neo4j

```
CALL db.schema.visualization();
```

We see that we have four node labels—Business, Review, Category, and User—connected by three relationship types: IN_CATEGORY (connecting businesses to the categories to which they belong), REVIEWS (connecting reviews to businesses), and

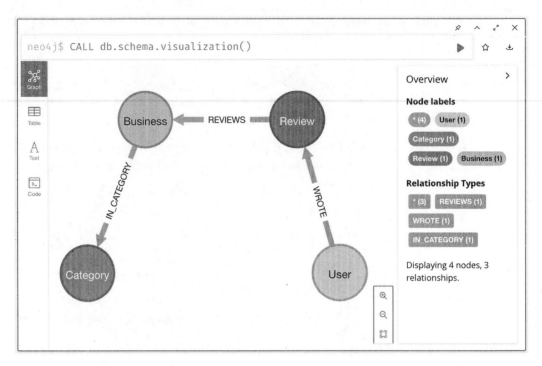

Figure 4.3   The graph schema of our sample dataset

WROTE (connecting users to reviews they have authored). We can also view the node properties stored on the various node labels, as shown in the next listing.

Listing 4.3   Inspecting the node properties stored in Neo4j

```
CALL db.schema.nodeTypeProperties()
```

This command will render a table, showing us the property names, their types, and whether or not they are found on all nodes of that label:

"nodeType"	"nodeLabels"	"propertyName"	"propertyTypes"	"mandatory"
":`User`"	["User"]	"name"	["String"]	true
":`User`"	["User"]	"userId"	["String"]	true
":`Review`"	["Review"]	"reviewId"	["String"]	true
":`Review`"	["Review"]	"text"	["String"]	false
":`Review`"	["Review"]	"stars"	["Double"]	true
":`Review`"	["Review"]	"date"	["Date"]	true
":`Category`"	["Category"]	"name"	["String"]	true
":`Business`"	["Business"]	"name"	["String"]	true
":`Business`"	["Business"]	"city"	["String"]	true
":`Business`"	["Business"]	"state"	["String"]	true
":`Business`"	["Business"]	"address"	["String"]	true
":`Business`"	["Business"]	"location"	["Point"]	true
":`Business`"	["Business"]	"businessId"	["String"]	true

We will make use of this table in a few moments when we construct GraphQL type definitions that describe this graph.

NODE.JS APP

Now that we have our Neo4j database loaded with our sample dataset, let's set up a new Node.js project for our GraphQL API:

```
npm init -y
```

We will also install our dependencies:

- @neo4j/graphql—A package to make it easier to use GraphQL and Neo4j together. The Neo4j GraphQL library translates GraphQL queries to a single Cypher query, eliminating the need to write queries in GraphQL resolvers and for batching queries. It also exposes the Cypher query language through GraphQL via the @cypher schema directive.
- apollo-server—Apollo Server is an open source GraphQL server that works with any GraphQL schema built with graphql.js, including the Neo4j GraphQL library. It also has options for working with many different Node.js webserver frameworks or the default Express.js.

- `graphql`—The GraphQL.js reference implementation for JavaScript is a peer dependency of both `@neo4j/graphql` and `apollo-server`. As of this writing, the `@neo4j/graphql` package is compatible with version 15.x of `graphql`; therefore, we will install the latest v15.x release.
- `neo4j-driver`—The Neo4j client drivers allow for connecting to a Neo4j instance, either local or remote, and executing Cypher queries over the Bolt protocol. Neo4j drivers are available in many different languages, and here we use the Neo4j JavaScript driver:

```
npm i @neo4j/graphql graphql neo4j-driver apollo-server
```

Now, create a new file called index.js, and let's add some initial code in the next listing.

Listing 4.4 index.js: Initial GraphQL API code

```
const { ApolloServer } = require("apollo-server");    ◁——  Importing our dependencies
const neo4j = require("neo4j-driver");
const { Neo4jGraphQL } = require("@neo4j/graphql");

const driver = neo4j.driver(          ◁——————  Creating a connection
  "bolt://localhost:7687",                      to our Neo4j database
  neo4j.auth.basic("neo4j", "letmein")
);
                                       This line serves as a placeholder for our
const typeDefs = /* GraphQL */ ``;  ◁—  GraphQL type definitions to be filled in later.

const neoSchema = new Neo4jGraphQL({ typeDefs, driver });  ◁—
                                                              Passing our GraphQL
neoSchema.getSchema().then((schema) => {    Our generated     type definitions and
  const server = new ApolloServer({       ◁— GraphQL schema is  database connection
    schema                                   passed to Apollo  as we instantiate the
  });                                        Server.           Neo4jGraphQL class
  server.listen().then(({url}) => {
    console.log(`GraphQL server ready at ${url}`);    ◁—  Here we start the
  });                                                       GraphQL server.
});
```

This is the basic structure for our GraphQL API application code. The credentials used when constructing the Neo4j driver instance will depend on whether you are using Neo4j Desktop, Neo4j Sandbox, or Neo4j Aura, as well as on your initial chosen password. Be sure to adjust the connection credentials for your specific Neo4j instance.

If we tried to run our GraphQL API application now, we would quickly see an error message complaining that we haven't provided GraphQL type definitions. We must provide GraphQL type definitions that define the GraphQL API, so the next step is to fill in our GraphQL type definitions.

4.3.2 Generated GraphQL schema from type definitions

Following the GraphQL-first approach described previously, our GraphQL type definitions will drive the API specification. In this case, we know what data we want to expose (our sample dataset loaded in Neo4j), so we can refer to the table of node properties shown previously and apply a simple rule as we create our GraphQL type definitions: Node labels become types, taking on the node properties as fields. We also need to define relationship fields in our GraphQL type definitions. Let's first look at the complete type definitions in the next listing and then explore how we define relationship fields.

Listing 4.5   index.js: GraphQL type definitions

```
const typeDefs = /* GraphQL */ `
  type Business {
  businessId: ID!
  name: String!
  city: String!
  state: String!
  address: String!
  location: Point!
  reviews: [Review!]! @relationship(type: "REVIEWS", direction: IN)
  categories: [Category!]!
    @relationship(type: "IN_CATEGORY", direction: OUT)
}

type User {
  userID: ID!
  name: String!
  reviews: [Review!]! @relationship(type: "WROTE", direction: OUT)
}

type Review {
  reviewId: ID!
  stars: Float!
  date: Date!
  text: String
  user: User! @relationship(type: "WROTE", direction: IN)
  business: Business! @relationship(type: "REVIEWS", direction: OUT)
}

type Category {
  name: String!
  businesses: [Business!]!
    @relationship(type: "IN_CATEGORY", direction: IN)
}
`;
```

@RELATIONSHIP GraphQL SCHEMA DIRECTIVE

In the property graph model used by Neo4j, every relationship has a direction and type. To represent this in GraphQL, we make use of GraphQL schema directives—specifically, the @relationship schema directive. A directive is similar to an annotation in our GraphQL type definitions. It is an identifier preceded by the @ character, and may then, optionally, contain a list of named arguments. Schema directives are GraphQL's built-in extension mechanism, indicating some custom logic for the GraphQL server implementation.

NC 949 7336

When defining relationship fields using the @relationship directive, the type argument indicates the relationship type stored in Neo4j, and the direction argument indicates the relationship direction. In addition to schema directives, directives can also be used in GraphQL queries to indicate specific behavior. We will see some examples of query directives when we explore managing client state using Apollo Client in our React application.

Now, let's run our API application:

```
node index.js
```

As output, we should see the address at which our API application is listening—in this case, on port 4000 on localhost:

```
?   node index.js
GraphQL server ready at http://localhost:4000/
```

Navigate to http://localhost:4000 in your web browser, and you should see the Apollo Studio landing page. Click the *Schema* icon in the upper-left corner of Apollo Studio in GraphQL to see the fully generated API (see figure 4.4). Spend a few minutes looking through the query field descriptions, and you'll notice arguments have been added to types for things like ordering, pagination, and filtering. You can also toggle between *Reference* and *SDL* views to see the full generated GraphQL SDL, based on our initial GraphQL type definitions.

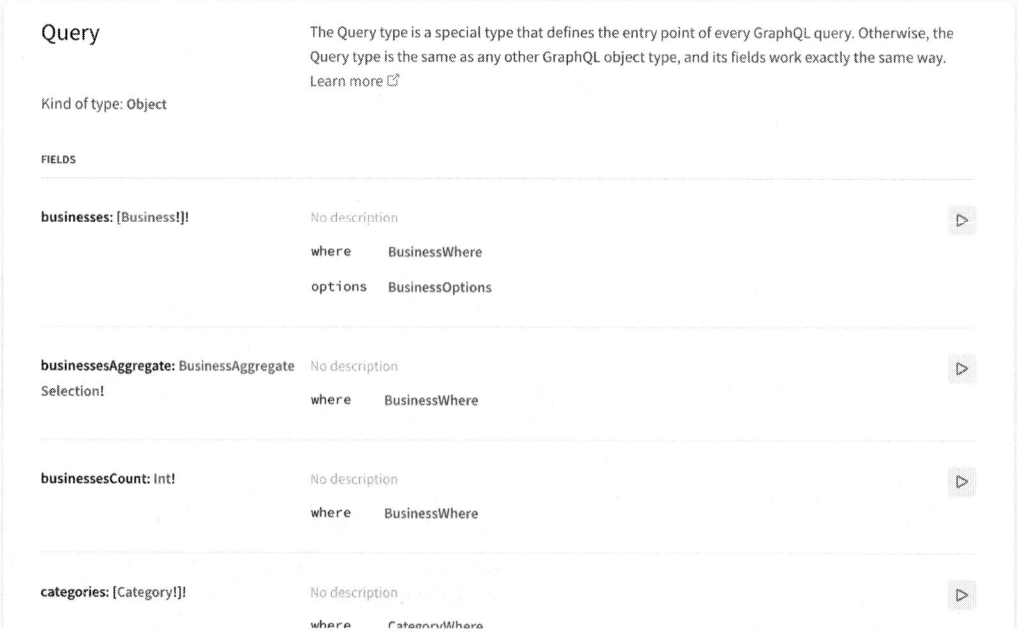

Figure 4.4   Apollo Studio showing our generated API

4.4   Basic GraphQL queries

Now that we have our GraphQL server powered by Apollo Server and the Neo4j GraphQL library up and running, let's start querying our API using Apollo Studio. Looking at the *Schema* tab in Apollo Studio, we can see the API entry points (in GraphQL parlance, each Query type field is an entry point to the API) available to us: Business, User, Review, and Category—one for each type defined in our type definitions. Let's start by querying for all businesses and returning only the name field, as the next listing shows.

Listing 4.6   GraphQL query to find all businesses

```
{
  businesses {
    name
  }
}
```

If we run this query in Apollo Studio, we should see a list of businesses names:

```
{
  "data": {
    "businesses": [
      {
        "name": "Missoula Public Library"
      },
      {
        "name": "Ninja Mike's"
      },
      {
        "name": "KettleHouse Brewing Co."
      },
      {
        "name": "Imagine Nation Brewing"
      },
      {
        "name": "Market on Front"
      },
      {
        "name": "Hanabi"
      },
      {
        "name": "Zootown Brew"
      },
      {
        "name": "Ducky's Car Wash"
      },
      {
        "name": "Neo4j"
      }
    ]
  }
}
```

Neat! This data has been fetched from our Neo4j instance for us, and we didn't even need to write any resolvers!

Let's turn on debug logging for the Neo4j GraphQL library so we can see the generated Cypher queries being sent to the database. To do this, we'll need to set a DEBUG environment variable. Let's stop our GraphQL server by pressing Ctrl-C in the terminal, and now when we start the GraphQL API application again, we'll set the DEBUG environment variable:

```
DEBUG=@neo4j/graphql:* node index.js
```

If we run our GraphQL query again and check the console output in the terminal, we can see the generated Cypher query logged to the terminal, as shown in the following listing.

Listing 4.7   Generated Cypher query

```
MATCH (`business`:`Business`)
RETURN `business` { .name } AS `business`
```

We can add additional fields to the GraphQL query, and those fields will be added to the generated Cypher query, returning only the data needed. For example, the GraphQL query adds the address of the business and the name field, as the next listing shows.

Listing 4.8   GraphQL query to return business name and address

```
{
  businesses {
    name
    address
  }
}
```

The Cypher translation of the GraphQL query now includes the address field as well, as shown in the following listing.

Listing 4.9   Generated Cypher query including address property

```
MATCH (`business`:`Business`)
RETURN `business` { .name , .address } AS `business`
```

And finally, when we examine the results of the GraphQL query, we now see an address listed for each business:

```
{
  "data": {
    "businesses": [
      {
        "name": "Missoula Public Library",
```

```
        "address": "301 E Main St"
      },
      {
        "name": "Ninja Mike's",
        "address": "200 W Pine St"
      },
      {
        "name": "KettleHouse Brewing Co.",
        "address": "313 N 1st St W"
      },
      {
        "name": "Imagine Nation Brewing",
        "address": "1151 W Broadway St"
      },
      {
        "name": "Market on Front",
        "address": "201 E Front St"
      },
      {
        "name": "Hanabi",
        "address": "723 California Dr"
      },
      {
        "name": "Zootown Brew",
        "address": "121 W Broadway St"
      },
      {
        "name": "Ducky's Car Wash",
        "address": "716 N San Mateo Dr"
      },
      {
        "name": "Neo4j",
        "address": "111 E 5th Ave"
      }
    ]
  }
}
```

Next, let's take advantage of some of the features of the generated GraphQL API.

4.5   Ordering and pagination

Each query field includes an input object argument `options`. We can specify values for `limit` and `sort` in this `options` argument to facilitate ordering and pagination. Here we search for the first three businesses ordered by the value of the `name` field.

Listing 4.10   Initial GraphQL API code including sort and limit

```
{
  businesses(options: { limit: 3, sort: { name: ASC } }) {
    name
  }
}
```

Ordering enums are generated for each type, offering ascending and descending options for each field. Running our query returns businesses now ordered by name, as shown in the next listing.

Listing 4.11   Paginated results

```
{
  "data": {
    "businesses": [
      {
        "name": "Ducky's Car Wash"
      },
      {
        "name": "Hanabi"
      },
      {
        "name": "Imagine Nation Brewing"
      }
    ]
  }
}
```

If we switch to the terminal, we can see the Cypher query generated from our GraphQL query, which now includes ORDER BY and LIMIT clauses that map to our first and orderBy GraphQL arguments, as the following listing shows. This means that the ordering and limiting is executed in the database, rather than in the client, so only the necessary data is returned from the database query.

Listing 4.12   Generated Cypher query including sort and limit

```
MATCH (`business`:`Business`)
WITH `business`
ORDER BY business.name ASC
RETURN `business` { .name } AS `business`
LIMIT toInteger($first)
```

Note that this query includes a $first parameter, rather than the value 3 inline in the query. Parameter usage is important here because it ensures a user is not able to inject potentially malicious Cypher code into the generated query and also ensures the query plan generated by Neo4j can be reused, increasing performance. To run this query in Neo4j Browser, first set a value for the first parameter with the :param command:

```
:param first => 3
```

4.6   Nested queries

Cypher can easily express the types of graph traversals in our GraphQL queries, and the Neo4j GraphQL library is capable of generating the equivalent Cypher queries for arbitrary GraphQL requests, including nested queries. Now we traverse from businesses to their categories, as the next listing shows.

Listing 4.13   GraphQL query including nested selection set

```
{
  businesses(options: { limit: 3, sort: { name: ASC } }) {
    name
    categories {
      name
    }
  }
}
```

And the result shows each business is connected to one or more categories:

```
{
  "data": {
    "businesses": [
      {
        "name": "Ducky's Car Wash",
        "categories": [
          {
            "name": "Car Wash"
          }
        ]
      },
      {
        "name": "Hanabi",
        "categories": [
          {
            "name": "Ramen"
          },
          {
            "name": "Restaurant"
          }
        ]
      },
      {
        "name": "Imagine Nation Brewing",
        "categories": [
          {
            "name": "Beer"
          },
          {
            "name": "Brewery"
          }
        ]
      }
    ]
  }
}
```

4.7   *Filtering*

The filter functionality is exposed by adding a where argument with associated inputs based on the GraphQL type definitions that expose filtering criteria. You can see the full list of filtering criteria in the documentation at neo4j.com/docs/graphql-manual/current/filtering/.

4.7.1   *where argument*

In the next listing, we use the where argument to search for businesses with names that contain Brew.

Listing 4.14   **GraphQL query filter for business names containing Brew**

```
{
  businesses(where: { name_CONTAINS: "Brew" }) {
    name
    address
  }
}
```

Our results now show businesses that match the filtering criteria, and only businesses that contain the string Brew in their name are returned:

```
{
  "data": {
    "businesses": [
      {
        "name": "KettleHouse Brewing Co.",
        "address": "313 N 1st St W"
      },
      {
        "name": "Imagine Nation Brewing",
        "address": "1151 W Broadway St"
      },
      {
        "name": "Zootown Brew",
        "address": "121 W Broadway St"
      }
    ]
  }
}
```

4.7.2   *Nested filter*

To filter based on the results of nested fields applied to the root, we can nest our filter arguments. In the next listing, we search for businesses that contain the name Brew and that have at least one review with at least a 4.75 rating.

Listing 4.15   GraphQL query using a nested filter

```
{
  businesses(
    where: { name_CONTAINS: "Brew", reviews_SOME: { stars_GTE: 4.75 } }
  ) {
    name
    address
  }
}
```

If we inspect the results of this GraphQL query, we can see two matching businesses:

```
{
  "data": {
    "businesses": [
      {
        "name": "KettleHouse Brewing Co.",
        "address": "313 N 1st St W"
      },
      {
        "name": "Zootown Brew",
        "address": "121 W Broadway St"
      }
    ]
  }
}
```

4.7.3   *Logical operators: AND, OR*

Filters can be wrapped in logical operators OR and AND. For example, we can search for
businesses in either the Coffee or Breakfast category by using an OR operator in the
filter argument, as shown in the next listing.

Listing 4.16   GraphQL query with a filter using logical operators

```
{
  businesses(
    where: {
      OR: [
        { categories_SOME: { name: "Coffee" } }
        { categories_SOME: { name: "Breakfast" } }
      ]
    }
  ) {
    name
    address
    categories {
      name
    }
  }
}
```

This GraphQL query yields businesses that are connected to either the `Coffee` or `Breakfast` category:

```
{
  "data": {
    "businesses": [
      {
        "name": "Market on Front",
        "address": "201 E Front St",
        "categories": [
          {
            "name": "Restaurant"
          },
          {
            "name": "Cafe"
          },
          {
            "name": "Coffee"
          },
          {
            "name": "Deli"
          },
          {
            "name": "Breakfast"
          }
        ]
      },
      {
        "name": "Ninja Mike's",
        "address": "200 W Pine St",
        "categories": [
          {
            "name": "Restaurant"
          },
          {
            "name": "Breakfast"
          }
        ]
      },
      {
        "name": "Zootown Brew",
        "address": "121 W Broadway St",
        "categories": [
          {
            "name": "Coffee"
          }
        ]
      }
    ]
  }
}
```

4.7.4   *Filtering in selections*

Filters can also be used throughout the selection set to apply the filter at the level of the selection. For example, let's say that in the next listing, we want to find all `Coffee` or `Breakfast` businesses but only view reviews containing the phrase `breakfast sandwich`.

Listing 4.17   GraphQL query with filter argument in the selection set

```
{
  businesses(
    where: {
      OR: [
        { categories_SOME: { name: "Coffee" } }
        { categories_SOME: { name: "Breakfast" } }
      ]
    }
  ) {
    name
    address
    reviews(where: { text_CONTAINS: "breakfast sandwich" }) {
      stars
      text
    }
  }
}
```

Since the filter was applied at the `reviews` selection, businesses that do not have any reviews containing the phrase `breakfast sandwich` are still shown in the results; however, only reviews containing that phrase are shown:

```
{
  "data": {
    "businesses": [
      {
        "name": "Market on Front",
        "address": "201 E Front St",
        "reviews": []
      },
      {
        "name": "Ninja Mike's",
        "address": "200 W Pine St",
        "reviews": [
          {
            "stars": 4,
            "text": "Best breakfast sandwich at the Farmer's Market."
          }
        ]
      },
      {
        "name": "Zootown Brew",
        "address": "121 W Broadway St",
```

```
      "reviews": []
    }
  ]
}
}
```

4.8 Working with temporal fields

Neo4j supports native temporal types as properties on nodes and relationships. These types include `Date`, `DateTime`, and `LocalDateTime`. With the Neo4j GraphQL library, you can use these temporal types in your GraphQL schema.

4.8.1 Using a Date type in queries

We're using a `Date` type on the `Review` type. The `Date` type is represented by a string with the format `yyyy-mm-dd` but is stored as a native `Date` type in the database with support for date operations. Let's query for the three most recent reviews in the next listing.

> **Listing 4.18   GraphQL query using a date field**

```
{
  reviews(options: { limit: 3, sort: { date: DESC } }) {
    stars
    date
    business {
      name
    }
  }
}
```

Since we specified the date field in our selection set, we see that in the results:

```
{
  "data": {
    "reviews": [
      {
        "stars": 3,
        "date": "2018-09-10",
        "business": {
          "name": "Imagine Nation Brewing"
        }
      },
      {
        "stars": 5,
        "date": "2018-08-11",
        "business": {
          "name": "Zootown Brew"
        }
      },
      {
        "stars": 4,
```

```
      "date": "2018-03-24",
      "business": {
        "name": "Market on Front"
      }
    }
  ]
}
}
```

4.8.2 Date and DateTime filters

Temporal fields are also included in the generated filtering enums, allowing for filtering using dates and date ranges. In the next listing, let's search for reviews created before January 1, 2017.

Listing 4.19 GraphQL query using a date filter

```
{
  reviews(
    where: { date_LTE: "2017-01-01" }
    options: { limit: 3, sort: { date: DESC } }
  ) {
    stars
    date
    business {
      name
    }
  }
}
```

We can see that the results are now ordered by the date field:

```
{
  "data": {
    "reviews": [
      {
        "stars": 5,
        "date": "2016-11-21",
        "business": {
          "name": "Hanabi"
        }
      },
      {
        "stars": 5,
        "date": "2016-07-14",
        "business": {
          "name": "KettleHouse Brewing Co."
        }
      },
      {
        "stars": 5,
        "date": "2016-03-04",
        "business": {
```

```
               "name": "Ducky's Car Wash"
            }
          }
        ]
      }
    }
```

4.9   Working with spatial data

Neo4j currently supports the spatial point type, which can represent both 2D (e.g., latitude and longitude) and 3D (e.g., x,y,z or latitude, longitude, height) points, using both geographic coordinate reference systems (e.g., latitude and longitude) and Cartesian coordinate reference systems. The Neo4j GraphQL library makes available two spatial types: `Point`, for points using the geographic coordinate reference system, and `CartesianPoint`, for points using the Cartesian coordinate reference system. You can read more about working with spatial data in the Neo4j GraphQL library in this documentation: http://mng.bz/qYKA.

4.9.1   The Point type in selections

`Point` type fields are object fields in the GraphQL schema, so let's retrieve the latitude and longitude fields for our matching businesses by adding those fields to our selection set in the next listing.

> **Listing 4.20   GraphQL query using a `Point` field**

```
{
  businesses(options: { limit: 3, sort: { name: ASC } }) {
    name
    location {
      latitude
      longitude
    }
  }
}
```

Now, in the GraphQL query result, we see longitude and latitude included for each business:

```
{
  "data": {
    "businesses": [
      {
        "name": "Ducky's Car Wash",
        "location": {
          "latitude": 37.575968,
          "longitude": -122.336041
        }
      },
      {
        "name": "Hanabi",
```

```
        "location": {
          "latitude": 37.582598,
          "longitude": -122.351519
        }
      },
      {
        "name": "Imagine Nation Brewing",
        "location": {
          "latitude": 46.876672,
          "longitude": -114.009628
        }
      }
    ]
  }
}
```

4.9.2 Distance filter

When querying using point data, we often want to find things that are close to other things. For example, what businesses are within 1.5 km of me? We can accomplish this using the generated where argument, as the following listing shows.

Listing 4.21 GraphQL query using a distance filter

```
{
  businesses(
    where: {
      location_LT: {
        distance: 3500
        point: { latitude: 37.563675, longitude: -122.322243 }
      }
    }
  ) {
    name
    address
    city
    state
  }
}
```

For points using the geographic coordinate reference system (latitude and longitude), distance is measured in meters:

```
{
  "data": {
    "businesses": [
      {
        "name": "Hanabi",
        "address": "723 California Dr",
        "city": "Burlingame",
        "state": "CA"
      },
      {
```

```
            "name": "Ducky's Car Wash",
            "address": "716 N San Mateo Dr",
            "city": "San Mateo",
            "state": "CA"
        },
        {
            "name": "Neo4j",
            "address": "111 E 5th Ave",
            "city": "San Mateo",
            "state": "CA"
        }
    ]
  }
}
```

4.10   *Adding custom logic to our GraphQL API*

So far, we've seen basic querying operations created by the Neo4j GraphQL library. Often, we want to add custom logic to our API. For example, we may want to calculate the most popular business or recommend businesses to users. There are two options for adding custom logic to your API using the Neo4j GraphQL library: the @cypher schema directive or implementing custom resolvers.

4.10.1 *The @cypher GraphQL schema directive*

The Neo4j GraphQL library exposes Cypher through GraphQL via the @cypher GraphQL schema directive. Annotate a field in your schema with the @cypher directive to map the results of that query to the annotated GraphQL field. The @cypher directive takes a single argument statement, which is a Cypher statement. Parameters are passed into this query at runtime, including this, which is the currently resolved node, as well as any field-level arguments defined in the GraphQL type definition.

> **NOTE** The @cypher directive and other features of the Neo4j GraphQL library require the use of the APOC standard library plugin. Be sure you've followed the steps to install APOC in the Project Setup section of this chapter.

COMPUTED SCALAR FIELDS

We can use the @cypher directive to define a custom scalar field, creating a computed field in our schema. In the next listing, we add an averageStars field to the Business type, which calculates the average stars of all reviews for the business, using the this variable.

> **Listing 4.22   index.js: Adding the averageStars field**

```
type Business {
  businessId: ID!
  averageStars: Float!
    @cypher(
      statement: "MATCH (this)<-[:REVIEWS]-(r:Review) RETURN avg(r.stars)"
    )
```

```
    name: String!
    city: String!
    state: String!
    address: String!
    location: Point!
    reviews: [Review!]! @relationship(type: "REVIEWS", direction: IN)
    categories: [Category!]!
      @relationship(type: "IN_CATEGORY", direction: OUT)
}
```

We need to restart our GraphQL server, since we have modified the type definitions:

```
DEBUG=@neo4j/graphql:* node index.js
```

Now let's include the `averageStars` field in our GraphQL query in the next listing.

Listing 4.23   GraphQL query, including `averageStars` field

```
{
  businesses {
    name
    averageStars
  }
}
```

We can see in the results that the computed value for `averageStars` is now included:

```
{
  "data": {
    "Business": [
      {
        "name": "Hanabi",
        "averageStars": 5
      },
      {
        "name": "Zootown Brew",
        "averageStars": 5
      },
      {
        "name": "Ninja Mike's",
        "averageStars": 4.5
      }
    ]
  }
}
```

If we check the terminal output to see the generated Cypher query, we will notice that the generated Cypher query includes the annotated Cypher query from our `@cypher` directive as a subquery, preserving the single database call to resolve the GraphQL request but still including our custom logic!

COMPUTED OBJECT AND ARRAY FIELDS

We can also use the @cypher schema directive to resolve object and array fields. Let's add a recommended business field to the Business type. We'll use a simple Cypher query to find common businesses that other users reviewed. For example, if a user likes Market on Front, we could recommend other businesses that were also reviewed by users who reviewed Market on Front.

Listing 4.24   Cypher query to find recommended businesses

```
MATCH (b:Business)<-[:REVIEWS]-(:Review)<-[:WROTE]-(u:User)
WHERE b.name = "Market on Front"
MATCH (u)-[:WROTE]->(:Review)-[:REVIEWS]->(rec:Business)
WITH rec, COUNT(*) AS score
RETURN rec ORDER BY score DESC
```

We can make use of this Cypher query in our GraphQL schema by including it in a @cypher directive on the recommended field in our Business type definition.

Listing 4.25   index.js: Adding the recommended field

```
type Business {
  businessId: ID!
  averageStars: Float!
    @cypher(
      statement: "MATCH (this)<-[:REVIEWS]-(r:Review) RETURN avg(r.stars)"
    )
  recommended(first: Int = 1): [Business!]!
    @cypher(
      statement: """
      MATCH (this)<-[:REVIEWS]-(:Review)<-[:WROTE]-(u:User)
      MATCH (u)-[:WROTE]->(:Review)-[:REVIEWS]->(rec:Business)
      WITH rec, COUNT(*) AS score
      RETURN rec ORDER BY score DESC LIMIT $first
      """
    )
  name: String!
  city: String!
  state: String!
  address: String!
  location: Point!
  reviews: [Review!]! @relationship(type: "REVIEWS", direction: IN)
  categories: [Category!]!
    @relationship(type: "IN_CATEGORY", direction: OUT)
}
```

We also define a first field argument, which is passed to the Cypher query included in the @cypher directive as a Cypher parameter and acts as a limit on the number of recommended businesses returned.

CUSTOM TOP-LEVEL QUERY FIELDS

Another helpful way to use the @cypher directive is as a custom query or mutation field. For example, let's see how we can add full-text query support to search for businesses. Applications often use full-text search to correct for things like misspellings in user input using fuzzy matching. In Neo4j, we can use full-text search by first creating a full-text index.

Listing 4.26   Cypher: Creating full-text index

```
CREATE FULLTEXT INDEX businessNameIndex FOR (b:Business) ON EACH [b.name]
```

Then, to query the index in this case we misspell libary, but including the ~ character enables fuzzy matching, ensuring we still find what we're looking for.

Listing 4.27   Cypher: Querying the full-text index

```
CALL db.index.fulltext.queryNodes("businessNameIndex", "libary~")
```

Wouldn't it be nice to include this fuzzy-matching full-text search in our GraphQL API? To do that, let's create a query field, called fuzzyBusinessByName, which takes a search string and searches for businesses, as shown in the following listing.

Listing 4.28   index.js: Adding a custom Query field

```
type Query {
  fuzzyBusinessByName(searchString: String): [Business]
    @cypher(
      statement: """
      CALL
      db.index.fulltext.queryNodes('businessNameIndex', $searchString+'~')
      YIELD node RETURN node
      """
    )
}
```

Again, since we've updated the type definitions, we must restart the GraphQL API application:

```
DEBUG=@neo4j/graphql:* node index.js
```

If we check the *Schema* tab in Apollo Studio, we will see a new Query field, fuzzyBusinessByName, and we can now search for business names using this fuzzy matching, as the next listing shows.

Listing 4.29   GraphQL query using our custom Query field

```
{
  fuzzyBusinessByName(searchString: "libary") {
    name
  }
}
```

Since we are using full-text search, even though we spelled libary incorrectly, we still find matching results:

```
{
  "data": {
    "fuzzyBusinessByName": [
      {
        "name": "Missoula Public Library"
      }
    ]
  }
}
```

The @cypher schema directive is a powerful way to add custom logic and advanced functionality to our GraphQL API. We can also use the @cypher directive for authorization features, accessing values, such as authorization tokens, from the request object—a pattern that will be discussed in a later chapter when we explore different options for adding authorization to our API. You can read more about the @cypher GraphQL schema directive in the documentation: http://mng.bz/7yom.

4.10.2   *Implementing custom resolvers*

While the @cypher directive is one way to add custom logic, in some cases we may need to implement custom resolvers that implement logic that is unable to be expressed in Cypher. For example, we may need to fetch data from another system or apply some custom validation rules. In these cases, we can implement a custom resolver and attach it to the GraphQL schema, so that resolver is called to resolve our custom field instead of relying on the Cypher query generated by the Neo4j GraphQL library to resolve the field.

   In our example, let's imagine there is an external system that can be used to determine current wait times at businesses. We want to add an additional waitTime field to the Business type in our schema and implement the resolver logic for this field to use this external system.

   To do this, we first add the field to our schema, adding the @ignore directive to ensure the field is excluded from the generated Cypher query, as the next listing shows. This is our way of telling the Neo4j GraphQL library that a custom resolver will be responsible for resolving this field, and we don't expect it to be fetched from the database automatically.

Listing 4.30   index.js: Adding the `waitTime` field

```
type Business {
  businessId: ID!
  waitTime: Int! @ignore
  averageStars: Float!
    @cypher(
      statement: "MATCH (this)<-[:REVIEWS]-(r:Review) RETURN avg(r.stars)"
    )
  name: String!
  city: String!
  state: String!
  address: String!
  location: Point!
  reviews: [Review!]! @relationship(type: "REVIEWS", direction: IN)
  categories: [Category!]! @relationship(type: "IN_CATEGORY", direction: OUT)
}
```

Next, we create a resolver map with our custom resolver, as shown in listing 4.31. We didn't have to create this previously because the Neo4j GraphQL library generated our resolvers for us. Our wait time calculation will involve just selecting a value at random, but we could implement any custom logic here to determine the `waitTime` value, such as making a request to a third-party API.

Listing 4.31   index.js: Creating a resolver map

```
const resolvers = {
  Business: {
    waitTime: (obj, args, context, info) => {
      const options = [0, 5, 10, 15, 30, 45];
      return options[Math.floor(Math.random() * options.length)];
    }
  }
};
```

Then, we add this resolver map to the parameters passed to the `Neo4jGraphQL` constructor, as the following listing shows.

Listing 4.32   index.js: Generating the GraphQL schema

```
const neoSchema = new Neo4jGraphQL({typeDefs, resolvers, driver})
```

Now, we restart the GraphQL API application, since we've updated the code:

```
DEBUG=@neo4j/graphql:* node index.js
```

After restarting, in Apollo Studio, if we check the schema for the business type, we will see our new field `waitTime` on the `Business` type. In the next listing, let's search for restaurants and see what their wait times are by including the `waitTime` field in the selection set.

Listing 4.33   GraphQL query using field with custom resolver

```
{
  businesses(where: { categories_SOME: { name: "Restaurant" } }) {
    name
    waitTime
  }
}
```

In the results, we now see a value for the wait time. Your results will, of course, vary, since the value is randomized:

```
{
  "data": {
    "businesses": [
      {
        "name": "Ninja Mike's",
        "waitTime": 30
      },
      {
        "name": "Market on Front",
        "waitTime": 5
      },
      {
        "name": "Hanabi",
        "waitTime": 45
      }
    ]
  }
}
```

4.11   *Introspecting GraphQL schema from an existing database*

Typically, when we start a new application, we don't have an existing database and follow the GraphQL-first development paradigm by starting with type definitions. However, in some cases, we may have an existing Neo4j database populated with data. In those cases, it can be convenient to generate GraphQL type definitions based on the existing database that can then be fed into the Neo4j GraphQL library to generate a GraphQL API for the existing database. We can do this with the use of the @neo4j/ introspector package.

First, we'll need to install the @neo4j/introspector package:

```
npm i @neo4j/introspector
```

This Node.js script will connect to our Neo4j database and introspect the GraphQL type definitions that describe this data, as shown in the next listing; then we will write those type definitions to a file named schema.graphql.

Listing 4.34   intropect.js: Introspecting GraphQL type definitions

```
const { toGraphQLTypeDefs } = require("@neo4j/introspector");
const neo4j = require("neo4j-driver");
const fs = require("fs");
const driver = neo4j.driver(
  "neo4j://localhost:7687",
  neo4j.auth.basic("neo4j", "letmein")
);
const sessionFactory = () =>
  driver.session({ defaultAccessMode: neo4j.session.READ });
// We create a async function here so we can use async/await
async function main() {
  const typeDefs = await toGraphQLTypeDefs(sessionFactory);
  fs.writeFileSync("schema.graphql", typeDefs);
  await driver.close();
}
main();
```

Then, we can load this schema.graphql file and pass the type definitions to the Neo4j-GraphQL constructor as the following listing shows.

Listing 4.35   Loading our GraphQL type definitions from schema.graphql

```
// Load GraphQL type definitions from schema.graphql file
const typeDefs = fs
  .readFileSync(path.join(__dirname, "schema.graphql"))
  .toString("utf-8");
```

So far, all of our GraphQL querying has been done using Apollo Studio, which is great for testing and development, but typically, our goal is to build an application that queries the GraphQL API. In the next few chapters, we'll start to build out the user interface for our business reviews application using React and Apollo Client. Along the way, we will learn more about GraphQL concepts, such as mutations, fragments, interface types, and more!

4.12   Exercises

1   Query the GraphQL API we created in this chapter, using Apollo Studio to find
   – Which users have reviewed the business named Hanabi.
   – Find any reviews that contain the word comfortable. What businesses are they reviewing?
   – Which users have given no 5-star reviews?
2   Add a @cypher directive field to the Category type that computes the number of businesses in each category. How many businesses are in the Coffee category?

3   Create a Neo4j Sandbox instance at https://sandbox.neo4j.com, choosing from any of the prepopulated datasets. Using the `@neo4j/introspector` package, create a GraphQL API for this Neo4j Sandbox instance without manually writing GraphQL type definitions. What data can you query for using GraphQL?

Refer to the book's GitHub repository to see the exercise solutions: http://mng.bz/mOYP.

Summary

- Common problems that arise when building GraphQL APIs include the $n + 1$ query problem, schema duplication, and a large amount of boilerplate data-fetching code.
- GraphQL database integrations, like the Neo4j GraphQL library, can help mitigate these problems by generating database queries from GraphQL requests, driving database schema from GraphQL type definitions, and autogenerating a GraphQL API from GraphQL type definitions.
- The Neo4j GraphQL library makes it easy to build GraphQL APIs backed by a Neo4j database by generating resolvers for data fetching and adding filtering, ordering, and pagination to the generated API.
- Custom logic can be added to our GraphQL API by using the `@cypher` schema directive to define custom logic for fields or by implementing custom resolvers and attaching them to the GraphQL schema.
- If we have an existing Neo4j database, we can use the `@neo4j/introspector` package to generate GraphQL type definitions and a GraphQL API on top of the existing database.

Part 2

Building the frontend

In part 1, we focused on the backend of our application, exploring the Neo4j graph database and building our GraphQL API using the Neo4j GraphQL library. Now, it's time to build the frontend React application.

In chapter 5, we will look at the React framework and concepts important for working with React as we begin building our frontend application. Then, in chapter 6, we add data fetching and client state management with React and GraphQL as we pull in data from the GraphQL API we built in previous chapters. After completing part 2, we will have a functioning initial version of our business review application and will be ready to explore adding authorization and deployment in part 3.

Building user interfaces
with React

5

This chapter covers

- An overview of the fundamental concepts of React
- Getting started with React, using the Create React App CLI tool
- Working with state in a React application, using React Hooks

So far in the book, we've been focused on the backend aspects of our application: building the GraphQL API and working with the database. Now it's time to turn our attention to the frontend. In chapter 1, we got a very brief overview of React and looked at a minimal code snippet of a React component. In this chapter, we return to React and begin building a React application that will be a client of our GraphQL API, searching for businesses and rendering results in the browser. Of course, it would be impossible to include everything you need to know for an introduction to React in a single chapter, so rather than aiming to provide a comprehensive introduction to React, the goal of this chapter is to explain the fundamental concepts of React that are necessary to get started building a simple application. We offer an opinionated approach to getting started, using the Create React App command-line tool. For more in-depth coverage of React, you may be interested in the documentation and tutorials found at https://reactjs.org/.

In this chapter, we will attempt to create the skeleton of our React application, using Create React App to handle build tooling and configuration. We'll then update the template application, creating the components necessary to search for businesses by category and view the results. Initially, our data will just be hardcoded in the application; then, in chapter 6, we'll add data-fetching logic to the React application, connecting the GraphQL API we created in previous chapters using Apollo Client (see figure 5.1). Let's get started!

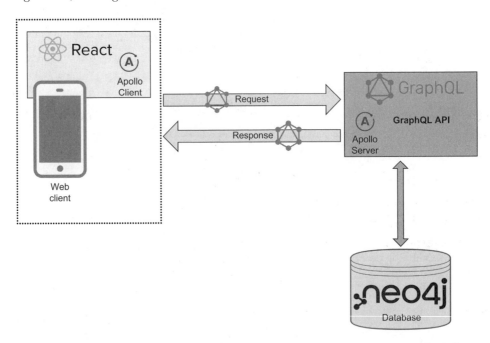

Figure 5.1   **This chapter focuses on building the React application that will become a client of our GraphQL API.**

5.1   *React overview*

React is fundamentally a JavaScript library for building user interfaces (UIs). React can be used to build UIs for the web (ReactDOM), native mobile applications (React Native), and other interfaces, such as virtual reality (React VR). React uses the concept of *components* to encapsulate model data and logic. Components can be reused and composed together to build complex UIs but provide a standard abstraction to help developers reason about their applications. Important React concepts to understand include JSX, React elements, props, state, hooks, and component hierarchy.

5.1.1   JSX and React elements

In React, an *element* is the most fundamental building block. Elements should not be confused with components; rather, components are composed of React elements. You can think of an element as something you might see visually displayed in the user interface. For example, consider the simple React element in the following listing.

Listing 5.1   A simple React element defined with JSX

```
const element = <h1>Welcome to GRANDstack</h1>;
```

At first glance, this appears to be an HTML snippet but with hints of JavaScript. In fact, this is a JSX example. JSX is used to create React elements.

> **NOTE** JSX is not required for working with React; however, using JSX is highly recommended, and the alternatives will not be covered in this book.

You can think of JSX as a combination of HTML and JavaScript. We can use JavaScript expressions within JSX by wrapping expressions in curly braces. For example, if we wanted to personalize our *Welcome to GRANDstack* greeting, we could use a JavaScript variable to define the name of the user.

Listing 5.2   Using JavaScript expressions within JSX

```
const name = "Bob Loblaw";
const element = <h1>Welcome to GRANDstack, {name}!</h1>
```

During build time, JSX is compiled into JavaScript and uses the `React.create-Element()` JavaScript function to create React elements, which are fundamentally represented as JavaScript objects that are rendered to the DOM.

React elements are important because they help React maintain what is called the virtual DOM—a representation of the DOM that allows React to apply DOM updates to the desired state. This means that rather than rerendering the entire DOM when the application changes, React only rerenders the pieces necessary.

5.1.2   React components

React allows us to construct the UI using smaller, reusable, composable pieces called *components*. Components are essentially functions that accept an input (*props*, or properties) and return React elements that make up the UI and are the building blocks of a React application. Listing 5.3 shows an example.

> **NOTE** We will only use functional React components. You may see references to so-called React class components; however, with the introduction of the React `Hooks` class, components are no longer required.

Listing 5.3   A simple React component

```
function Greeting(props) {
  return <h1>Welcome to GRANDstack, {props.name}</h1>;
}
```

Components make use of two types of model data: *props* and *state*. Props are immutable; if we need to change values within our component that should trigger a rerender, then we need to work with state data.

5.1.3   Component hierarchy

React components can be composed of other components. This allows us to encapsulate and reuse logical components as we build our UI.

Listing 5.4   Composing React components

```
function Greeting(props) {
  return <h1>Welcome to GRANDstack, {props.name}</h1>;
}

function Popup() {
  const name = "Bob Loblaw";
  return <Greeting name={name} />
}
```

5.2   Create React App

Create React App is a command-line tool for creating React applications. It bundles together build tooling and requires no initial configuration. It is the easiest way to get started with React, as it automatically configures webpack, Babel, ESLint, and other tools, allowing developers to start writing React applications without struggling to set up and configure build tooling. You can learn more about Create React App at create -react-app.dev/.

5.2.1   Creating a React application with Create React App

Let's create a React application using Create React App. We'll do this in the directory alongside api, where we've been building our GraphQL API. We'll start by building some initial functionality for our business review application, starting with a business search. The initial version of our React application should allow the user to search for businesses by category and display business details. For now, we'll hardcode our data in a JavaScript object; then, in the next chapter, we'll connect the React application to our GraphQL API as a data source. To get started with Create React App, run the following command in the terminal at the directory level, alongside the API directory with our GraphQL API code:

```
npx create-react-app web-react --use-npm
```

The command npx is included with npm as of version 5.2.0, and can be used for executing npm packages and commands. One great feature of npx is that it will automatically download the package for us if we don't have it installed locally, ensuring that we always run the latest version.

So far, we've been using npm; by default, Create React App uses the yarn package manager CLI, so we'll use the --use-npm command flag when calling create-react-app. After running this command, we should see output telling us we've created a new React project and some helpful commands we can use to get started with our project:

```
Success! Created web-react at /Users/lyonwj/business-reviews/web-react
Inside that directory, you can run several commands:

  npm start
    Starts the development server.

  npm run build
    Bundles the app into static files for production.

  npm test
    Starts the test runner.

  npm run eject
    Removes this tool and copies build dependencies, configuration files
    and scripts into the app directory. If you do this, you can't go back!

We suggest that you begin by typing:

  cd web-react
  npm start

Happy hacking!
```

Let's take a look at what Create React App has created for us:

```
.
├── README.md
├── package-lock.json
├── package.json
├── public
│   ├── favicon.ico
│   ├── index.html
│   ├── logo192.png
│   ├── logo512.png
│   ├── manifest.json
│   └── robots.txt
└── src
    ├── App.css
    ├── App.js
    ├── App.test.js
    ├── index.css
    ├── index.js
    ├── logo.svg
```

```
      ├──  serviceWorker.js
      └──  setupTests.js
└──  node_modules
      ├──  ...
```

The README.md file contains comprehensive documentation for working with the React application we've just created and Create React App. The node_modules directory contains all the dependencies of our application, which were installed automatically. Inside the public directory, we can find static content that is served from the root when our application is started. In the src directory, we'll find the JavaScript and CSS code that defines a skeleton React application. First, let's examine the package.json file in the next listing to see the dependencies included and the scripts that are available.

Listing 5.5   package.json

```json
{
  "name": "web-react",
  "version": "0.1.0",
  "private": true,
  "dependencies": {
    "@testing-library/jest-dom": "^5.15.1",
    "@testing-library/react": "^11.2.7",
    "@testing-library/user-event": "^12.8.3",
    "react": "^17.0.2",
    "react-dom": "^17.0.2",
    "react-scripts": "4.0.3",
    "web-vitals": "^1.1.2"
  },
  "scripts": {
    "start": "react-scripts start",
    "build": "react-scripts build",
    "test": "react-scripts test",
    "eject": "react-scripts eject"
  },
  "eslintConfig": {
    "extends": [
      "react-app",
      "react-app/jest"
    ]
  },
  "browserslist": {
    "production": [
      ">0.2%",
      "not dead",
      "not op_mini all"
    ],
    "development": [
      "last 1 chrome version",
      "last 1 firefox version",
      "last 1 safari version"
    ]
  }
}
```

We can see the dependencies of our application included so far: the React library as well as a package called `react-scripts`. The `react-scripts` package is used to start, run, build, and test our application, as we can see in the "scripts" section of the package.json file. Let's go ahead and run our application:

```
cd web-react
npm start
```

The `npm start` command creates a development build of the application and starts a local webserver serving our React application. A watcher is used, so any changes we make to the source files trigger a live reload of the application; this means we typically won't need to restart the web server after making changes to the code to see our changes reflected in the application:

```
Compiled successfully!

You can now view web-react in the browser.

  Local:            http://localhost:3000
  On Your Network:  http://192.168.1.3:3000

Note that the development build is not optimized.
To create a production build, use npm run build.
```

If running our application is successful, we see a message telling us how to open our application in a web browser (see figure 5.2).

Figure 5.2   Our initial React application running in the web

Let's open that src/App.js file and look at our initial application in the next listing.

Listing 5.6   src/App.js: Initial code

```
import logo from './logo.svg';
import './App.css';

function App() {
  return (
    <div className="App">
      <header className="App-header">
        <img src={logo} className="App-logo" alt="logo" />
        <p>
          Edit <code>src/App.js</code> and save to reload.
        </p>
        <a
          className="App-link"
          href="https://reactjs.org"
          target="_blank"
          rel="noopener noreferrer"
        >
          Learn React
        </a>
      </header>
    </div>
  );
}

export default App;
```

We are exporting an App component, but where is it used? If we open src/ index.js, we can see how the App component is used (see the next listing). It is passed to React-DOM.render, telling ReactDOM to render the App component in an HTML element with the ID of root.

Listing 5.7   src/index.js

```
import React from 'react';
import ReactDOM from 'react-dom';
import './index.css';
import App from './App';
import reportWebVitals from './reportWebVitals';

ReactDOM.render(
  <React.StrictMode>
    <App />
  </React.StrictMode>,
  document.getElementById('root')
);

// If you want to start measuring performance in your app, pass a function
// to log results (for example: reportWebVitals(console.log))
```

```
// or send to an analytics endpoint. Learn more: https://bit.ly/CRA-vitals
reportWebVitals();
```

Let's update the src/App.js file in the next listing. To start off, we'll create a simple form with a select dropdown to search for businesses by category.

Listing 5.8   src/App.js: Adding sample data and a simple form

```
const businesses = [                          ◁──────────   For now, our business data is
  {                                                          defined as a JavaScript array.
    businessId: "b1",
    name: "San Mateo Public Library",
    address: "55 W 3rd Ave",
    category: "Library",
  },
  {
    businessId: "b2",
    name: "Ducky's Car Wash",
    address: "716 N San Mateo Dr",
    category: "Car Wash",
  },
  {
    businessId: "b3",
    name: "Hanabi",
    address: "723 California Dr",
    category: "Restaurant",
  },
];                             Our React component is at the top of the
                               component hierarchy and is not passed any
function App() {    ◁───────   props data; therefore, it takes no arguments.
  return (
    <div>
      <h1>Business Search</h1>
      <form>
        <label>
          Select Business Category:
          <select value="All">
            <option value="All">All</option>
            <option value="Library">Library</option>
            <option value="Restaurant">Restaurant</option>
            <option value="Car Wash">Car Wash</option>
          </select>
        </label>
        <input type="submit" value="Submit" />
      </form>

      <h2>Results</h2>
      <table>
        <thead>
          <tr>
            <th>Name</th>
            <th>Address</th>
            <th>Category</th>
          </tr>
```

```
      </thead>
      <tbody>
        {businesses.map((b, i) => (        ◁────┐   We map over our businesses array,
          <tr key={i}>                              creating a row in the table for each
            <td>{b.name}</td>                        business.
            <td>{b.address}</td>
            <td>{b.category}</td>
          </tr>
        ))}
      </tbody>
    </table>
  </div>
  );
}
```

```
export default App;
```

For now, we just define our businesses as a JavaScript array, but later we'll need to pop-ulate our application with data from our GraphQL API. Initially, all results are dis-played in a simple HTML table (see figure 5.3).

Business Search

Select Business Category: [All ⌄] [Submit]

Results

Name	Address	Category
San Mateo Public Library	55 W 3rd Ave	Library
Ducky's Car Wash	716 N San Mateo Dr	Car Wash
Hanabi	723 California Dr	Restaurant

Figure 5.3   Our React application after updating src/App.js

We render a table, but our form doesn't really work. We can't select a category, and nothing changes in our table when we try. Let's update our app to filter results based on the category we've selected. To do that, we need to understand state, and along the way, we'll learn about props! Since we're exclusively using functional React compo-nents, we'll need to make use of React Hooks to work with state.

5.3   State and React Hooks

React Hooks were introduced in React version 16.8 and provide a way of working with state (and other React concepts) while keeping React components as functions instead of classes. Previously, you may have seen React class components that included calls to a setState function, lifecycle methods, and constructors. With Hooks, none of that is required; instead, we can manage state through single function calls.

We'll introduce Hooks in a hands-on way, updating our React application to add filtering functionality to allow us to filter our result table for businesses by category. Along the way, we'll see how to use the State React Hook to manage state within our component.

Let's create a new React component that will be responsible for rendering our result table, called `BusinessResults`. To do that, first create a new file called Business-Results.js in the same directory as App.js, as shown in the next listing.

Listing 5.9 src/BusinessResults.js

```
function BusinessResults(props) {            ◁──┐  The component is passed
  const { businesses } = props;    ◁──────────┘  props data as an argument.

  return (
    <div>
      <h2>Results</h2>                          The props argument contains the business
      <table>                                   data to be rendered in the result table.
        <thead>
          <tr>
            <th>Name</th>
            <th>Address</th>
            <th>Category</th>
          </tr>
        </thead>
        <tbody>
          {businesses.map((b, i) => (
            <tr key={i}>
              <td>{b.name}</td>
              <td>{b.address}</td>
              <td>{b.category}</td>
            </tr>
          ))}
        </tbody>
      </table>
    </div>
  );
}

export default BusinessResults;
```

We move the result table into this src/BusinessResults.js file, passing in the businesses to be rendered by the component as props. Instead of rendering all businesses to the table, the component renders whatever data is passed through the props argument. Now, in our `App` component, we can import this new `BusinessResults` component and pass our array of business data as props to the component, as shown next.

Listing 5.10 src/App.js: Using the `BusinessResults` component

```
import BusinessResults from "./BusinessResults";   ◁──┐  Importing the BusinessResults
                                                      │  component
const businesses = [
```

```
    {
      businessId: "b1",
      name: "San Mateo Public Library",
      address: "55 W 3rd Ave",
      category: "Library",
    },
    {
      businessId: "b2",
      name: "Ducky's Car Wash",
      address: "716 N San Mateo Dr",
      category: "Car Wash",
    },
    {
      businessId: "b3",
      name: "Hanabi",
      address: "723 California Dr",
      category: "Restaurant",
    },
];

function App() {
  return (
    <div>
      <h1>Business Search</h1>
      <form>
        <label>
          Select Business Category:
          <select value="All">
            <option value="All">All</option>
            <option value="Library">Library</option>
            <option value="Restaurant">Restaurant</option>
            <option value="Car Wash">Car Wash</option>
          </select>
        </label>
        <input type="submit" value="Submit" />
      </form>

      <BusinessResults businesses={businesses} />    ◁─┐  Passing the businesses array as
    </div>                                              │  props to the BusinessResults
  );                                                    │  component
}

export default App;
```

We've imported a new component, BusinessResults, and we're passing in our businesses array, so the BusinessResults component can take care of rendering the results. Our App component now just needs to concern itself with allowing the user to choose the category to search.

After making this change, our application looks exactly the same in the web browser, and our select form still doesn't work. In the next listing, let's make our dropdown actually do something!

Listing 5.11   src/App.js: Using a state variable

```
import React, { useState } from "react";        ⟵—— Import the useState hook.
import BusinessResults from "./BusinessResults";

const businesses = [
  {
    businessId: "b1",
    name: "San Mateo Public Library",
    address: "55 W 3rd Ave",
    category: "Library",
  },
  {
    businessId: "b2",
    name: "Ducky's Car Wash",
    address: "716 N San Mateo Dr",
    category: "Car Wash",
  },
  {
    businessId: "b3",
    name: "Hanabi",
    address: "723 California Dr",
    category: "Restaurant",
  },
];
```

Call the useState hook to create a new state variable and the function to update its value.

```
function App() {

  const [selectedCategory, setSelectedCategory] = useState("All");     ⟵—┐

  return (
    <div>
      <h1>Business Search</h1>
      <form>
        <label>
          Select Business Category:
          <select
           value={selectedCategory}        ⟵—┐
           onChange={(event) => setSelectedCategory(event.target.value)}  ⟵—┐
          >
            <option value="All">All</option>
            <option value="Library">Library</option>
            <option value="Restaurant">Restaurant</option>
            <option value="Car Wash">Car Wash</option>
          </select>
        </label>
        <input type="submit" value="Submit" />
      </form>

      <BusinessResults
        businesses={
          selectedCategory === "All"
            ? businesses
            : businesses.filter((b) => {
                return b.category === selectedCategory;
```

Bind the selected value of the dropdown to our new state variable.

Update the value of our state variable when the user selects a new option in the form.

```
                    })
            }
          />      ◄
        </div>
      );
    }
```

Filter the business results passed to the BusinessResults component based on the selected category.

```
export default App;
```

First, we import the `useState` hook and use it to create a new state variable `selected-Category`. The call to `useState` also returns a function (which we call `setSelected-Category`) that is used to update the value of `selectedCategory`. We bind this variable to the selected option of the select input by passing `selectedCategory` for the `value` prop to the `select` element and using the `setSelectedCategory` function to update the value of `selectedCategory` when a new option is selected. Now the user can select a value in the form and see the result table showing only businesses in the selected category (see figure 5.4).

Business Search

Select Business Category | All ✓ Library | Restaurant | Car Wash | Submit

Results

Name	Address	Category
San Mateo Public Library	55 W 3rd Ave	Library

Figure 5.4   Our React application after adding state and filtering functionality

Now that we have a very basic React application, our next step will be adding data-fetching functionality to connect to our GraphQL API. We'll do that in the next chapter, using Apollo Client React Hooks, and explore more React functionality along the way!

5.4   Exercises

1 Move the search logic into a new component called `BusinessSearch`, and render that component from within the `App` component.

2 Allow the business search to include filtering by city in addition to the business category. You'll need to add the city to the sample data and include it in the table results.

3 How would you handle searching by multiple categories? Modify the sample data to include multiple categories. Change form handling to allow selecting multiple categories. Update the filtering logic to pass the correct business search results to the `BusinessResults` component.

Summary

- React is a JavaScript library for creating UIs and uses the concept of components to encapsulate logic. Components can be composed to create complex UIs.
- JSX is a syntax used to create React elements and allows us to use an HTML-like syntax when working with UI code.
- React components use model data in two forms: props and state. Props (or properties) are immutable data passed to components as part of React's one-way data flow. State data is local and private to a single component and, when changed, triggers a rerender of the component tree.
- Create React App is a command-line tool for creating React applications. It bundles together build tooling and requires no initial configuration.
- React Hooks allow the developer to work with state within a component, while still keeping components as functions.

Client-side GraphQL with React and Apollo Client

This chapter covers

- Connecting a React application to a GraphQL endpoint, using Apollo Client
- Caching and updating data on the client, using Apollo Client
- Updating data in the application, using GraphQL mutations
- Using Apollo Client to manage React client state data

In the previous chapter, we created a React application, using Create React App, that allowed users to search for businesses by category. We used a single JavaScript object hardcoded into the application as the source of our data, so our application had limited functionality. In this chapter, we explore connecting our React application to the GraphQL API we created in previous chapters and introduce a new tool to our GraphQL toolbox: Apollo Client.

Apollo Client is a data management JavaScript library that enables developers to manage both local and remote data with GraphQL. It is used to fetch, cache, and modify application data and offers a number of frontend framework integrations, including React, to enable updating your UI as data changes.

We'll use the React Hooks API for Apollo Client to populate our React app with data from our GraphQL API, issuing data-fetching GraphQL queries using Apollo Client. We'll then explore GraphQL mutation operations for updating data via our GraphQL API, seeing how to handle changing application data. Finally, we'll see how to use Apollo Client for managing the local state of our React application, called *client state management*, by adding local-only fields to our GraphQL API. Let's get started!

6.1 Apollo Client

Apollo Client is much more than just a library that sends and receives graph data. As the Apollo Client docs say:

> *Apollo Client is a comprehensive state management library for JavaScript that enables you to manage both local and remote data with GraphQL. Use it to fetch, cache, and modify application data, all while automatically updating your UI. ... Apollo Client helps you structure code in an economical, predictable, and declarative way that's consistent with modern development practices. The core @apollo/client library provides built-in integration with React, and the larger Apollo community maintains integrations for other popular view layers.*

> —https://www.apollographql.com/docs/react/

We'll take advantage of these features of Apollo Client as we add it to our React application, first adding data-fetching logic, and then using Apollo Client to manage local state data in our React application.

6.1.1 Adding Apollo Client to our React Application

Since we're using React, we'll focus on the React-specific integration for Apollo Client. First, we'll install Apollo Client using npm, create an Apollo Client instance connected to our GraphQL API, and then start issuing data-fetching queries in our React application, using the `useQuery` React Hook provided by Apollo Client.

Since we'll be querying our GraphQL API, make sure that our Neo4j database and GraphQL API application from previous chapters are both running. If they are not, we'll see errors indicating that Apollo Client isn't able to reach the GraphQL endpoint.

INSTALLING APOLLO CLIENT

As of this writing, Apollo Client 3.5.5 is the latest release of Apollo Client, and most of the tools we need to add GraphQL support to our React application are included in a single package. Previous Apollo Client releases bundled React Hooks separately; however, the React integration is now included by default.

Open a terminal, make sure you're in the `web-react` directory, and run the following command to install Apollo Client. We also need to install the `graphql.js` peer dependency for Apollo Client. We are using the most recent version of Apollo Client as of this writing, which is v3.5.5:

```
npm install @apollo/client graphql
```

Now that Apollo Client is installed, we can create an Apollo Client instance and start issuing GraphQL queries. First, we'll see how to do this in a generic way, and then we'll add this functionality to our React application.

CREATING AN APOLLO CLIENT INSTANCE

To create a new Apollo Client instance, we need to pass the URI for the GraphQL API we'd like to connect to as well as the cache we'd like to use to the Apollo Client constructor, as the next listing shows. The most common cache type is Apollo's `InMemoryCache`.

Listing 6.1 Creating an Apollo Client instance

```
import { ApolloClient, InMemoryCache } from "@apollo/client";

const client = new ApolloClient({
  uri: "http://localhost:4000",
  cache: new InMemoryCache(),
});
```

We can, then, use this client instance to execute GraphQL operations.

MAKING A QUERY WITH APOLLO CLIENT

First, let's look at listing 6.2 to see how to execute a GraphQL query using the client API. In our React application, most of the time we'll want to take advantage of the React Hooks API for Apollo Client, so this code won't be part of our application.

Listing 6.2 Executing a query using Apollo Client

```
import { ApolloClient, InMemoryCache, gql } from "@apollo/client";

const client = new ApolloClient({
  uri: "http://localhost:4000",
  cache: new InMemoryCache(),
});

client
  .query({
    query: gql`
      {
        businesses {
          name
        }
      }
    `
  })
  .then(result => console.log(result));
```

Note that we wrap our GraphQL query with the `gql` template literal tag. The purpose of this is to parse GraphQL query strings into the standard GraphQL abstract syntax tree (AST) understood by GraphQL clients. Here we are executing a GraphQL query operation to fetch businesses, returning only the name of each business and logging to the console.

This minimal Apollo Client example is depicted in figure 6.1. Our Apollo Client instance sends a GraphQL query operation to the GraphQL server, which responds with data and is then stored in the Apollo Client cache. Subsequent requests for the same data will read from the cache instead of sending a request to the GraphQL server. Later in the chapter, we'll cover how to work with the Apollo Client cache directly.

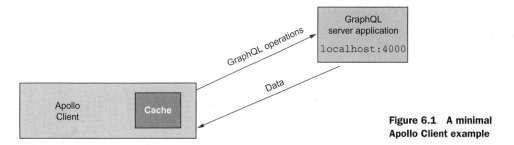

Figure 6.1 A minimal Apollo Client example

Now that we understand the basics of Apollo Client, let's see how to implement them in our React application.

INJECTING APOLLO CLIENT INTO THE COMPONENT HIERARCHY

The first thing we'll need to do is inject the client instance into the React component hierarchy, making it available in each of our components. To do this, we'll make a few changes to the web-react/src/index.js file, which was generated by Create React App.

Listing 6.3   web-react/src/index.js: Creating an Apollo Client instance

```
import React from "react";
import ReactDOM from "react-dom";
import "./index.css";
import App from "./App";
import reportWebVitals from "./reportWebVitals";
import {
  ApolloClient,
  InMemoryCache,
  ApolloProvider,
} from "@apollo/client";

const client = new ApolloClient({        ⟵── Create an Apollo Client instance.
  uri: "http://localhost:4000",
  cache: new InMemoryCache(),
});

ReactDOM.render(                                    Use the Apollo Provider component
  <React.StrictMode>                                to inject the client instance into the
    <ApolloProvider client={client}>    ⟵──┘       React component hierarchy.
      <App />
```

```
    </ApolloProvider>
   </React.StrictMode>,
   document.getElementById("root")
);

// If you want to start measuring performance in your app, pass a function
// to log results (for example: reportWebVitals(console.log))
// or send to an analytics endpoint. Learn more: https://bit.ly/CRA-vitals
reportWebVitals();
```

Once we create an Apollo Client instance that is connected to our GraphQL API, we wrap our App component with the Apollo Provider component, passing our client instance as a prop to the `ApolloProvider` component. This will allow any of the components in our React application to access the client instance and execute GraphQL operations. We'll do that via the React Hooks API in any of our components that require data fetching logic (see figure 6.2).

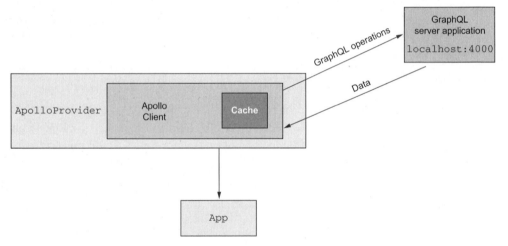

Figure 6.2   **Injecting our Apollo Client instance into the React component hierarchy**

6.1.2   *Apollo Client hooks*

The Apollo Client React integration includes React hooks for working with data. The useQuery React hook is the primary method for executing GraphQL queries. To learn how to use the useQuery hooks, let's start updating our App component to search data in the GraphQL API, instead of using the hardcoded data array.

> **Listing 6.4   web-react/src/App.js: Adding a GraphQL query**

```
import React, { useState } from "react";
import BusinessResults from "./BusinessResults";

import { gql, useQuery } from "@apollo/client";   ◁——— Import the useQuery hook.
```

```
const GET_BUSINESSES_QUERY = gql`        ◁────┐  Define the GraphQL query
  {                                            │  to search for businesses.
    businesses {
      businessId
      name
      address
      categories {
        name
      }
    }
  }
`;

function App() {
  const [selectedCategory, setSelectedCategory] = useState("All");

  const { loading, error, data } = useQuery(GET_BUSINESSES_QUERY);    ◁──────
                                               The useQuery hook exposes
  if (error) return <p>Error</p>;              the various lifecycle states
  if (loading) return <p>Loading...</p>;       of running the GraphQL
                                                              operation.
  return (
    <div>
      <h1>Business Search</h1>
      <form>
        <label>
          Select Business Category:
          <select
            value={selectedCategory}
            onChange={(event) => setSelectedCategory(event.target.value)}
          >
            <option value="All">All</option>
            <option value="Library">Library</option>
            <option value="Restaurant">Restaurant</option>
            <option value="Car Wash">Car Wash</option>
          </select>
        </label>
        <input type="submit" value="Submit" />      We pass the GraphQL
      </form>                                        response to the
                                                     BusinessResults
      <BusinessResults businesses={data.businesses} />  ◁──┘  component.
    </div>
  );
}

export default App;
```

First, we import the useQuery hook and gql template literal tag. Then, we define the
GraphQL query to search for businesses and return the data we need to render the
results in our results table. Next, we pass this GraphQL query to the useQuery hook,
which returns state objects that let us inspect the various states of the GraphQL operation: loading, error, and data. While the query is loading, we can display an indication
to the user that we're fetching data. If our GraphQL query returned an error, we can

render some error result to the user. Finally, once the `data` object is populated, we know that our GraphQL query has completed successfully, and we can pass that data as props to the `BusinessResults` component, which is responsible for rendering our results table (see figure 6.3).

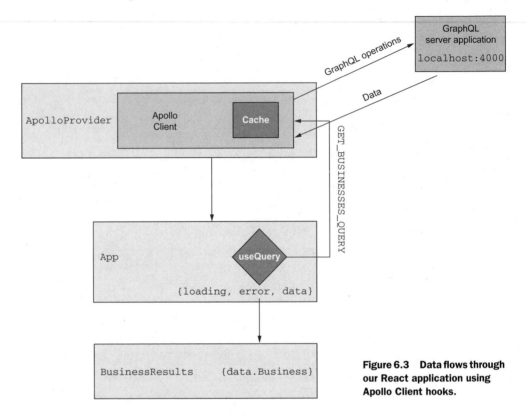

Figure 6.3   Data flows through our React application using Apollo Client hooks.

We'll also need to make a slight adjustment to the `BusinessResults` component, since we now have multiple categories to display per business.

Listing 6.5   web-react/src/BusinessResults.js: Displaying business categories

```
function BusinessResults(props) {
  const { businesses } = props;

  return (
    <div>
      <h2>Results</h2>
      <table>
        <thead>
          <tr>
            <th>Name</th>
            <th>Address</th>
            <th>Category</th>
```

```
          </tr>
        </thead>
        <tbody>
          {businesses.map((b, i) => (
            <tr key={i}>
              <td>{b.name}</td>
              <td>{b.address}</td>
              <td>
                {b.categories.reduce(
                  (acc, c, i) => acc + (i === 0 ? " " : ", ") + c.name,
                  ""
                )}
              </td>
            </tr>
          ))}
        </tbody>
      </table>
    </div>
  );
}
```

> We use the reduce function to create a single string representation of our categories.

```
export default BusinessResults;
```

Now, if we take a look at our React application, we should see our business results table populated with businesses. The data is coming from the GraphQL API (see figure 6.4).

Business Search

Select Business Category: [All ▾] [Submit]

Results

Name	Address	Category
Missoula Public Library	301 E Main St	Library
Ninja Mike's	200 W Pine St	Restaurant, Breakfast
KettleHouse Brewing Co.	313 N 1st St W	Beer, Brewery
Imagine Nation Brewing	1151 W Broadway St	Beer, Brewery
Market on Front	201 E Front St	Coffee, Restaurant, Cafe, Deli, Breakfast
Hanabi	723 California Dr	Restaurant, Ramen
Zootown Brew	121 W Broadway St	Coffee
Ducky's Car Wash	716 N San Mateo Dr	Car Wash
Neo4j	111 E 5th Ave	Graph Database

Figure 6.4   **Our React application after connecting to our GraphQL API**

Of course, our application is not yet fully functional, since we're just showing *all* businesses. Instead, we need to filter based on the user input of category. To do that, we'll pass the selected category as a GraphQL variable.

6.1.3   *GraphQL variables*

GraphQL variables allow us to pass dynamic arguments as part of our GraphQL operation. Let's modify web-react/src/App.js to search for businesses that only match the category selected by the user, passing the selected category as a GraphQL variable. We'll make use of the filtering functionality covered in chapter 4, using the where argument to filter for businesses with a connection to the user-selected category.

Listing 6.6   web-react/src/App.js: Using GraphQL variables

```
import React, { useState } from "react";
import BusinessResults from "./BusinessResults";

import { gql, useQuery } from "@apollo/client";

const GET_BUSINESSES_QUERY = gql`
  query BusinessesByCategory($selectedCategory: String!) {
    businesses(
      where: { categories_SOME: { name_CONTAINS: $selectedCategory } }
    ) {
      businessId
      name
      address
      categories {
        name
      }
    }
  }
`;

function App() {
  const [selectedCategory, setSelectedCategory] = useState("");

  const { loading, error, data } = useQuery(GET_BUSINESSES_QUERY, {
    variables: { selectedCategory },
  });

  if (error) return <p>Error</p>;
  if (loading) return <p>Loading...</p>;

  return (
    <div>
      <h1>Business Search</h1>
      <form>
        <label>
          Select Business Category:
          <select
            value={selectedCategory}
            onChange={(event) => setSelectedCategory(event.target.value)}
          >
            <option value="">All</option>
            <option value="Library">Library</option>
            <option value="Restaurant">Restaurant</option>
```

```
            <option value="Car Wash">Car Wash</option>
          </select>
        </label>
        <input type="submit" value="Submit" />
      </form>

      <BusinessResults businesses={data.businesses} />
    </div>
  );
}

export default App;
```

When working with GraphQL variables, we first need to replace the static value with $selectedCategory. Then, we declare $selectedCategory as one of the variables accepted by the query. We then pass the value for $selectedCategory in the call to useQuery. Now, our search results are updated when we change the selected category, showing only the results for that category (see figure 6.5).

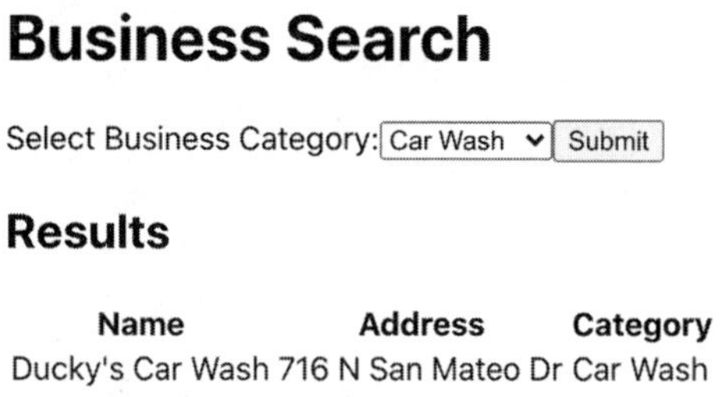

Business Search

Select Business Category: [Car Wash ▾] [Submit]

Results

Name	Address	Category
Ducky's Car Wash	716 N San Mateo Dr	Car Wash

Figure 6.5   Enabling filtering by category, using GraphQL

6.1.4   GraphQL fragments

So far, when creating a selection set, we've listed all the fields and nested fields we want to include in the query. Often, different components in our application use the same (or subsets of) selection sets in GraphQL queries. *GraphQL fragments* allow us to reuse selection sets, or pieces of selection sets, across GraphQL queries. To use fragments in our GraphQL queries, we first declare the fragment, assigning it a name and the type on which it is valid, as shown in the following listing.

Listing 6.7   Declaring a GraphQL fragment

```
fragment businessDetails on Business {
    businessId
    name
    address
    categories {
        name
    }
}
```

Here we've defined a fragment called `businessDetails`, which can be used to select fields of the `Business` type and includes all the fields needed to render our results table. Then, to use the fragment in a selection set, we include the fragment name in the selection set, preceded by ...., as the next listing shows.

Listing 6.8   Using a fragment in a GraphQL query

```
query BusinessesByCategory($selectedCategory: String!) {
  businesses(
    where: { categories_SOME: { name_CONTAINS: $selectedCategory } }
  ) {
    ...businessDetails
    }
  }
}
```

Our query results will be the same, but we can now reuse this `businessDetails` fragment in other queries.

USING FRAGMENTS WITH APOLLO CLIENT

To use fragments with Apollo Client, we can declare our fragments in separate variables and include them in our GraphQL queries, using placeholders in the template literal. This allows us to store fragments and share them across components. If we need to change the fields in the selection set, we only need to do that where we declare the fragment, and then any queries using that fragment will be updated.

Next, we declare our `businessDetails` fragment in a `BUSINESS_DETAILS_FRAGMENT` variable, and we then include it in our GraphQL query, using a template literal placeholder, as shown in the next listing.

Listing 6.9   web-react/src/App.js: Using a GraphQL fragment

```
...

const BUSINESS_DETAILS_FRAGMENT = gql`
  fragment businessDetails on Business {
    businessId
    name
    address
    categories {
      name
    }
  }
`;

const GET_BUSINESSES_QUERY = gql`
  query BusinessesByCategory($selectedCategory: String!) {
    businesses(
      where: { categories_SOME: { name_CONTAINS: $selectedCategory } }
    ) {
      ...businessDetails
    }
```

```
    }

    ${BUSINESS_DETAILS_FRAGMENT}
  `;
```

...

6.1.5   Caching with Apollo Client

Apollo Client stores GraphQL results in a normalized, in-memory cache. This means that if the same GraphQL query is run again, instead of sending data to the server, the results from the cache will be read instead, reducing unnecessary network requests and improving the perceived performance of the application. We can verify that the results are cached by opening our browser's developer tools and inspecting the network tab while selecting different categories from the dropdown.

UPDATING CACHED RESULTS

Caching is great for performance when our application data isn't changing very often, but how do we handle updating data that's been cached? What if we don't want to use cached data in our application and instead want to show fresh data from the server? Fortunately, Apollo Client has options for updating cached results. We'll explore two options for updating cached query results: polling and refetching.

Polling allows for synchronizing results periodically at a specified interval. With Apollo Client, polling can be enabled on a per-query basis by specifying a value for `pollInterval`, specified in milliseconds. Next, we set the query results to update every 500 milliseconds, as shown in the next listing.

Listing 6.10   web-react/src/App.js: Setting a poll interval

```
const { loading, error, data } = useQuery(GET_BUSINESSES_QUERY, {
    variables: { selectedCategory },
    pollInterval: 500
  });
```

Instead of updating results at a fixed interval, *refetching* allows us to update query results explicitly, often in response to a user action, such as clicking a button or submitting a form. To use refetching with Apollo client, call the `refetch` function returned by the `useQuery` hook, as the following listing shows.

Listing 6.11   web-react/src/App.js: Using the `refetch` function

```
import React, { useState } from "react";
import BusinessResults from "./BusinessResults";

import { gql, useQuery } from "@apollo/client";

const GET_BUSINESSES_QUERY = gql`
  query BusinessesByCategory($selectedCategory: String!) {
```

```
        businesses(
          where: { categories_SOME: { name_CONTAINS: $selectedCategory } }
        ) {
          businessId
          name
          address
          categories {
            name
          }
        }
      }
`;

function App() {
  const [selectedCategory, setSelectedCategory] = useState("");

  const { loading, error, data, refetch } = useQuery(
    GET_BUSINESSES_QUERY,
    {
      variables: { selectedCategory },
    }
  );

  if (error) return <p>Error</p>;
  if (loading) return <p>Loading...</p>;

  return (
    <div>
      <h1>Business Search</h1>
      <form>
        <label>
          Select Business Category:
          <select
            value={selectedCategory}
            onChange={(event) => setSelectedCategory(event.target.value)}
          >
            <option value="">All</option>
            <option value="Library">Library</option>
            <option value="Restaurant">Restaurant</option>
            <option value="Car Wash">Car Wash</option>
          </select>
        </label>
        <input type="button" value="Refetch" onClick={() => refetch()} />
      </form>

      <BusinessResults businesses={data.businesses} />
    </div>
  );
}

export default App;
```

The refetch function is returned by the useQuery hook.

Calling the refetch function when the button is clicked

Now that we're ready to handle changing data in our application, let's see how to update our API data using GraphQL mutations.

6.2 GraphQL mutations

GraphQL mutations are GraphQL operations that can write or update data. We introduced the concept of mutations in chapter 2, but up until now, we haven't actually used any mutations. In this section, we'll explore the mutations generated by the Neo4j GraphQL library, allowing us to create, update, and delete nodes and relationships.

6.2.1 Creating nodes

A create mutation is generated for each type in our GraphQL type definitions, mapping to a node label in Neo4j. To create nodes, we call the appropriate create mutation, passing in the property values for the new node as arguments. Note that if fields are defined using !, that means that the field is nonnullable and must be included in order to create the node. Let's add a new business to the database: Philz Coffee.

Listing 6.12 GraphQL mutation to create business

```
mutation {
  createBusinesses(
    input: {
      businessId: "b10"
      name: "Philz Coffee"
      address: "113. S B St"
      city: "San Mateo"
      state: "CA"
      location: { latitude: 37.567109, longitude: -122.323680 }
    }
  ) {
    businesses {
      businessId
      name
      address
      city
    }
    info {
      nodesCreated
    }
  }
}
```

Running this mutation in Apollo Studio will create a new business node in the database:

```
{
  "data": {
    "createBusinesses": {
      "businesses": [
        {
          "businessId": "b10",
          "name": "Philz Coffee",
          "address": "113. S B St",
          "city": "San Mateo"
```

```
        }
      ],
      "info": {
        "nodesCreated": 1
      }
    }
  }
}
```

6.2.2   *Creating relationships*

To create relationships in the database, we can use the update operations generated by the Neo4j GraphQL library. In the next listing, let's connect our new Philz Coffee node to the Coffee category node. To do that, we use the IDbusinessID to refer to the business node in the input for the mutation.

> **Listing 6.13   GraphQL mutation to create a relationship**

```
mutation {
  updateBusinesses (
    where: { businessId: "b10" }
    connect: { categories: { where: { node: { name: "Coffee" } } } }
  ) {
    businesses {
      name
      categories {
        name
      }
    }
    info {
      relationshipsCreated
    }
  }
}
```

Note the use of the connect argument. This argument allows us to create relationships between nodes that already exist. We could also create a new category node by using the create argument; however, in this case, our coffee category node already exists in the database. These connect and create arguments are also available when creating nodes and make up a powerful feature of the Neo4j GraphQL library, called *nested mutations*. By nesting create or connect operations, we can execute many write operations in a single GraphQL mutation:

```
{
  "data": {
    "updateBusinesses": {
      "businesses": [
        {
          "name": "Philz Coffee",
          "categories": [
            {
```

```
          "name": "Coffee"
        }
      ]
    }
  ],
  "info": {
    "relationshipsCreated": 1
  }
}
}
}
}
```

6.2.3 *Updating and deleting*

Let's say the Philz Coffee shop moves from B St. to an address right next door to the Neo4j office, and we need to update the address. To do that, we use the update-Businesses mutation, using the businessId field to reference the node and then passing in any values that need to be updated to the update argument, as shown next.

Listing 6.14   GraphQL mutation to update business address

```
mutation {
  updateBusinesses(
    where: { businessId: "b10" }
    update: { address: "113 E 5th Ave" }
  ) {
    businesses {
      name
      address
      categories {
        name
      }
    }
  }
}

{
  "data": {
    "updateBusinesses": {
      "businesses": [
        {
          "name": "Philz Coffee",
          "address": "113 E 5th Ave",
          "categories": [
            {
              "name": "Coffee"
            }
          ]
        }
      ]
    }
  }
}
```

Or if we need to delete the node from the database completely, we can use the deleteBusinesses mutation, as the following listing shows.

Listing 6.15   GraphQL mutation to delete a business node

```
mutation {
  deleteBusinesses(where: { businessId: "b10" }) {
    nodesDeleted
  }
}


{
  "data": {
    "deleteBusinesses": {
      "nodesDeleted": 1
    }
  }
}
```

While you execute these mutation operations in Apollo Studio, try the polling and refetching technique mentioned in the previous section to see how the React application reacts to changing backend data as the mutations are executed.

6.3   *Client state management with GraphQL*

We said earlier that Apollo Client is a comprehensive data management library, and that includes not only working with data from our GraphQL server, but also managing local data. Local data can include the state of our React application—for example, user preferences that we don't want to send to the server because they are only relevant to the client.

Apollo Client allows us to add local-only fields to our GraphQL queries, which can then be managed and cached by Apollo Client to help manage the state of our React application. This is helpful because it allows us to use the same API for working with local data as we do for remote data: GraphQL!

6.3.1   *Local-only fields and reactive variables*

In Apollo Client, *local-only fields* can be defined and included in our GraphQL schema. These fields are not defined in the server's schema, but rather are specific to the client application only. The values for these fields are computed locally using logic that we can define, such as storing and reading from localStorage in the browser.

Reactive variables enable us to read and write local values outside of GraphQL. These are useful when we want to update their values without executing a GraphQL operation (e.g., in response to user action) but read local-only fields as part of a GraphQL data-fetching operation alongside other data-fetching logic from the GraphQL server. Also, modifying a reactive variable triggers an update of any query that uses its value.

Let's combine a local-only field with a reactive variable to add a *starred businesses* function to our application. We'll add a *Stars* button next to each business in the results list, allowing the user to select their starred businesses. When a use has starred a business, it will show as bold, letting the user know it is one of their preferred businesses.

As shown in listing 6.16, to do this, we first add a *field policy* for a local-only field to the `InMemoryCache` instance that we're using in Apollo Client. A field policy specifies how to compute a local-only field. Here we add an `isStarred` field that will be a local-only field. We also create a new reactive variable that will be used to store a list of starred businesses. In this case, the field policy for the `isStarred` field checks to see if the business being resolved is included in the list of starred businesses.

Listing 6.16 web-react/src/index.js: Using a reactive variable

```
import React from "react";
import ReactDOM from "react-dom";
import "./index.css";
import App from "./App";
import reportWebVitals from "./reportWebVitals";
import {
  ApolloClient,
  InMemoryCache,          Import the makeVar
  ApolloProvider,         function to create a
  makeVar,            ◁── new reactive variable.
} from "@apollo/client";
                                        Create a new reactive
                                        variable, setting the initial
export const starredVar = makeVar([]);  ◁── value equal to an empty array.

const client = new ApolloClient({
  uri: "http://localhost:4000",    Include a field policy in the InMemoryCache
  cache: new InMemoryCache({        constructor arguments.
    typePolicies: {         ◁──
      Business: {                   The field policy defines how the value is
        fields: {                   computed for a local-only field called
          isStarred: {       ◁──   isStarred on the business type.
            read(_, { readField }) {
              return starredVar().includes(readField("businessId"));  ◁──
            },
          },                                Return true if the list of starred
        },                        businesses includes the current business.
      },
    },
  }),
});

ReactDOM.render(
  <React.StrictMode>
    <ApolloProvider client={client}>
      <App />
    </ApolloProvider>
  </React.StrictMode>,
  document.getElementById("root")
);

// If you want to start measuring performance in your app, pass a function
```

```
// to log results (for example: reportWebVitals(console.log))
// or send to an analytics endpoint. Learn more: https://bit.ly/CRA-vitals
reportWebVitals();
```

Now, we can include the isStarred field in our GraphQL query, as shown in the next listing. We'll need to include the @client directive to indicate this is a local-only field and won't be fetched from the GraphQL server.

Listing 6.17   web-react/src/App.js: Using a local-only GraphQL field

```
...

const GET_BUSINESSES_QUERY = gql`
  query BusinessesByCategory($selectedCategory: String!) {
    businesses(
      where: { categories_SOME: { name_CONTAINS: $selectedCategory } }
    ) {
      businessId
      name
      address
      categories {              Add the isStarred field to the selection
        name                    set, indicating this is a local-only field
      }                         using the @client directive.
      isStarred @client  ⊲─┘
    }
  }
`;

...
```

Finally, we need a way to update the starredVar reactive variable. In the next listing, we add a *Star* button next to each business. When the user clicks this button, the value of starredVar is updated to include the businessId of the selected business.

Listing 6.18   web-react/src/BusinessResults.js: Using our reactive variable

```
import { starredVar } from "./index";

function BusinessResults(props) {
  const { businesses } = props;          We fetch the value of starredVar
  const starredItems = starredVar();  ⊲─┘ to find all starred businesses.

  return (
    <div>
      <h2>Results</h2>
      <table>
        <thead>
          <tr>
            <th>Name</th>
            <th>Address</th>
            <th>Category</th>
          </tr>
        </thead>
        <tbody>
```

```
            {businesses.map((b, i) => (
              <tr key={i}>
                <td>
                  <button
                    onClick={() =>
                      starredVar([...starredItems, b.businessId])
                    }
                  >
                    Star
                  </button>
                </td>
                <td style={b.isStarred ? { fontWeight: "bold" } : null}>
                  {b.name}
                </td>
                <td>{b.address}</td>
                <td>
                  {b.categories.reduce(
                    (acc, c, i) => acc + (i === 0 ? " " : ", ") + c.name,
                    ""
                  )}
                </td>
              </tr>
            ))}
          </tbody>
        </table>
      </div>
    );
}
```

When clicked, add the businessId to the list of starred businesses.

If the business has been starred, then use a bold style for the business name.

```
export default BusinessResults;
```

And because this is a reactive variable, any active query that depends on the isStarred local-only field is automatically updated in the UI (see figure 6.6)!

Business Search

Select Business Category: [All ▾] [Submit]

Results

Star	Name	Address	Category
Star	Missoula Public Library	301 E Main St	Library
Star	Ninja Mike's	200 W Pine St	Restaurant, Breakfast
Star	KettleHouse Brewing Co.	313 N 1st St W	Beer, Brewery
Star	Imagine Nation Brewing	1151 W Broadway St	Beer, Brewery
Star	Market on Front	201 E Front St	Coffee, Restaurant, Cafe, Deli, Breakfast
Star	**Hanabi**	723 California Dr	Restaurant, Ramen
Star	Zootown Brew	121 W Broadway St	Coffee
Star	**Ducky's Car Wash**	716 N San Mateo Dr	Car Wash
Star	**Neo4j**	111 E 5th Ave	Graph Database

Figure 6.6   Our React application after connecting to our GraphQL API

Now that we've explored mutations, we need to think about how we can secure our application, so not just anyone can add data and update our application. In the next chapter, we explore how to add authentication to secure our application, both on the frontend and backend.

6.4   Exercises

1 What other GraphQL fragments could we use across our application? Write some fragments, and try using them in your queries in Apollo Studio. When would it make sense to use multiple fragments in the same query?

2 Using GraphQL mutations, create relationships connecting business and category nodes to add businesses to additional categories. For example, add the newly created Philz Coffee business to the `Restaurant` and `Breakfast` categories. Add your favorite business and corresponding categories to the graph.

3 Turn the *Star* button into a toggle. If the business is already starred, remove it from the starred list.

Summary

- Apollo Client is a data management library that enables developers to manage both local and remote data with GraphQL and includes integrations for frontend frameworks, like React.
- GraphQL mutations are operations that allow for creating and updating data and are generated for each type by the Neo4j GraphQL library.
- Apollo Client can be used for managing local state by adding local-only fields to the GraphQL schema and by defining field policies that specify how to read, store, and update that local data.

Part 3

Full stack considerations

After building the initial version of our full stack business review application, it is now time to turn our attention to securing our application and deploying it using cloud services. In chapter 7, we will add authorization and authentication to our GraphQL API and explore using the Auth0 service. In chapter 8, we will use Netlify, AWS Lambda, and Neo4j AuraDB to deploy our full stack application. Finally, in chapter 9, we will close the book with a look at how to leverage abstract types in GraphQL, cursor-based pagination, and handling relationship properties in GraphQL. After completing this part of the book, we will have a secure full stack GraphQL application deployed to the cloud.

Adding authorization and authentication

This chapter covers

- Adding authentication and authorization to our application, including both the GraphQL API and our frontend React application
- Using JSON Web Tokens (JWTs) to encode user identity and permissions
- Expressing and enforcing authorization rules in our GraphQL schema using the `@auth` GraphQL schema directive
- Using Auth0 as a JWT provider and the Auth0 React SDK to add Auth0 support to our application

Authentication (verifying a user's identity) and *authorization* (verifying resources users can access) are needed to secure any application—ensuring users have the permissions that they should and protecting data and actions of the application, both on the frontend and backend. So far, both our frontend React application and GraphQL API are open for anyone to access all features and functionality, including modifying, creating, and deleting data.

GraphQL itself is not opinionated about authorization, leaving it up to the developer to choose the most appropriate approach to implement in their application. In this chapter, we show how to implement authorization and authentication features in our application, using JWTs, GraphQL schema directives, and Auth0. First, we'll take a look at a *naive* approach to adding authorization to our GraphQL API by adding an authorization check in our resolvers. Then, we explore how to use the @auth GraphQL schema directive with the Neo4j GraphQL library to protect our GraphQL API, adding authorization rules in the schema. We then add support for the Auth0 authorization service and see how we can make use of JSON Web Tokens to encode user identity and permissions in our application.

7.1 Authorization in GraphQL: A naive approach

Let's first take a look at a naive approach to adding authorization to a GraphQL API in listing 7.1 as a starting point, using just a single static authorization token. When receiving a request by the GraphQL server, we'll check for a token contained in the authorization header of the request. We'll pass this token through to the GraphQL resolver, where we'll check for a certain value of the token to determine whether the request is properly authenticated and send back the appropriate response only if the token is valid. Note that this example is meant to convey concepts and does not represent best practices!

Listing 7.1   api/naive.js: A naive GraphQL authorization implementation

```
const { ApolloServer } = require("apollo-server");

const peopleArray = [
  {
    name: "Bob",
  },
  {
    name: "Lindsey",
  },
];

const typeDefs = /* GraphQL */ `
  type Query {
    people: [Person]
  }

  type Person {
    name: String
  }
`;

const resolvers = {
  Query: {
    people: (obj, args, context, info) => {
```

```
      if (
        context &&
        context.headers &&
        context.headers.authorization === "Bearer authorized123"
      ) {
        return peopleArray;
      } else {
        throw new Error("You are not authorized.");
      }
    },
  },
};
```

> Checking for a specific auth token value

```
const server = new ApolloServer({
  resolvers,
  typeDefs,
  context: ({ req }) => {
    return { headers: req.headers };
  },
});
```

> Adding the HTTP request headers to the GraphQL context object

```
server.listen().then(({ url }) => {
  console.log(`GraphQL server ready at ${url}`);
});
```

Our GraphQL server has a single resolver, `Query.people`, which includes the logic for checking the value of an authorization token, passed through the context object. This token comes from the request header and is passed into the context object at query time (see figure 7.1).

Let's give it a try. We can now start the GraphQL server:

```
node naive.js
```

In Apollo Studio, let's issue a GraphQL query to find all Person objects and return the name field of each:

```
{
    people {
        name
    }
}
```

Our request is rejected since we haven't included the appropriate authorization token, and our result is an error message: *You are not authorized.* Let's add the appropriate authorization header to the GraphQL request with our authorization token. We can do this in Apollo Studio by clicking *Headers* in the lower-left corner and selecting *New header* with the key *Authorization* and value *Bearer authorized123*:

```
{
    "Authorization": "Bearer authorized123"
}
```

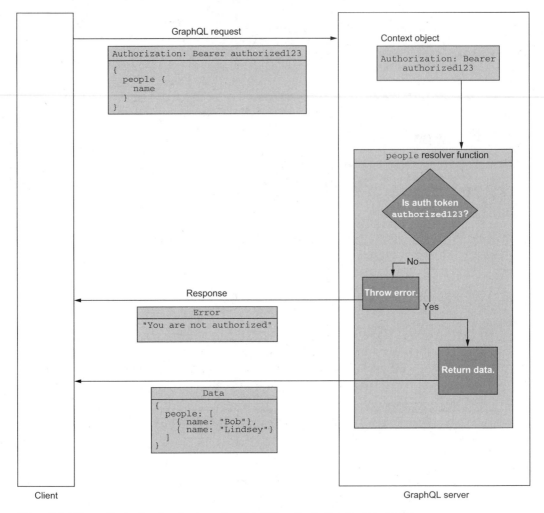

Figure 7.1   The authorization flow for our naive GraphQL authorization implementation

Now, when we execute the same GraphQL operation—this time with the authorization token attached as a header in the request—we see the results we're expecting:

```
{
  "data": {
    "people": [
      {
       name: "Bob",
      },
      {
       name: "Lindsey",
      },
    ]
  }
}
```

This naive approach shows a few important concepts, such as how to take the authorization header from a request and pass it through to the context object of the GraphQL resolver, as well as how to add an authorization header in Apollo Studio. However, there are a few problems with this approach that we wouldn't want to implement in a real-world application:

1   *We don't validate the token.* How do we know the user making the request is who they say they are and if they actually have the permissions they state in the token? We're just taking their word for it!

2   *Our authorization rules are mixed with data-fetching logic in the GraphQL resolver.* This might seem like something that works for a simple example, but imagine what will happen as we add more types and authorization rules—it will be difficult to track and maintain.

We'll address the first issue by using cryptographically-signed JWTs to encode and validate the users' identity and permissions expressed in the authorization header. We'll address the second issue by using the `@auth` GraphQL schema directive with the Neo4j GraphQL library; by adding declarative authorization rules to our schema, we have a single source of truth for our authorization rules.

7.2   JSON Web Tokens

JSON Web Token, commonly referred to as JWT, is an open standard for cryptographically signing a JSON object that can be used for trusted communication between parties. A compact token is generated and signed using public/private key pairs to verify that the token was generated by a party holding the private key, and therefore, the integrity of the information contained in the token can be cryptographically verified by decoding it, using the public key counterpart of the private key used to sign it.

The information encoded in a JWT (the payload) is a series of *claims* about an entity, typically a user. Standard claims in a JWT include

- `iss`—The issuer of the token
- `exp`—The expiration date of the token
- `sub`—The subject, usually some sort of ID referencing the user to which these claims apply
- `aud`—The audience, often used when authenticating against an API

We can also add additional claims to a JWT to express information about the user, such as what roles they have in the application (i.e., Is the user an admin or editor?) or more fine-grained permissions they should be granted, such as the permission to read, create, update, or delete certain types of data in the application.

Many identity and access management services support the JWT standard. They can even be used self-contained, if you choose to provide your own authorization service. In this chapter, we will make use of the Auth0 service.

First, let's create a JWT to encode some claims about a user, and then we'll modify the previous naive GraphQL API to verify the token and ensure the user should be given access to the GraphQL API. To do this, we'll use the online JWT debugger at https://jwt.io.

We'll need a random string to use as the signing key. Later, we'll use this in our GraphQL server to verify the incoming JWTs:

```
Dpwm9XXKqk809WXjCsOmRSZQ5i5fXw8N
```

Enter this value in the *VERIFY SIGNATURE* section of the JWT Debugger. Next, we need to add some claims to the payload of our token (see figure 7.2):

```
{
    "sub": "1234567890",
    "name": "William Lyon",
    "email": "will@grandstack.io",
    "iat": 1638331785
}
```

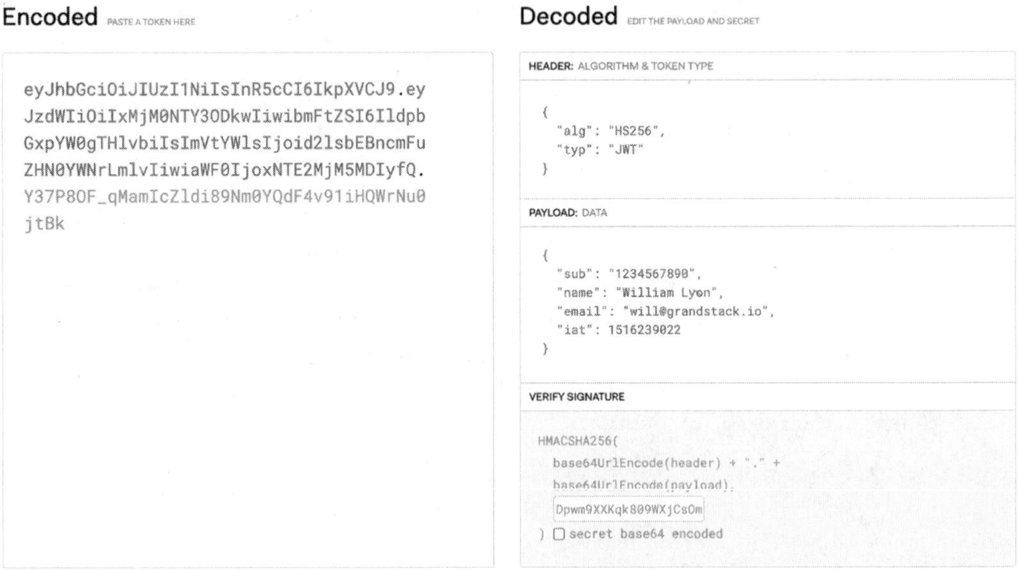

Encoded PASTE A TOKEN HERE

```
eyJhbGciOiJIUzI1NiIsInR5cCI6IkpXVCJ9.ey
JzdWIiOiIxMjM0NTY3ODkwIiwibmFtZSI6Ildpb
GxpYW0gTHlvbiIsImVtYWlsIjoid2lsbEBncmFu
ZHN0YWNrLmlvIiwiaWF0IjoxNTE2MjM5MDIyfQ.
Y37P8OF_qMamIcZldi89Nm0YQdF4v91iHQWrNu0
jtBk
```

Decoded EDIT THE PAYLOAD AND SECRET

HEADER: ALGORITHM & TOKEN TYPE

```
{
  "alg": "HS256",
  "typ": "JWT"
}
```

PAYLOAD: DATA

```
{
  "sub": "1234567890",
  "name": "William Lyon",
  "email": "will@grandstack.io",
  "iat": 1516239022
}
```

VERIFY SIGNATURE

```
HMACSHA256(
    base64UrlEncode(header) + "." +
    base64UrlEncode(payload),
    Dpwm9XXKqk809WXjCsOm
) ☐ secret base64 encoded
```

Figure 7.2   Creating a signed JWT using jwt.io

After creating our JWT, let's return to the naive GraphQL server and add support for verifying the token. First, we'll install the `jsonwebtoken` package:

```
npm install jsonwebtoken
```

Next, we'll update the resolver logic to decode the JWT using our random client secret, as shown in the next listing.

Listing 7.2   api/naive.js: Verifying a JWT in the GraphQL server

```
const { ApolloServer } = require("apollo-server");
const jwt = require("jsonwebtoken");

const peopleArray = [
  {
    name: "Bob",
  },
  {
    name: "Lindsey",
  },
];

const typeDefs = /* GraphQL */ `
  type Query {
    people: [Person]
  }

  type Person {
    name: String
  }
`;

const resolvers = {
  Query: {
    people: (obj, args, context, info) => {
      if (context.user) {
        return peopleArray;
      } else {
        throw new Error("You are not authorized");
      }
    },
  },
};

const server = new ApolloServer({
  resolvers,
  typeDefs,
  context: ({ req }) => {
    let decoded;
    if (req && req.headers && req.headers.authorization) {
      try {
        decoded = jwt.verify(                         ⟵——————┐  Verifying the token using
          req.headers.authorization.slice(7),               │  our random client secret
          "Dpwm9XXKqk809WXjCsOmRSZQ5i5fXw8N"         ———————┘
        );
      } catch (e) {
        // token not valid
        console.log(e);
      }
    }
    return {
      user: decoded,
    };
```

```
  },
});

server.listen().then(({ url }) => {
  console.log(`GraphQL server ready at ${url}`);
});
```

If the token can be verified, meaning it was signed by the appropriate key, then we continue fetching data in the resolver. If the token is not valid, then the resolver throws an error, and no data is fetched (see figure 7.3).

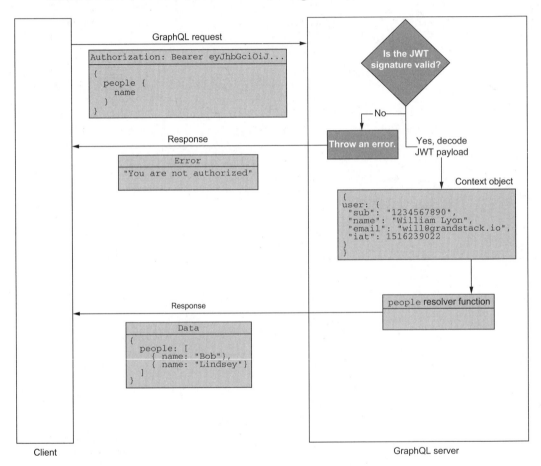

Figure 7.3 Introducing JWT into our authorization flow

This example uses the HS256 algorithm, which means the client and server share the same key. Later, when we switch to Auth0 as the provider for our tokens, we'll make use of the more secure RS256 algorithm in which a public/private key pair is used instead.

After restarting the GraphQL server to pick up our changes, we'll open Apollo Studio and add the JWT token to the authorization header. If we try to make the request without a token or using an invalid token, we receive this error: *You are not authorized.* This ensures the GraphQL server only executes valid requests—those containing a JWT signed using the private key corresponding to the public key (see figure 7.4).

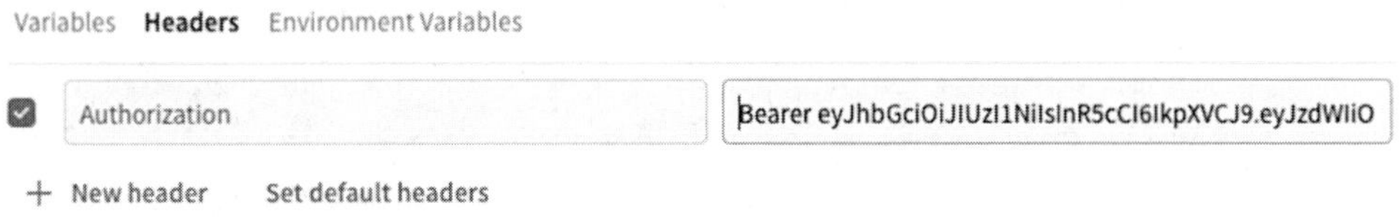

Variables **Headers** Environment Variables

| ☑ | Authorization | Bearer eyJhbGciOiJIUzI1NiIsInR5cCI6IkpXVCJ9.eyJzdWIiO |

+ New header   Set default headers

Figure 7.4 Adding a JWT as an Authorization header in Apollo Studio

Earlier, we mentioned two issues with our naive approach to authorization. The first was that we didn't have a way to validate the authorization token. We've solved that problem by using and validating a JWT, so now, it's time to address our commingled authorization rules. We'll use directives to declare our authorization rules in our GraphQL schema and ensure they are enforced using the Neo4j GraphQL library.

7.3 The @auth GraphQL schema directive

Let's leave behind the simple, naive GraphQL server example and return to our business reviews application to explore how to add authorization rules to our GraphQL schema. As we saw previously with the @cypher schema directive, GraphQL schema directives allow us to indicate that some custom server-side logic should be applied when resolving the GraphQL request.

The Neo4j GraphQL library includes the @auth GraphQL schema directive, which allows for defining authorization rules to protect fields or types in the GraphQL schema. Before we can use the @auth schema directive, we'll need to specify the method used to verify the JWT as well as the secret that should be used to verify the token. Let's set an environment variable with the value of our JWT secret:

```
export JWT_SECRET=Dpwm9XXKqk809WXjCsOmRSZQ5i5fXw8N
```

Now, we'll need to update the configuration for the Neo4j GraphQL Library to specify that this token should be used when verifying authorization tokens, as shown in listing 7.3. To do this, we will read the JWT_SECRET environment variable we just set and pass this in a plugins object alongside our type definitions and resolvers. We'll also need to install the graphql-plugin-auth package to enable the usage of authorization plugins with the Neo4j GraphQL Library:

```
npm i @neo4j/graphql-plugin-auth
```

Listing 7.3   api/index.js: Configuring authorization for the Neo4j GraphQL library

```
const {
  Neo4jGraphQLAuthJWTPlugin,
} = require("@neo4j/graphql-plugin-auth");

const neoSchema = new Neo4jGraphQL({
  typeDefs,
  resolvers,
  driver,
  plugins: {
    auth: new Neo4jGraphQLAuthJWTPlugin({
      secret: process.env.JWT_SECRET,      ◁——— Validate JWTs using a secret.
    }),
  },
});
```

We can also configure JWT decoding and verification using a JSON Web Key Set (JWKS) URL, a more secure approach than using a shared secret. We will use this method to configure JWT verification with the Neo4j GraphQL library when we use Auth0, but for now, configuring using the shared secret is fine, as shown in the next listing. In addition, we also need to pass through the HTTP request object that includes the authorization header and the user's auth token.

Listing 7.4   api/index.js: Pass through the request object with the auth token

```
neoSchema.getSchema().then((schema) => {      Pass the HTTP request object to the context
  const server = new ApolloServer({          function so the JWT can be decoded in the
    schema,                                   resolvers generated by the Neo4j GraphQL
    context: ({ req }) => ({ req }),   ◁——   library.
  });
  server.listen().then(({ url }) => {
    console.log(`GraphQL server ready at ${url}`);
  });
});
```

7.3.1   *Rules and operations*

When using the @auth GraphQL schema directive, there are two aspects we need to consider: rules and operations. Both of these are specified as arguments to the @auth directive. There are several types of authorization rules that can be defined, depending on how, exactly, we want to protect fields and types. Perhaps we only want certain fields to be accessible to users who have signed in. Or perhaps we want only administrators in our application to be able to edit certain types. Or perhaps only authors of a review should be able to update it. These are all authorization rules that can be specified using the @auth directive. The following rule types are available with the @auth schema directive:

- isAuthenticated is the most basic rule we can use. A GraphQL request accessing the protected type or field must have a valid JWT.

- The `roles` rule specifies one or more roles, which must be contained in the JWT payload.
- The `allow` rule will compare values from the JWT payload to values in the database, ensuring they are equal for a valid request.
- The `bind` rule is used to ensure equality between a value in the JWT payload and in a GraphQL mutation operation before committing to the database.
- The `where` rule is similar to `allow`, in that a value from the JWT payload is used; however, instead of checking for equality, a predicate is added to the generated database query to filter for data matching the rule.

When adding rules using the `@auth` directive, one or more operations can be optionally specified, indicating which operations the rule should be applied to. If no operations are specified, then the rule will be applied to all operations. The following operations can be used:

- CREATE
- READ
- UPDATE
- DELETE
- CONNECT
- DISCONNECT

Let's see the `@auth` directive in action to help us understand how these rules and operations should be used in our business reviews application.

7.3.2 The isAuthenticated authorization rule

The `isAuthenticated` rule can be used on either GraphQL types or fields and indicates that to access that type or field, the GraphQL request must have a valid JWT attached. The validity of the JWT is determined by whether or not it can be verified using the JWT secret value as the key—indicating that the token was signed by the private key and created by the appropriate authority. The `isAuthenticated` logic is used to gate some area of the application that requires the user to authenticate to the application but does not require any specific permissions—the user only needs to be an authenticated user.

For the purposes of our business reviews application, let's say we want to allow any user to search for businesses but only show the `averageStars` field to authenticated users, encouraging users to sign up with our application. Let's update our GraphQL type definitions to include this authorization rule.

> **Listing 7.5 api/index.js: Updating the Business type**

```
type Business {
  businessId: ID!
  waitTime: Int! @computed
  averageStars: Float
```

```
    @auth(rules: [{ isAuthenticated: true }])          ◄──────────────┐
    @cypher(                                                           │
      statement: "MATCH (this)<-[:REVIEWS]-(r:Review) RETURN avg(r.stars)"
    )                                               We add the @auth schema directive to
  recommended(first: Int = 1): [Business]            protect the averageStars field, using an
    @cypher(                                                       isAuthenticated rule.
      statement: """
      MATCH (this)<-[:REVIEWS]-(:Review)<-[:WROTE]-(u:User)
      MATCH (u)-[:WROTE]->(:Review)-[:REVIEWS]->(rec:Business)
      WITH rec, COUNT(*) AS score
      RETURN rec ORDER BY score DESC LIMIT $first
      """
    )
  name: String!
  city: String!
  state: String!
  address: String!
  location: Point!
  reviews: [Review!]! @relationship(type: "REVIEWS", direction: IN)
  categories: [Category!]!
    @relationship(type: "IN_CATEGORY", direction: OUT)
}
```

We've now protected the averageStars field, which means we'll need to include a valid JWT in the header of any GraphQL request with that field, as shown in the next listing.

Listing 7.6   Requesting the protected `averageStars` field in a GraphQL query

```
{
  businesses {
    name
    categories {
      name
    }
    averageStars
  }
}


"errors": [
    {
      "message": "Unauthenticated",
```

If we don't include the averageStars field in the selection set, our request returns the expected fields. Experiment with sending an invalid token and requests with and without the averageStars field. Here we include a valid token in the request's authorization header to allow us to view the averageStars field:

```
{
"Authorization":"Bearer eyJhbGciOiJIUzI1NiIsInR5cCI6IkpXVCJ9.eyJzdWIiOiIxM
jM0NTY3ODkwIiwibmFtZSI6IldpbGxpYW0gTHlvbiIsImVtYWlsIjoid21sbEBncmFuZHN0YWNr
LmlvIiwiaWF0IjoxNTE2MjM5MDIyfQ.Y37P8OF_qMamIcZldi89Nm0YQdF4v91iHQWrNu0jtBk"
}
```

7.3.3 The roles authorization rule

The roles rule allows us to add requirements for the type of permissions required for one or more operations. Rather than just having a valid signed token, to access a field or type protected by a roles rule, the token must include one of the specified roles in the role claim encoded in the token. Let's take a look at an example in the next listing.

Listing 7.7 api/index.js: Protecting the user type with a roles authorization rule

```
extend type User @auth(rules: [{roles: ["admin"]}])
```

Here we use the extend GraphQL keyword in our type definitions to add additional directives or fields to a type already defined in our type definitions. Using this syntax is equivalent to including the directive when first defining the type, but using type extensions allows us to separate our type definitions into multiple files if we desire (see figure 7.5).

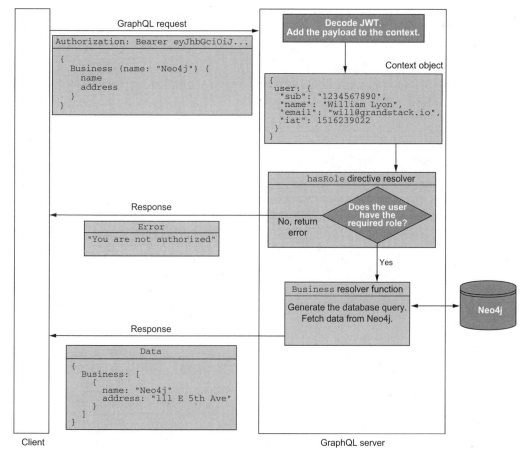

Figure 7.5 Authorization flow, using the @auth GraphQL schema directive

Now, any GraphQL operation that accesses the User type must have the admin role, including any that traverse to a user, as the next listing shows.

Listing 7.8   GraphQL query accessing user information

```
query  {
  businesses(where: {name: "Neo4j"}) {
    name
    categories {
      name
    }
    address
    reviews {
      text
      stars
      date
      user {
        name
      }
    }

  }
}
```

Executing the previous query will result in the following error message, since our token does not include the admin role:

```
"errors": [
  {
    "message": "Forbidden"
  }
]
```

We'll need to include the roles in the claims in the token. Return to the online JWT builder at https://jwt.io, and add the roles array to the claims:

```
{
  "sub": "1234567890",
  "name": "William Lyon",
  "email": "will@grandstack.io",
  "iat": 1516239022,
  "roles": ["admin"]
}
```

Now, if we update the token used in the authorization header in Apollo Studio using this new JWT and run the GraphQL query again, we will be able to access user information.

Remember that if we don't specify specific operations (e.g., create, read, and update) when adding our authorization rules, then the rule applies to all operations that include the type or field in question. If we want to limit the authorization rule to only being applied to certain operations, we must explicitly specify them when defining the rules, using the `@auth` schema directive.

The first two `@auth` rules we examined (`isAuthenticated` and `roles`) used only values from the JWT payload (or, simply, the presence of a valid token, in the case of `isAuthenticated`). The next three rules we will explore will use values from the database (our application data) to enforce authorization rules.

7.3.4 The allow authorization rule

Previously, we created a rule that protected the user type by requiring the `admin` role for the authenticated user. Let's add an additional authorization rule to allow users to read their own user information.

> **Listing 7.9 api/index.js: Allowing users to access their own user information**

```
extend type User
  @auth(
    rules: [
      { operations: [READ], allow: { userId: "$jwt.sub" } }
      { roles: ["admin"] }
    ]
  )
```

Note that we have combined our new allow rule with the existing roles rule. Since the `rules` argument takes an array of rules, these act as `or` logic. To access the user type, the claims in the request's JWT must conform to at least one of the authorization rules defined in the `rules` array. In this case, the authenticated user must be either an admin or match the `userId` of the user being requested. To test our new rule, let's create a new JWT for the user Jenny with the following payload:

```
{
  "sub": "u3",
  "name": "Jenny",
  "email": "jenny@grandstack.io",
  "iat": 1516239022,
  "roles": [
    "user"
  ]
}
```

We can create this using the web interface at jwt.io; just be sure to use the same JWT secret when signing the token:

eyJhbGciOiJIUzI1NiIsInR5cCI6IkpXVCJ9.eyJzdWIiOiJ1MyIsIm5hbWUiOiJKZW5ueSIsImVtYWlsIjoiamVubnlAZ3JhbmRzdGFjay5pbyIsImlhdCI6MTUxNjIzOTAyMiwicm9sZXMiOlsidXNlciJdfQ.ctal5qgshR4-hqchxsYxxHVGPsE0JNxydGy3Pga27nA

Now, using this JWT to execute a GraphQL request as the user `Jenny`, we can query for this user's details in the following listing.

Listing 7.10   Query for a single user's details

```
query {
  users(where: { name: "Jenny" }) {
    name
    userId
  }
}
```

Since the `sub` claim in our JWT matches the `userId` of the user we are requesting, we see the result data:

```
{
  "data": {
    "users": [
      {
        "name": "Jenny",
        "userId": "u3"
      }
    ]
  }
}
```

In this case, our GraphQL query is filtering for the user, using the `where` argument to ensure we are only querying for the data that we have access to. What happens if we ask for user data that we don't have access to? For example, what if we asked for all user information?

Listing 7.11   Query for all user details

```
query {
  users {
    name
    userId
  }
}
```

Since our user is not an admin and we are requesting user objects for which the `userId` will not match the `sub` claim in our JWT, we will see a `Forbidden` error.

Let's see how we can avoid these types of errors by automatically filtering the query results for only the data the authenticated user has access to. To accomplish this, we will use a `where` authorization rule. This means the client doesn't need to worry about adding a filter to avoid asking for data the authenticated user doesn't have access to.

7.3.5   *The where authorization rule*

In the previous section, we used an `allow` authorization rule to ensure that users are only able to access their own data. However, this approach was problematic in that it put the burden on the client to add the appropriate filters to ensure the GraphQL request was not asking for data the user was not authorized to see. Let's instead use a where rule in the next listing, so we don't need to worry about requesting data that the authenticated user is not authorized to see.

Listing 7.12 api/index.js: Using a `where` authorization rule

```
extend type User
  @auth(
    rules: [
      { operations: [READ], where: { userId: "$jwt.sub" } }
      { operations: [CREATE, UPDATE, DELETE], roles: ["admin"] }
    ]
  )
```

We still need to ensure that only admin users are able to create, update, or delete users, so we add those operations to the `roles` rule, as shown in listing 7.13. Now, whenever a read request for the user type is executed, a predicate in the generated database query is added to filter for only the currently authenticated user, matching the sub claim of the JWT to the `userId` node property value in the database.

Listing 7.13 GraphQL query requesting user information

```
query {
  users {
    name
    userId
  }
}

{
  "data": {
    "users": [
      {
        "name": "Jenny",
        "userId": "u3"
      }
    ]
  }
}
```

If we examine the generated Cypher query sent to the database we can see the predicate that is appended, ensuring the node's `userId` property value in the database matches the JWT sub value, as shown in the following listing.

Listing 7.14 Generated Cypher query

```
MATCH (this:User)
WHERE this.userId IS NOT NULL AND this.userId = "u3"
RETURN this { .name, .userId } as this
```

7.3.6 *The bind authorization rule*

The bind rule is used to enforce authorization rules when creating or updating data and can also be used across relationships. In listing 7.15, let's use a bind rule to ensure that when reviews are created or updated, they are connected to the currently authenticated user. We don't want to allow users to falsely create reviews written by other users!

Listing 7.15 api/index.js: Using a `bind` authorization rule

```
extend type Review
  @auth(
    rules: [
      {
        operations: [CREATE, UPDATE]
        bind: { user: { userId: "$jwt.sub" } }
      }
    ]
  )
```

Let's write a GraphQL mutation to create a new business review in the next listing.

Listing 7.16 Creating a new review

```
mutation {
  createReviews(
    input: {
      business: { connect: { where: { node: { businessId: "b10" } } } }
      date: "2022-01-22"
      stars: 5.0
      text: "Love the Philtered Soul!"
      user: { connect: { where: { node: { userId: "u3" } } } }
    }
  ) {
    reviews {
      business {
        name
      }
      text
      stars
    }
  }
}
```

This executes with no problem, adding the review node to the database and the appropriate relationships:

```
{
  "data": {
    "createReviews": {
      "reviews": [
        {
          "business": {
            "name": "Philz Coffee"
          },
          "text": "Love the Philtered Soul!",
          "stars": 5
        }
      ]
    }
  }
}
```

However, if instead of connecting the review to the currently authenticated user (in this case, the user with `userId u3`), the mutation tries to connect to user `u1` or to no user at all, then the mutation operation will fail, and a `Forbidden` error will be returned.

Be sure to refer to the documentation for more examples of how to use the `@auth` GraphQL schema directive to add complex authorization rules to your GraphQL API: neo4j.com/docs/graphql-manual/current/auth.

So far, we've been using the JWT Builder website to create our JWTs; this is fine for development and testing, but we need something more for production.

7.4 Auth0: JWT as a service

Auth0 is an authentication and authorization service that can authenticate users with several methods, such as social sign-in or email and password. It also includes functionality to maintain a database of users, and we can use it to define rules and permissions for our users. I like to think of Auth0 as a JWT-as-a-service provider. Even though Auth0 has lots of functionality and services, at the end of the day, I'm often just interested in getting a user's auth token (as a JWT) and using that to authorize the user in my APIs and applications.

Auth0 is also a good service for learning and development because it offers a free tier with no credit card required to sign up. In this section, we will configure Auth0 to protect our API and then use the Auth0 React SDK to add Auth0 support to our application. You can create an Auth0 account for free at https://auth0.com.

7.4.1 Configuring Auth0

Once we've signed in to Auth0, we'll need to create an API and an Application in our Auth0 tenant (see figure 7.6). First, create the API and give it a name.

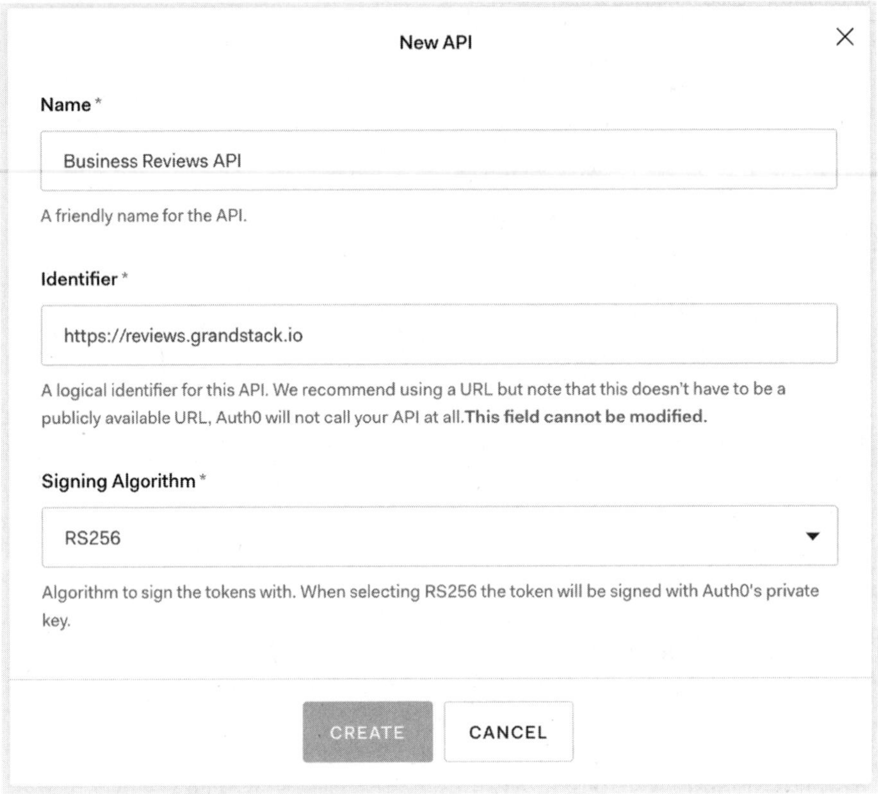

Figure 7.6   Creating an API in Auth0

We won't make use of this feature in our application, but we can, optionally, enable role-based access control (RBAC) for our API (see figure 7.7). This will allow us to add fine-grained permissions to the JWTs generated by Auth0 that can be used by the `roles` `@auth` schema directive rule for role-based access control.

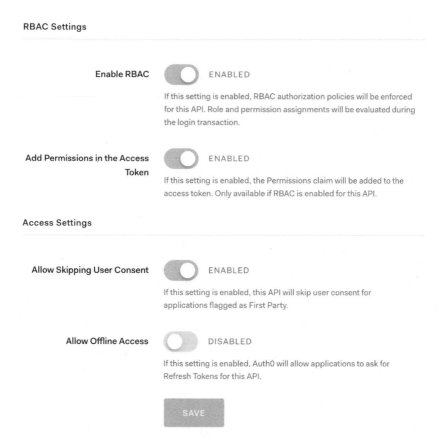

Figure 7.7 Enabling RBAC for our API in Auth0

If we do enable RBAC, we'll also need to define all possible permissions that can be used in our API. I've added the necessary permissions for creating, reading, updating, and deleting businesses in our API (see figure 7.8).

You can read more about using the `roles` authorization rule to enable RBAC in the Neo4j GraphQL Library documentation here: http://mng.bz/5Q5z.

Now, we need to create our Application in the Auth0 dashboard. Select *Create Application*. We'll need to choose a name for our application—I used *Business Reviews*. We're also asked to choose the type of application. Since we're building a React application, choose *Single Page Web Application,* and click the *Create* button.

Business Reviews API

CUSTOM API   Identifier   `https://reviews.grandstack.io`

Quick Start   Settings   **Permissions**   Machine to Machine Applications   Test

Add a Permission (Scope)

Define the permissions (scopes) that this API uses.

Permission (Scope) *   Description *

| read:appointments | | Read your appointments | | + ADD |

List of Permissions (Scopes)

These are all the permissions (scopes) that this API uses.

Permission	Description	
`read:business`	Read business data	🗑
`create:business`	Create business nodes	🗑
`update:business`	Update existing businesses	🗑
`delete:business`	Delete business nodes	🗑

Figure 7.8   Adding permissions to the API in Auth0

We'll keep most default settings, but we must update the entries for *Allowed Callback URLs* and *Allowed Logout URLs*. Add http://localhost:3000 to each of these text boxes under the *Settings* tab for our new application, and then select *Save Changes*.

Next, we'll need to update the configuration in our GraphQL API, specifying the method used to verify the JWTs generated by Auth0, as shown in listing 7.17. Up to now, we've been using a simple secret stored in an environment variable (`JWT_SECRET`) to verify the JWT. This is fine for local development and testing, but we'll want to use a more secure method now that we're using Auth0 and preparing to deploy our application to the web.

Navigate to *Advanced Settings* and then *Endpoints*. Look for the JWKS URL, and copy this value. Then, in the code for our GraphQL API, change the method used for validating the JWT to `jwksEndpoint` using the URL for your Auth0 application. This will allow our GraphQL API to fetch the public key from Auth0 to validate the token, which is a much more secure method than using a shared secret.

Listing 7.17   api/index.js: Using the Auth0 JSON Web Key Set (JWKS) endpoint

```
const {
  Neo4jGraphQLAuthJWKSPlugin,
} = require("@neo4j/graphql-plugin-auth");
```
← Now we use the **Neo4jGraphQLAuthJWKSPlugin** class.

```
...

const neoSchema = new Neo4jGraphQL({
  typeDefs,
  resolvers,
  driver,
  plugins: {
    auth: new Neo4jGraphQLAuthJWKSPlugin({
      jwksEndpoint: "https://grandstack.auth0.com/.well-known/jwks.json",
    }),
  },
});
```
← Be sure to use your endpoint, as found in Auth0's Advanced Settings.

We're now ready to start integrating Auth0 into our React application.

7.4.2   Auth0 React

First, let's install the Auth0 SDK for React. This package includes React-specific integrations for adding Auth0 support to any React applications.

We'll install the `auth0-react` library using `npm`. First, be sure you're in the `web-react` directory:

```
npm install @auth0/auth0-react
```

Now, let's add the initial Auth0 setup to our React application in the next listing.

Listing 7.18   web-react/src/index.js: Adding the Auth0 provider component

```
import React from "react";
import ReactDOM from "react-dom";
import "./index.css";
import App from "./App";
import reportWebVitals from "./reportWebVitals";
import {
  ApolloClient,
  InMemoryCache,
  ApolloProvider,
  makeVar,
} from "@apollo/client";
import { Auth0Provider } from "@auth0/auth0-react";
```
← Import the Auth0 Provider component.

```
export const starredVar = makeVar([]);

const client = new ApolloClient({
  uri: "http://localhost:4000",
  cache: new InMemoryCache({
    typePolicies: {
```

```
    Business: {
      fields: {
        isStarred: {
          read(_, { readField }) {
            return starredVar().includes(readField("businessId"));
          },
        },
      },
    },
  }),
});
```

```
ReactDOM.render(
  <React.StrictMode>                          Wrap our App component with
    <Auth0Provider                            the Auth0Provider component.
      domain="grandstack.auth0.com"
      clientId="4xw3K3cjvw0hyT4Mjp4RuOVSxvVYcOFF"
      redirectUri={window.location.origin}
      audience="https://reviews.grandstack.io"
    >
      <ApolloProvider client={client}>
        <App />
      </ApolloProvider>
    </Auth0Provider>
  </React.StrictMode>,
  document.getElementById("root")
);
```

```
// If you want to start measuring performance in your app, pass a function
// to log results (for example: reportWebVitals(console.log))
// or send to an analytics endpoint. Learn more: https://bit.ly/CRA-vitals
reportWebVitals();
```

We add the `Auth0Provider` component, injecting it into the component hierarchy by wrapping our `ApolloProvider` and `App` components. We also include the domain, client ID, and audience information for our Auth0 tenant, application, and API that we just created. This information can be found in the Auth0 dashboard for your Auth0 application.

In the next listing, we'll add login and logout buttons to our application using Auth0. Clicking the login button will walk the user through Auth0's authentication flow.

Listing 7.19   web-react/src/App.js: Adding login and logout buttons

```
import React, { useState } from "react";
import BusinessResults from "./BusinessResults";
import { gql, useQuery } from "@apollo/client";        Import the useAuth0
import { useAuth0 } from "@auth0/auth0-react";          React hook.

const GET_BUSINESSES_QUERY = gql`
  query BusinessesByCategory($selectedCategory: String!) {
    businesses(
```

```
        where: { categories_SOME: { name_CONTAINS: $selectedCategory } }
    ) {
      businessId
      name
      address
      categories {
        name
      }
      isStarred @client
    }
  }
`;

function App() {
  const [selectedCategory, setSelectedCategory] = useState("");
  const { loginWithRedirect, logout, isAuthenticated } = useAuth0();    ◄
```

Access functions to work with authentication flow and user data.

```
  const { loading, error, data, refetch } = useQuery(
    GET_BUSINESSES_QUERY,
    {
      variables: { selectedCategory },
    }
  );

  if (error) return <p>Error</p>;
  if (loading) return <p>Loading...</p>;

  return (
    <div>
      {!isAuthenticated && (
```

Add the login and logout buttons.

```
        <button onClick={() => loginWithRedirect()}>Log In</button>
      )}
      {isAuthenticated && (
        <button onClick={() => logout()}>Log Out</button>
      )}
      <h1>Business Search</h1>
      <form>
        <label>
          Select Business Category:
          <select
            value={selectedCategory}
            onChange={(event) => setSelectedCategory(event.target.value)}
          >
            <option value="">All</option>
            <option value="Library">Library</option>
            <option value="Restaurant">Restaurant</option>
            <option value="Car Wash">Car Wash</option>
          </select>
        </label>
        <input type="button" value="Refetch" onClick={() => refetch()} />
      </form>

      <BusinessResults businesses={data.businesses} />
    </div>
  );
```

```
}

export default App;
```

The Auth0 React package includes a `useAuth0` hook, which gives us access to functions that can trigger the authentication flow, determine whether the user is currently authenticated, and access user information. Now, we have a button with the option to log in, or if we're already logged in, then we have the option to log out.

Clicking *Log In*, we're presented with a number of options for sign-in, including GitHub, Google, Twitter, or email and password authentication (see figure 7.9). One benefit of using an authentication service is that we don't really need to concern ourselves with the specifics of the auth flow, since this is handled by Auth0.

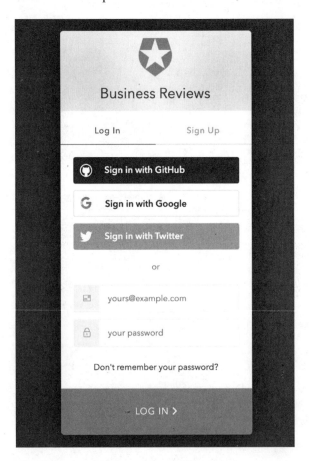

Figure 7.9   Sign-in options via Auth0

Notice the use of the `isAuthenticated` variable provided by the `useAuth0` hook. Once they log in, we can also access user information. Let's now add a profile component to show the user's name and avatar image once they've logged in. Create a new file, Profile .js, in the web-react/src directory, as shown in the next listing.

Listing 7.20 web-react/src/Profile.js: Adding a user profile component

```
import { useAuth0 } from "@auth0/auth0-react";

const Profile = () => {
  const { user, isAuthenticated } = useAuth0();
  return (
    isAuthenticated && (
      <div style={{ padding: "10px" }}>
        <img
          src={user.picture}
          alt="User avatar"
          style={{ width: "40px" }}
        />
        <strong>{user.name}</strong>
      </div>
    )
  );
};

export default Profile;
```

Now, let's include this profile component in our main App component to display the profile when the user is logged in.

Listing 7.21 web-react/src/App.js: Adding profile component

```
import Profile from "./Profile";

...

    {!isAuthenticated && (
      <button onClick={() => loginWithRedirect()}>Log In</button>
    )}
    {isAuthenticated && <button onClick={() => logout()}>Log Out</button>}
    <Profile />                ◄—————  Adding the Profile component
    <h1>Business Search</h1>

...
```

OK, we're able to have users sign in to our application and show their profile information, as shown in figure 7.10, but how do we make authenticated requests to our GraphQL API? We saw when using Apollo Studio that we need to attach the authorization token as a header in the GraphQL request.

Log Out

William Lyon

Business Search

Select Business Category: All ▼ Submit

Results

Star	Name	Address	Category
Star	Missoula Public Library	301 E Main St	Library
Star	Ninja Mike's	200 W Pine St	Restaurant, Breakfast
Star	KettleHouse Brewing Co.	313 N 1st St W	Beer, Brewery
Star	Imagine Nation Brewing	1151 W Broadway St	Beer, Brewery
Star	Market on Front	201 E Front St	Coffee, Restaurant, Cafe, Deli, Breakfast
Star	Hanabi	723 California Dr	Restaurant, Ramen
Star	Zootown Brew	121 W Broadway St	Coffee
Star	Ducky's Car Wash	716 N San Mateo Dr	Car Wash
Star	Neo4j	111 E 5th Ave	Graph Database

Figure 7.10   **The authenticated view of our React application**

To access the token, we will use the `getAccessTokenSilently` function from the `auth0-react` library. Then, we will attach this token to the Apollo Client instance, as shown in the next listing.

Listing 7.22   **web-react/src/index.js: Adding the access token in our GraphQL request**

```
import React from "react";
import ReactDOM from "react-dom";
import "./index.css";
import App from "./App";
import reportWebVitals from "./reportWebVitals";
import {
  ApolloClient,
  InMemoryCache,
  ApolloProvider,
  makeVar,
  createHttpLink,
} from "@apollo/client";
import { setContext } from "@apollo/client/link/context";
import { Auth0Provider, useAuth0 } from "@auth0/auth0-react";

export const starredVar = makeVar([]);

const AppWithApollo = () => {        ◄──
```

Create a wrapper component that will be responsible for adding the authorization token.

```
    const { getAccessTokenSilently, isAuthenticated } = useAuth0();

    const httpLink = createHttpLink({
      uri: "http://localhost:4000",
    });
```

Use Apollo Client's setContext function to add the JWT to the GraphQL request.

```
    const authLink = setContext(async (_, { headers }) => {     ◁─┐
      // Only try to fetch access token if user is authenticated
      const accessToken = isAuthenticated
        ? await getAccessTokenSilently()
        : undefined;
      if (accessToken) {
        return {
          headers: {
            ...headers,
            authorization: accessToken ? `Bearer ${accessToken}` : "",
          },
        };
      } else {
        return {
          headers: {
            ...headers,
            // We could set additional headers here or a "default"
            // authorization header if needed
          },
        };
      }
    });

    const client = new ApolloClient({
      link: authLink.concat(httpLink),
      cache: new InMemoryCache({
        typePolicies: {
          Business: {
            fields: {
              isStarred: {
                read(_, { readField }) {
                  return starredVar().includes(readField("businessId"));
                },
              },
            },
          },
        },
      }),
    });

    return (
      <ApolloProvider client={client}>
        <App />
      </ApolloProvider>
    );
  };

ReactDOM.render(
  <React.StrictMode>
```

```
<Auth0Provider
  domain="grandstack.auth0.com"
  clientId="4xw3K3cjvw0hyT4Mjp4RuOVSxvVYcOFF"
  redirectUri={window.location.origin}
  audience="https://reviews.grandstack.io"          Inject the AppWithApollo
>                                                    component into the React
  <AppWithApollo />        ◁                         component hierarchy.
</Auth0Provider>
</React.StrictMode>,
document.getElementById("root")

reportWebVitals();
```

Now, each request to the GraphQL API will include the authorization token in the header if the user is authenticated. We can verify this by opening the browser developer tools and inspecting the GraphQL network request (see figure 7.11).

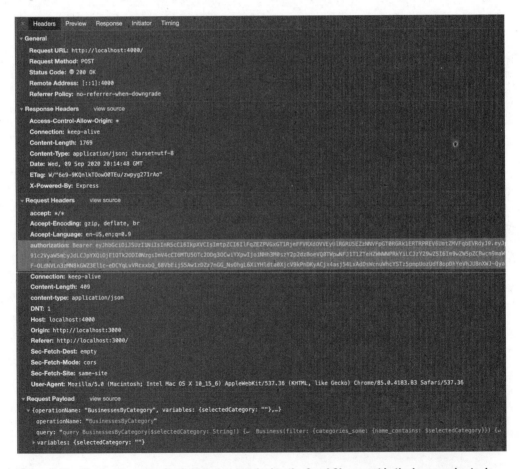

Figure 7.11   Viewing the authorization header attached to the GraphQL request in the browser dev tools window

We can copy this token and decode its payload using `jwt.io`. Here's what my decoded token looks like:

```json
{
  "iss": "https://grandstack.auth0.com/",
  "sub": "github|1222454",
  "aud": [
    "https://reviews.grandstack.io",
    "https://grandstack.auth0.com/userinfo"
  ],
  "iat": 1599684745,
  "exp": 1599771145,
  "azp": "4xw3K3cjvw0hyT4Mjp4RuOVSxvVYcOFF",
  "scope": "openid profile email"
}
```

Of course, our application doesn't look any different, since we aren't requesting any protected fields in our GraphQL query. Let's add the averageStars field, which is protected by the isAuthenticated rule, to the GraphQL query when the user is logged in.

Listing 7.23 web-react/src/App.js: Including the `averageStars` field in the selection set

```javascript
function App() {
  const [selectedCategory, setSelectedCategory] = useState("");
  const { loginWithRedirect, logout, isAuthenticated } = useAuth0();

  const GET_BUSINESSES_QUERY = gql`
  query BusinessesByCategory($selectedCategory: String!) {
    businesses(
      where: { categories_SOME: { name_CONTAINS: $selectedCategory } }
    ) {
      businessId
      name
      address
      categories {
        name
      }
      ${isAuthenticated ? "averageStars" : ""}    ⟵── Add the averageStars field when
      isStarred @client                                the user is authenticated.
    }
  }
`;

  const { loading, error, data, refetch } = useQuery(
    GET_BUSINESSES_QUERY,
    {
      variables: { selectedCategory },
    }
  );

  if (error) return <p>Error</p>;
  if (loading) return <p>Loading...</p>;
```

And now we will update the `BusinessResults` component to include `averageStars` when the use is authenticated.

Listing 7.24   web-react/src/BusinessResults.js: Display the `averageStars` field

```
import React from "react";
import { starredVar } from "./index";
import { useAuth0 } from "@auth0/auth0-react";

function BusinessResults(props) {
  const { businesses } = props;
  const starredItems = starredVar();
  const { isAuthenticated } = useAuth0();

  return (
    <div>
      <h2>Results</h2>
      <table>
        <thead>
          <tr>
            <th>Star</th>
            <th>Name</th>
            <th>Address</th>
            <th>Category</th>
            {isAuthenticated ? <th>Average Stars</th> : null}
          </tr>
        </thead>
        <tbody>
          {businesses.map((b) => (
            <tr key={b.businessId}>
              <td>
                <button
                  onClick={() =>
                    starredVar([...starredItems, b.businessId])
                  }
                >
                  Star
                </button>
              </td>

              <td style={b.isStarred ? { fontWeight: "bold" } : null}>
                {b.name}
              </td>
              <td>{b.address}</td>
              <td>
                {b.categories.reduce(
                  (acc, c, i) => acc + (i === 0 ? " " : ", ") + c.name,
                  ""
                )}
              </td>
              {isAuthenticated ? <td>{b.averageStars}</td> : null}
            </tr>
          ))}
        </tbody>
```

Add the Average Stars header only when the user is authenticated.

Show the Average Stars value when authenticated.

```
      </table>
    </div>
  );
}
```

```
export default BusinessResults;
```

Now, we'll see the average stars for each business only when the user is authenticated. We've added authentication and authorization to our application and added support for Auth0. Now that we're confident our application is secure, we'll take a look at deploying our application and database in the next chapter.

7.5 Exercises

1 Create a new query field called `qualityBusinesses` that uses a `@cypher` schema directive to return businesses that have at least two reviews each with four or more stars. Protect this field, using a `roles` rule and the `@auth` schema directive to require a role of `analyst`. Create a JWT that includes this role in the claims, and use Apollo Studio to query this new `qualityBusinesses` field.

2 In this chapter, we used a GraphQL mutation to create a new business review. Update the React application to include a form to allow the currently authenticated user to create new business reviews.

Summary

- Authorization rules can be expressed declaratively in the GraphQL schema using the `@auth` GraphQL schema directive.
- JWT is a standard for encoding and transmitting JSON objects and is commonly used for authorization tokens in web applications, such as GraphQL APIs.
- Auth0 is an identity and access management service that can be used to handle JWT generation and user authentication. Auth0 can be integrated into a React application, using the Auth0 React SDK.

Deploying our full stack GraphQL application

8

This chapter covers

- Deploying our full stack GraphQL application so it is accessible to users on the web
- Using serverless deployment and cloud-managed services like Netlify, AWS Lambda, and Neo4j Aura
- A framework for evaluating various deployment options to help us reconcile the inherent tradeoffs

While developing our application so far, we have been running it locally on our machine for testing. Now, it's time to deploy our application so we can share it with the world and have users interact with it. There are many different ways to deploy applications, especially with the growth and evolution of cloud-managed services that offer improved developer experiences and usage pricing. There is not a single best deployment option for any application, as each choice has tradeoffs; ultimately, the developer must decide what options make the most sense for them and their use case.

In this chapter, we explore an opinionated approach to deploying our full stack GraphQL application, taking advantage of third-party service providers, like Netlify, AWS Lambda, and Neo4j Aura. This approach of leveraging managed services, outsourcing much of the operations of these services to the provider, is often referred to as *serverless*. We evaluate the advantages and disadvantages of this deployment approach, using a framework focused on operations, scale, and developer experience. Finally, we review alternative options for deployment and discuss the tradeoffs introduced.

8.1 Deploying our full stack GraphQL application

Serverless computing is a paradigm that describes a way of allocating computing resources and execution on demand; it's a way for developers to ship their application without concerning themselves with provisioning and maintaining servers. Services like the AWS Lambda Function as a Service (FaaS) platform are said to be *serverless*—not because no servers are involved in the process of serving an application, but rather, the developer need not think about servers, and instead, the relevant abstraction becomes the *function*, or unit of code. Usage of the term *serverless* has expanded to describe not just computing runtimes like AWS Lambda and Google App Engine but also databases and other managed cloud services.

The first deployment paradigm we will examine takes advantage of *managed services*. A managed service is a way of outsourcing responsibility for operating software, infrastructure, or networking to a cloud service provider. This means developers can spend less time maintaining and operating things like the database, scaling up web-servers, installing security updates, and renewing SSL certificates and can, instead, focus on building aspects of their application in which they have a competitive advantage, such as the core business competency and business logic. Our approach has special appeal for full stack developers, who may not be experts or care to take on responsibility for managing databases, servers, dealing with SSL certificates, DNS configuration, and other aspects needed for operating a full stack web application.

8.1.1 Advantages of this deployment approach

Embracing managed services offers advantages over alternative approaches. Here we highlight the advantages of developer productivity, usage-based pricing, scalability, and maintenance and operations.

DEVELOPER PRODUCTIVITY

Many managed services pride themselves on offering an improved developer experience that abstracts away many unnecessary complexities or concerns that are unrelated to the goals of the developer: building and shipping their application. Tooling like web consoles to configure services and command line interfaces (CLIs) that can be integrated into developer workflows enable developers to be more productive.

USAGE PRICING

Incurring costs based on the usage of the service is a core tenet of this paradigm. If an application has very little usage, it will incur little cost for the developer. This allows developers to build, deploy, and test their applications with little upfront cost, since their costs are not fixed.

SCALABILITY

Services should scale on demand driven by usage. For example, a FaaS runtime like AWS Lambda executes in response to events, such as the invocation of an API endpoint. Each function invocation is stateless and runs concurrently, allowing for greater elasticity and on-demand scaling than a single web server.

MAINTENANCE AND OPERATIONS

By using managed services, the responsibility for ensuring that the service operates in a healthy, secure, and high-performing state is outsourced to the service provider. This benefit often resonates with the full-stack developer who is typically responsible for many components of the overall application.

8.1.2 Disadvantages of our deployment approach

Of course, managed services are not a silver bullet that will solve all our problems, and they can introduce some disadvantages. These disadvantages include vendor lock-in, performance optimization, and usage-based pricing (a double-edged sword!).

VENDOR LOCK-IN

Outsourcing the responsibility for maintaining and updating the service to a service provider means the developer is at the mercy of the service provider to provide continuous operation of the service—and at a reasonable cost. Services can sometimes be discontinued or deprecated, as many services have specific APIs, libraries, or paradigms that may be costly for a developer to adapt to an alternative.

PERFORMANCE OPTIMIZATIONS

Since many services operate in a multitenant architecture, performance cannot always be guaranteed to be consistent, as resources may be shared or allocated to other users. Given the on-demand nature of many services, there may be some overhead, as resources are provisioned to respond to increased usage.

USAGE PRICING

Usage pricing can be both an advantage and a disadvantage. If the cost structure and usage patterns are not understood, or if there is a surge in unanticipated usage, then an unexpected increase in costs could be most unwelcome.

8.1.3 Overview of our approach to full stack GraphQL

Our deployment approach will take advantage of three managed services (see figure 8.1):

1 *Neo4j Aura database as a service*—For deploying a managed, scalable graph database in the cloud. By using Neo4j Aura, we eliminate the need to think about how to manage our database instance. Operations and maintenance, such as regular backups and updates, are handled for us by the service.

2 *Netlify Build*—For building, deploying, and updating our React application and serving it globally through a content delivery network (CDN). Using the Netlify platform will not only give us access to a global CDN to ensure our site loads fast, regardless of where in the world our users are located, but Netlify also

offers a smooth developer experience and integration with version control systems, such as GitHub.

3 *AWS Lambda (via Netlify Functions)*—For deploying our GraphQL API as a scalable serverless function. Using AWS Lambda for our GraphQL API means we don't have to think about hosting and managing webservers and scaling servers up and down as incoming requests grow.

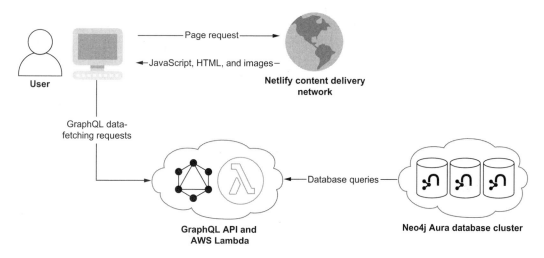

Figure 8.1 **A full stack GraphQL deployment from the user's perspective**

8.2 Neo4j Aura database as a service

Neo4j Aura is Neo4j's managed cloud service, offering Neo4j database clusters as a cloud service. Neo4j Aura offers scalable, highly available Neo4j clusters without dealing with operations or maintenance. Developers can provision Neo4j clusters with the click of a button and have access to Neo4j developer tooling, like Neo4j Browser, Neo4j Bloom, and the APOC standard library. There are two flavors of Neo4j Aura: AuraDB and AuraDS. AuraDB is Neo4j's standard database-as-a-service offering, which is suitable for backing web applications and API services. AuraDS is Neo4j's hosted graph data science platform and includes features specific to data science workloads. For our purposes, we will be using Neo4j AuraDB.

8.2.1 Creating a Neo4j Aura cluster

Since Neo4j Aura is a managed service, we'll need to first sign up by either logging in with a Google account or creating an account using email and password at neo4j.com/aura and then selecting *Sign Up Now*. Since I use Gmail, I'll choose to sign in with Google. After signing in, we'll see the Neo4j Aura Dashboard.

The Neo4j Aura Dashboard is our mission control central for our Neo4j clusters in the cloud. We can monitor our databases, provision new databases, import data, scale databases up or down, and access developer tooling.

YW 278 7482

However, since we haven't created any Neo4j Aura clusters yet, our dashboard looks empty. Let's create a new cluster by clicking the *Create a database* button (see figure 8.2). There is an AuraDB Free tier that offers a Neo4j instance without any cost or requirement to input a credit card, so I'll choose this option. For larger applications, we can choose the AuraDB Professional tier, which offers additional features and the ability to scale the resources available to our database instance.

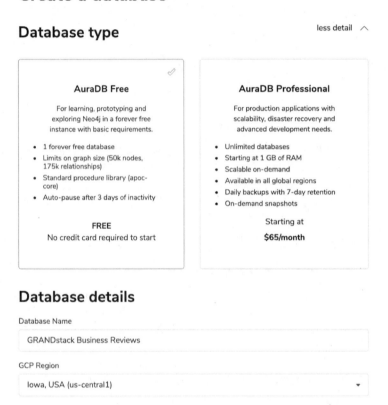

Create a database

Database type

less detail ⌃

AuraDB Free

For learning, prototyping and exploring Neo4j in a forever free instance with basic requirements.

- 1 forever free database
- Limits on graph size (50k nodes, 175k relationships)
- Standard procedure library (apoc-core)
- Auto-pause after 3 days of inactivity

FREE
No credit card required to start

AuraDB Professional

For production applications with scalability, disaster recovery and advanced development needs.

- Unlimited databases
- Starting at 1 GB of RAM
- Scalable on-demand
- Available in all global regions
- Daily backups with 7-day retention
- On-demand snapshots

Starting at
$65/month

Database details

Database Name

GRANDstack Business Reviews

GCP Region

Iowa, USA (us-central1)   ▾

Starting dataset

Learn about graphs with a movie dataset

Beginner

Load or create your own data in a blank database

✕ Cancel   ✅ Create Database

Figure 8.2   Configuring a Neo4j AuraDB deployment

Be sure to select the *AuraDB Free* database type. Next, we'll need to choose a name for our database. I went with *GRANDstack Business Reviews*. We can choose from different regions where our database will be deployed. I just left the default, but feel free to select the location closest to you. In the *Starting dataset* option, we can choose to start with a predefined dataset or load our own data. Since we'll be working with our own data, select *Load or create your own data in a blank database*. After selecting the configuration options, we'll be presented with a random password, which we'll use to access our Neo4 Aura instance (see figure 8.3).

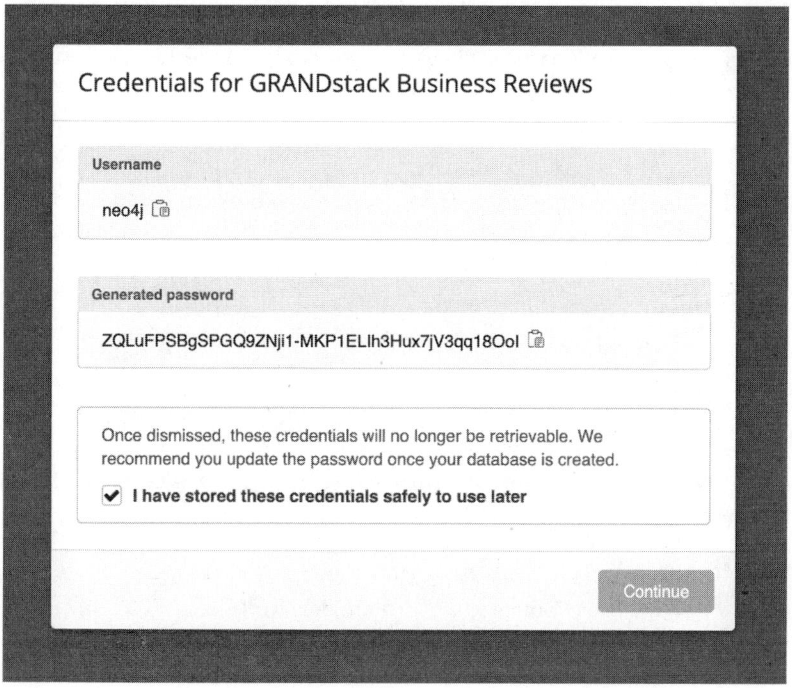

Figure 8.3 Database credentials for our Neo4j AuraDB deployment

Be sure to save the password somewhere safe. We'll change it, but we will need it to log in with Neo4j Browser in a moment.

Clicking *Continue* will take us back to the Neo4j Aura dashboard, but now, we'll see details for the database cluster we've just deployed with options to *Explore*, *Query*, or *Import* (see figure 8.4). The *Explore* button will launch Neo4j Browser, which we've used in previous chapters to execute Cypher queries and visualize the results. The *Query* button will launch Neo4j Bloom, a visual graph exploration tool, which we will explore in a moment. Finally, the *Import* button will launch the Neo4j Data Importer, a tool for loading data into Neo4j from flat files such as CSV format.

Figure 8.4   The Neo4j AuraDB dashboard, showing our new database

If we click on the database name, we can see more detailed information and options specific to our database. For our cluster, we can see the following details:

- *Connection URI*—This is the connection string used to connect to our Neo4j cluster using the Neo4j client drivers.
- *Tier*—This tells us the service tier for this database (Free, Professional, or Enterprise).
- *Cloud provider*—This is the cloud platform where this cluster is deployed. In this case, it is Google Cloud Platform.
- *Region*—This is the geographical region of the data center where the cluster is deployed.
- *Memory*—This is the current size of the database, which can be scaled up or down at any time.

We also have the *Open with* dropdown button to access Neo4j Browser or Neo4j Bloom developer tools.

8.2.2   *Connecting to a Neo4j Aura cluster*

Now that we've provisioned our Neo4j Aura cluster, we're ready to connect to it using the Neo4j JavaScript driver. First, let's change the initial password for the `neo4j` database user. To do this, we'll launch Neo4j Browser by clicking the *Query* button. This will open Neo4j Browser, which we're familiar with from previous chapters. Refer back to chapter 3 for an overview of how to use Neo4j Browser. We'll be prompted to sign in using the `neo4j` database user and initial password we were assigned.

After signing in, let's change our password for user `neo4j`. To do this, we'll need to execute a Cypher command against the *system* database. Any administrative commands, like changing user passwords, need to be done against this system database. First, we tell Neo4j Browser to switch to the system database:

```
:use system
```

Then, we'll use the `ALTER CURRENT USER` Cypher command to change the password of the default `neo4j` user:

```
ALTER CURRENT USER SET PASSWORD FROM
"<OUR_RANDOM_INITIAL_PASSWORD_HERE>" TO "<NEW_SECRET_PASSWORD_HERE>"
```

Be sure to replace <OUR_RANDOM_INITIAL_PASSWORD_HERE> with the initial password and <NEW_SECRET_PASSWORD_HERE> with a new secure password. For the remaining examples, we'll use the password *graphqlapi*, but using a stronger password is encouraged. To switch back to the default *neo4j* database, we can use the command :use neo4j.

> **NOTE** Commands like :use are utility commands specific to Neo4j Browser and are not Cypher commands. For more information on using these commands in Neo4j Browser, run :help or :help commands.

Now that we've changed our database user's password, let's test whether we can connect to our Neo4j Aura cluster, using the Neo4j JavaScript driver. From the Aura dashboard, if we click on our database name, we can see code samples showing how to connect to our Neo4j Aura instance using different language drivers (see figure 8.5).

Figure 8.5 The Connect tab in Neo4j Aura, showing code examples in various languages

In listing 8.1, let's adapt the JavaScript example to simply count the number of nodes in the database and return the results. We'll create a new file in the API directory, called aura-connect.js, with our simplified JavaScript example.

> **NOTE** Note the neo4j+s:// URI scheme used in the code sample. Previously, we used bolt://, which indicated a connection to a specific Neo4j instance. With Neo4j Aura, we've deployed a cluster—a series of Neo4j instances that talk to each other to replicate and distribute data—so we use the neo4j scheme to tell the driver to route requests to different machines in the cluster, instead of to a single machine. The +s tells the driver we want to use a secure encrypted connection.

Listing 8.1   aura-connect.js: Querying our Neo4j Aura instance

```javascript
(async () => {
  const neo4j = require("neo4j-driver");

  // be sure to change these connection details for your Neo4j instance
  const uri = "neo4j+s://97a0fe69.databases.neo4j.io";
  const user = "neo4j";
  const password = "graphqlapi";

  const driver = neo4j.driver(uri, neo4j.auth.basic(user, password));
  const session = driver.session();

  try {
    const readQuery = `MATCH (n)
                       RETURN COUNT(n) AS num`;
    const readResult = await session.readTransaction((tx) =>
      tx.run(readQuery)
    );
    readResult.records.forEach((record) => {
      console.log(`Found ${record.get("num")} nodes in the database`);
    });
  } catch (error) {
    console.error("Something went wrong: ", error);
  } finally {
    await session.close();
  }

  await driver.close();
})();
```

This code imports the Neo4j JavaScript driver, creating an instance of the driver with our Neo4j Aura credentials, executing a Cypher query in a read transaction, and then logging the results of the query to the console. If we run this file, we should verify that we are able to connect to our Neo4j Aura database and that the database is currently empty:

```
$ node aura-connect.js
Found 0 nodes in the database
```

Our next step is to upload data from our local Neo4j instance that we've been using to develop our application to our Neo4j Aura database.

8.2.3   Uploading data to Neo4j Aura

Previously, we used the `:play grandstack` Neo4j Browser guide to load some initial data to import our business reviews data, but in this case, we may have added user information, new reviews, or updated businesses. Let's discuss the process of dumping and loading data from a local Neo4j database into our new Neo4j Aura cluster.

There are a few different ways to import data into Neo4j Aura, but we will use the push-to-cloud tool. If you select the *Import* tab in the Neo4j Aura dashboard, you'll be presented with a wizard-like interface to walk you through the steps of uploading a local Neo4j database into your Neo4j Aura cloud database. We'll go through those steps now.

First, we want to make sure our local Neo4j database is in a stopped state. We can verify this in Neo4j Desktop and click the *Stop* button if it is not (see figure 8.6).

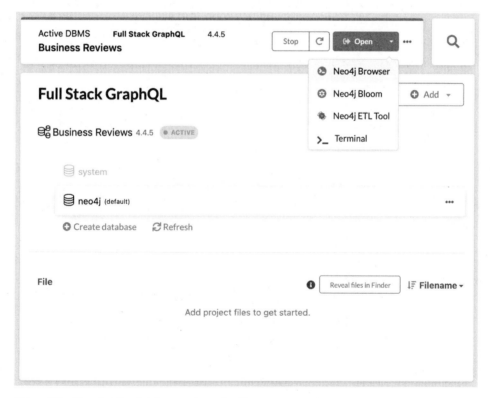

Figure 8.6   Stopping the database and opening the management pane

Next, we'll open a terminal in Neo4j Desktop that will allow us to run the `neo4j-admin` command for this specific Neo4j instance. The `neo4j-admin` command line tool has several useful features, such as a high-volume data import from CSV files, generating recommended memory configuration, and the push-to-cloud command, which we will use to upload this database to our Neo4j Aura instance.

Select the drop-down arrow next to the *Open* button, and choose *Terminal* to open a new window with a command prompt. The working directory for this new command prompt is set to the directory where this particular Neo4j instance has been installed:

```
$ pwd
/Users/lyonwj/Library/Application Support/com.Neo4j.Relate/Data/dbmss/
dbms-54c2c495-211d-408d-8c9e-6a65cce61d91
```

Now, we're ready to use the push-to-cloud command to upload this database to Neo4j Aura. We'll specify the Bolt URI of our Neo4j Aura instance as well as the --overwrite flag to indicate we want to replace any data we may have already created in the Neo4j Aura instance. We'll be prompted for database user and password, and then our local database will be exported and uploaded to our Neo4j Aura database:

```
$ bin/neo4j-admin push-to-cloud --bolt-uri \
neo4j+s://97a0fe69.databases.neo4j.io  --database neo4j --overwrite

Neo4j aura username (default: neo4j):neo4j
Neo4j aura password for neo4j:
Done: 68 files, 879.4KiB processed.
Dumped contents of database 'neo4j' into '/Users/lyonwj/Library/Application
Support/com.Neo4j.Relate/Data/dbmss/
dbms-54c2c495-211d-408d-8c9e-6a65cce61d91/dump-of-neo4j-1612960685687'
Upload
..................... 10%
..................... 20%
..................... 30%
..................... 40%
..................... 50%
..................... 60%
..................... 70%
..................... 80%
..................... 90%
..................... 100%
We have received your export and it is currently being loaded into your
Aura instance.
You can wait here, or abort this command and head over to the console to
be notified of when your database is running.
Import progress (estimated)
..................... 10%
..................... 20%
..................... 30%
..................... 40%
..................... 50%
..................... 60%
..................... 70%
..................... 80%
..................... 90%
..................... 100%
Your data was successfully pushed to Aura and is now running.
```

Now, we can verify the data was uploaded to our Neo4j Aura instance. If we run our aura-connect.js script again, we should see that we have a total of 36 nodes in the database:

```
$ node aura-connect.js
Found 36 nodes in the database
```

8.2.4 Exploring the graph with Neo4j Bloom

We can also visually inspect and explore the data we've just uploaded to Neo4j Aura. Let's return to the Neo4j Aura dashboard, and this time we'll open the database using *Neo4j Bloom*. Neo4j Bloom is a graph exploration application for visually interacting with Neo4j graphs and is included with Neo4j Aura. From the Neo4j Aura dashboard, click the *Explore* button. A new tab will open, and we'll be prompted to log in, using our database username and password.

Once we are signed in, Neo4j Bloom will connect to our Neo4j Aura instance and allow us to visually explore our graph data. First, we'll need to configure a *perspective* (see figure 8.7). In Neo4j Bloom, a perspective defines the domain or view of the graph data that should be exposed and how that data should be styled. For our purposes, the default-generated perspective should be sufficient, so select *Create Perspective* to generate a perspective from the database, and then select the perspective to use it for visualization.

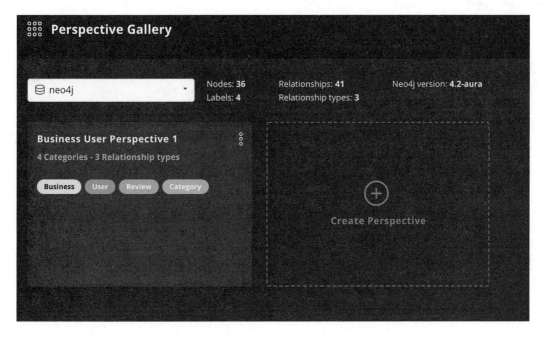

Figure 8.7   Creating a perspective in Neo4j Bloom

Once we've created the perspective, we can begin our visual exploration of the graph. This main view in Neo4j Bloom is called the scene and serves as a kind of canvas for us to paint on with our graph data, based on the data we select. To bring data into the scene, we use natural language, like search terms in the search bar that will be translated to graph patterns (see figure 8.8). For example, if we begin to type User name: Will WROTE Review, we can see helpful autocomplete graph patterns start to be suggested for us. Selecting one of these patterns will execute the search and populate the scene with data matching the graph search pattern.

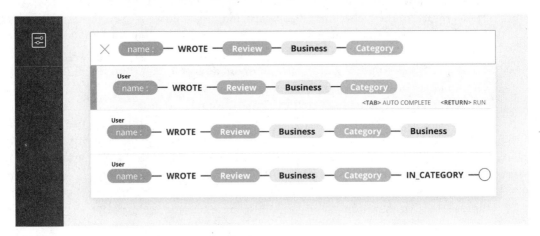

Figure 8.8   Natural language search in Neo4j Bloom

We said earlier that perspectives can configure how the visualization is styled (see figure 8.9). One such styling we can configure is the icons used to represent nodes in the visualization. By selecting a category in the legend panel, we can apply styling, such as the color, size, icon, or caption of the node.

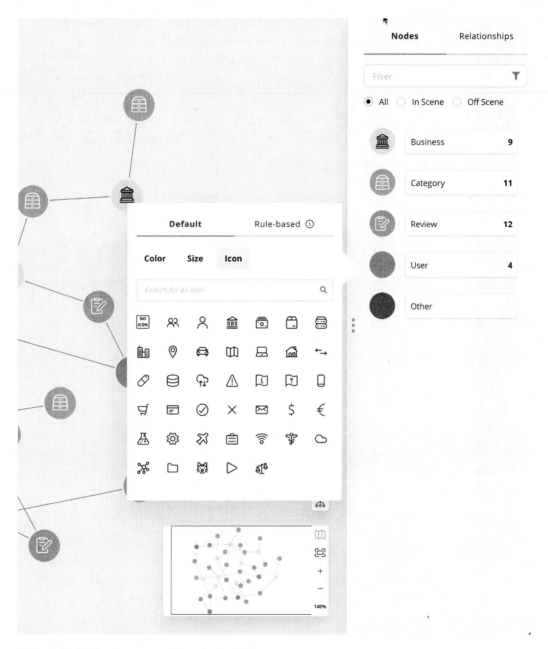

Figure 8.9   Configuring category icons in Neo4j Bloom

The visualization is interactive and can be used to explore the graph or validate that the data uploaded is as we expected. Selecting nodes will allow us to view their properties (see figure 8.10). We can also right-click on nodes or relationships to further expand or filter the data shown in the scene.

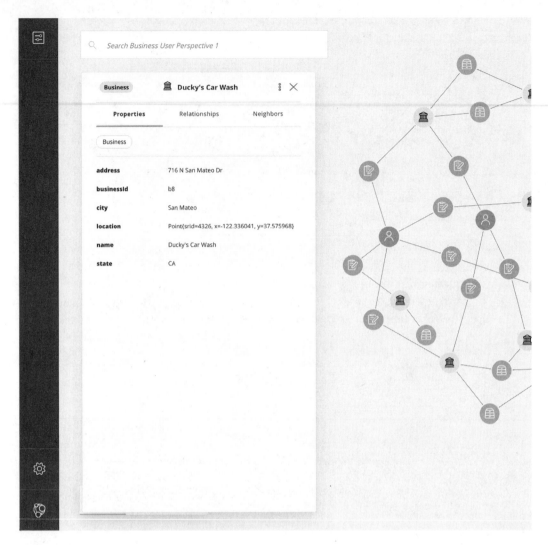

Figure 8.10   View node details in Neo4j Bloom

At this point, we've provisioned our Neo4j Aura cluster, changed the password, uploaded our data, explored the data, and verified and explored our graph in Neo4j Bloom. Now, let's turn our attention to deploying our React application and GraphQL API using Netlify and AWS Lambda.

8.3   *Deploying a React application with Netlify Build*

To deploy our React application, we'll make use of Netlify. Netlify is a cloud platform focused on a smooth developer experience and workflow for building and deploying web applications. Netlify combines an automated build system, global content delivery network, serverless functions, edge handlers, and other features, all wrapped up in a platform focused on a smooth developer experience and workflow.

Services with similar features include Vercel, DigitalOcean App Platform, Cloudflare Pages, and Azure Static Web Apps. Netlify also has a free tier, so we can deploy our application and try out the service without needing to input a credit card or incur any charges.

Netlify also enables us to trigger builds and deployments via commits and pull requests to a Git version control system, like GitHub or GitLab. We'll make use of GitHub in this section to trigger Netlify deployments and show a great feature of Netlify, called preview builds, that allows us to deploy and test the application from a pull request.

8.3.1 Adding a site to Netlify

Let's start by navigating to netlify.com and clicking the *Sign up* button to create a free Netlify account. Since we'll be taking advantage of the GitHub integration to deploy and update our application from GitHub, we can sign in to Netlify using our GitHub account, and our Netlify account will then be linked to GitHub (see figure 8.11). We can also sign in with another option, such as email and password, and choose to link our Netlify account to GitHub later on.

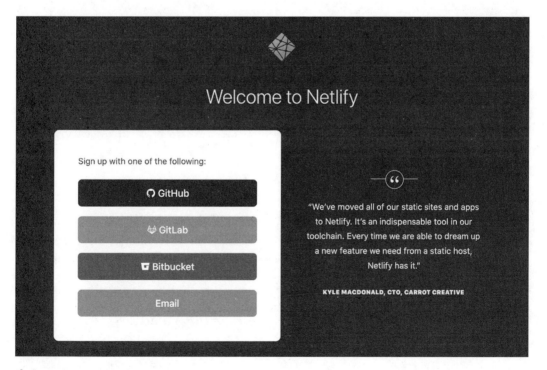

Figure 8.11   Signing in to Netlify

Once we've signed in, we are presented with an overview of the web sites we've added to Netlify (see figure 8.12). Since we just created our account, this page is a bit sparse.

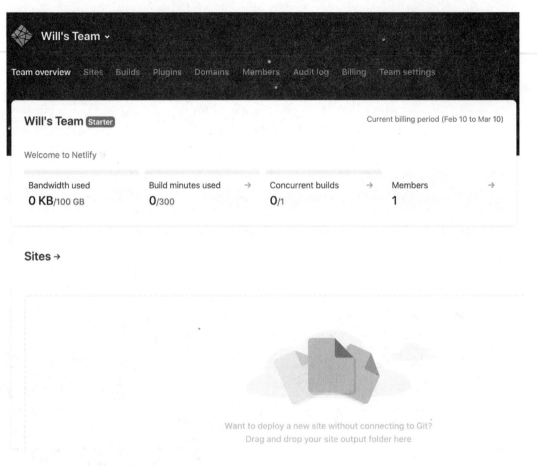

Figure 8.12   The Netlify dashboard

To add our first site to Netlify, let's create a GitHub repository for our application so we can add it as a site to Netlify to start deployments. We'll need to create a new GitHub repository for our application (see figure 8.13). To do that, first navigate to github.com/new. We'll need to choose a name for our repository—I chose grandstack-business-reviews. We can also choose to make our repository private if we don't want to expose it to the world.

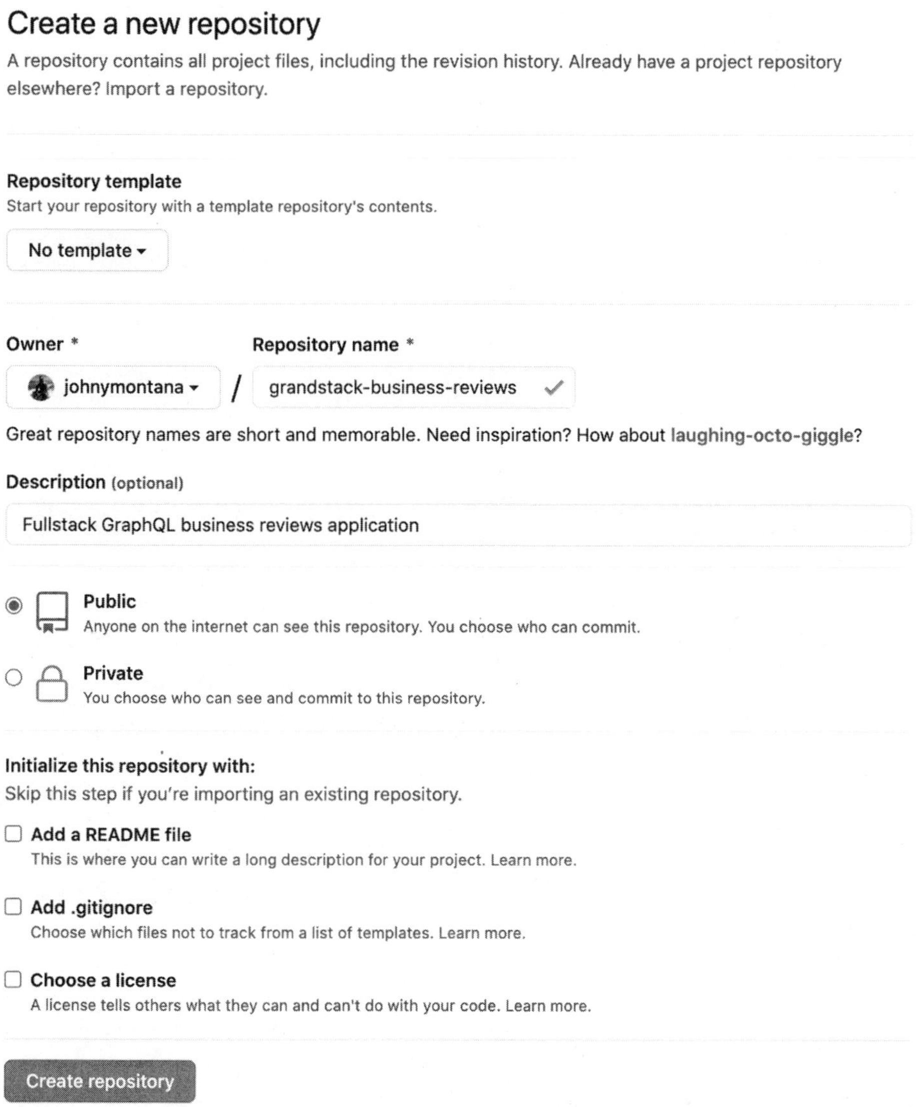

Create a new repository

A repository contains all project files, including the revision history. Already have a project repository elsewhere? Import a repository.

Repository template

Start your repository with a template repository's contents.

No template ▾

Owner *   **Repository name** *

🔵 johnymontana ▾ / grandstack-business-reviews ✓

Great repository names are short and memorable. Need inspiration? How about laughing-octo-giggle?

Description (optional)

Fullstack GraphQL business reviews application

◉ 📖 **Public**
Anyone on the internet can see this repository. You choose who can commit.

○ 🔒 **Private**
You choose who can see and commit to this repository.

Initialize this repository with:

Skip this step if you're importing an existing repository.

☐ **Add a README file**
This is where you can write a long description for your project. Learn more.

☐ **Add .gitignore**
Choose which files not to track from a list of templates. Learn more.

☐ **Choose a license**
A license tells others what they can and can't do with your code. Learn more.

Create repository

Figure 8.13   Creating a new GitHub repository

We've now created an empty GitHub repository, and it's time to add our business reviews application code to the repository. This screen shows the common terminal commands used to initialize a git repository, commit code, and push to GitHub (see figure 8.14). There is also a Desktop client that can be used with GitHub; however, we'll use the command line to do this.

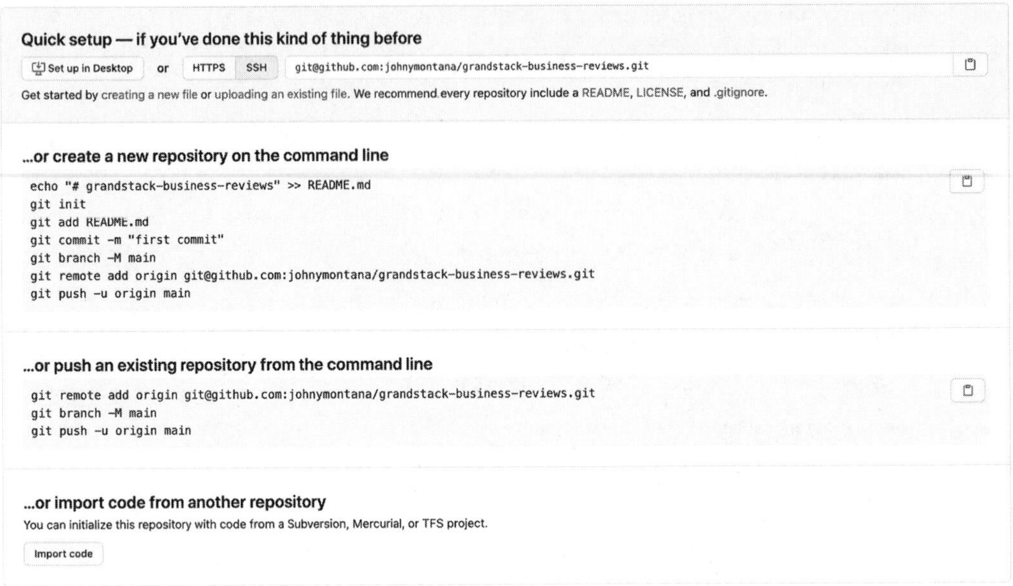

Figure 8.14   Instructions for pushing a local Git repository to GitHub

Let's open a terminal and navigate to the web-react directory that holds the React application we've been building. First, we initialize a blank GitHub repository:

```
$ git init
```

We can view the status of our local working directory with the `git status` command:

```
$ git status

On branch main
No commits yet

Untracked files:
  (use "git add <file>..." to include in what will be committed)
    .gitignore
    README.md
    package-lock.json
    package.json
    public/
    src/

nothing added to commit but untracked files present (use "git add" to track)
```

In this case, we have haven't made any commits to the repository yet, so let's stage our code to be added. To do this, we'll use the `git add` command:

```
$ git add -A
```

The `-A` flag indicates we want to stage all files in the project to be added. We typically don't want to add *all* files to the repository; things like the node_modules directory and secrets shouldn't be checked into version control. The `create-react-app` tool we used earlier to create the skeleton of our React application also created a .gitignore file that includes rules for files to be excluded from git. Thanks to this file, we can safely make use of the -A flag when staging files for a commit. Now, as we run `git status` again, we'll see all the files to be added to the repository in our commit:

```
$ git status
On branch main
No commits yet

Changes to be committed:
  (use "git rm --cached <file>..." to unstage)
    new file:   .gitignore
    new file:   README.md
    new file:   package-lock.json
    new file:   package.json
    new file:   public/favicon.ico
    new file:   public/index.html
    new file:   public/logo192.png
    new file:   public/logo512.png
    new file:   public/manifest.json
    new file:   public/robots.txt
    new file:   src/App.css
    new file:   src/App.js
    new file:   src/App.test.js
    new file:   src/BusinessResults.js
    new file:   src/Profile.js
    new file:   src/index.css
    new file:   src/index.js
    new file:   src/logo.svg
    new file:   src/serviceWorker.js
    new file:   src/setupTests.js
```

Let's make our commit with the `git commit` command. Every commit also includes a message that indicates the reason or functionality introduced in the commit. This message can be added using the -m flag, or we can omit that flag and then be prompted for a commit message:

```
$ git commit -m "initial commit"
[main (root-commit) 0bb81ca] initial commit
 20 files changed, 14609 insertions(+)
 create mode 100644 .gitignore
 create mode 100644 README.md
 create mode 100644 package-lock.json
 create mode 100644 package.json
 create mode 100644 public/favicon.ico
 create mode 100644 public/index.html
 create mode 100644 public/logo192.png
 create mode 100644 public/logo512.png
 create mode 100644 public/manifest.json
 create mode 100644 public/robots.txt
 create mode 100644 src/App.css
 create mode 100644 src/App.js
```

```
create mode 100644 src/App.test.js
create mode 100644 src/BusinessResults.js
create mode 100644 src/Profile.js
create mode 100644 src/index.css
create mode 100644 src/index.js
create mode 100644 src/logo.svg
create mode 100644 src/serviceWorker.js
create mode 100644 src/setupTests.js
```

Next, we connect our local Git repository with the remote GitHub repository we created:

```
$ git remote add origin \
git@github.com:johnymontana/grandstack-business-reviews.git
```

And finally, we push our local commit up to the remote GitHub repository with the git push command:

```
$ git push -u origin main

Enumerating objects: 24, done.
Counting objects: 100% (24/24), done.
Delta compression using up to 16 threads
Compressing objects: 100% (24/24), done.
Writing objects: 100% (24/24), 175.60 KiB | 1.60 MiB/s, done.
Total 24 (delta 0), reused 0 (delta 0)
To github.com:johnymontana/grandstack-business-reviews.git
 * [new branch]      main -> main
Branch 'main' set up to track remote branch 'main' from 'origin'.
```

If we refresh the GitHub web page for our repository, we'll now see the code we've committed and a history of the commits (see figure 8.15).

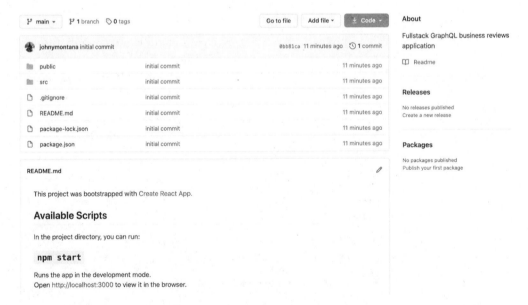

Figure 8.15   Viewing our new repository on GitHub

Now, we're ready to deploy our React application with Netlify. Return to the Netlify dashboard, and click on *Add site from Git*. We'll be prompted to select the Git provider we want to connect to and then the repository we want to add. Select GitHub, and choose the repository we just created and pushed our code to (see figure 8.16).

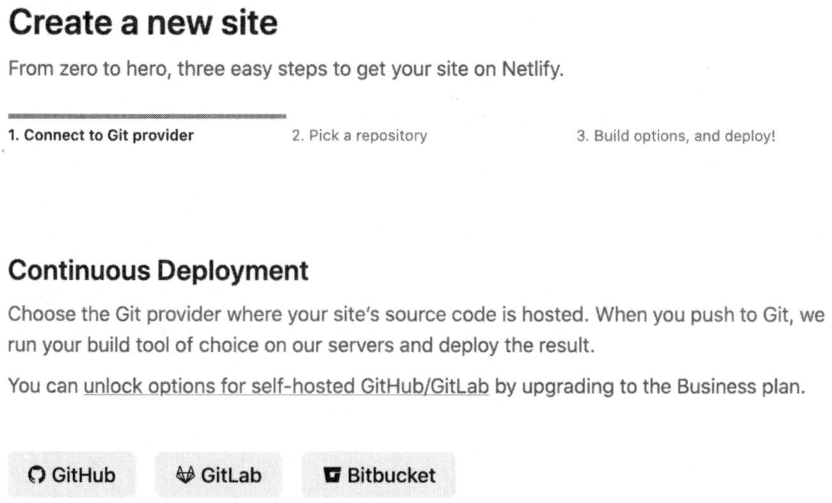

Create a new site

From zero to hero, three easy steps to get your site on Netlify.

1. Connect to Git provider   2. Pick a repository   3. Build options, and deploy!

Continuous Deployment

Choose the Git provider where your site's source code is hosted. When you push to Git, we run your build tool of choice on our servers and deploy the result.

You can unlock options for self-hosted GitHub/GitLab by upgrading to the Business plan.

⬢ GitHub   ⬢ GitLab   ⬢ Bitbucket

Figure 8.16   Adding a new site in Netlify

Netlify will inspect the code to determine that this is a React application built using the command npm run build, and the content should be served from the /build directory. We shouldn't need to make any changes here, as the defaults will typically be sufficient to build and deploy our React application. We can change these build settings later if needed (see figure 8.17).

Netlify will now pull down our code from GitHub to build and deploy the site. We can view the build logs from the dashboard as this happens. Each site in Netlify is assigned a URL and SSL certificate, so we can immediately preview our application

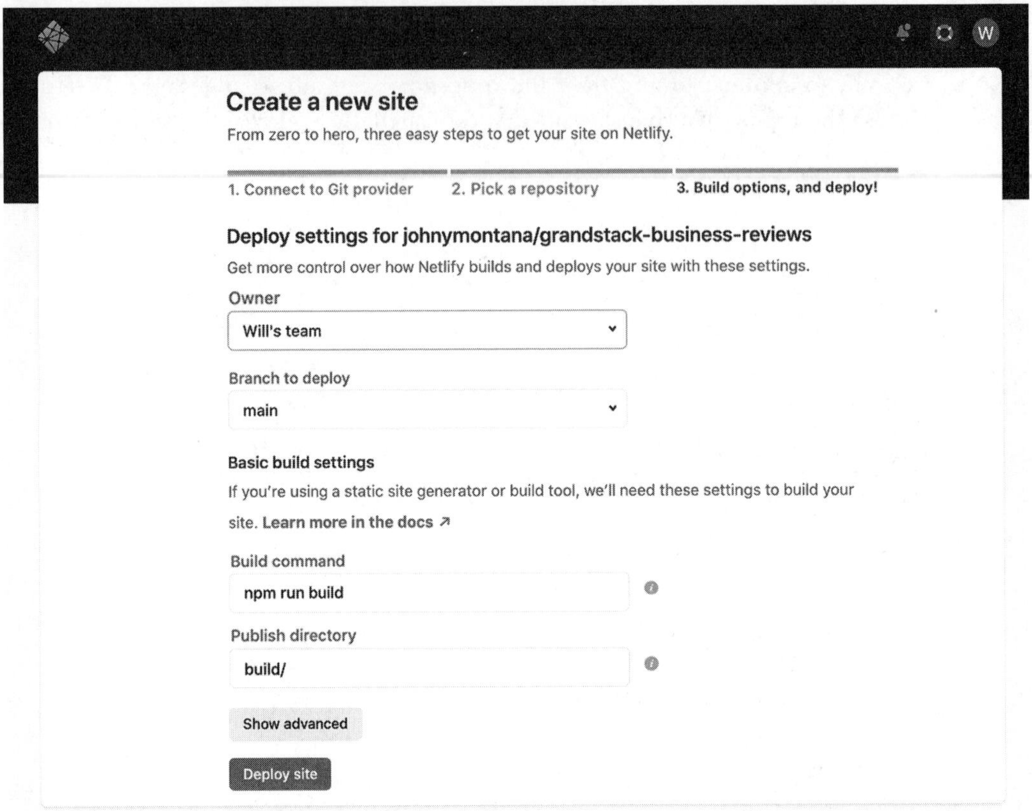

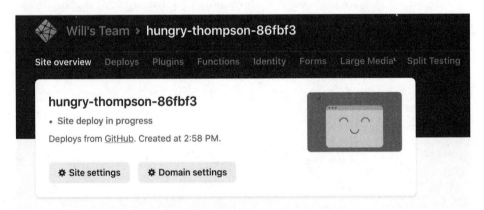

Figure 8.17   Configuring our new Netlify site

once it's been built and deployed without needing to add a custom domain (see figure 8.18).

Figure 8.18   Configuring the deploy settings in Netlify

Once the build is finished, we can navigate to our application in a web browser (see figure 8.19). In this case, the URL is https://hungry-thompson-86fbf3.netlify.app/.

Business Search

Select Business Category: [All ▼] [Submit]

Results

Star	Name	Address	Category
[Star]	Missoula Public Library	301 E Main St	Library
[Star]	Ninja Mike's	200 W Pine St	Restaurant, Breakfast
[Star]	KettleHouse Brewing Co.	313 N 1st St W	Beer, Brewery
[Star]	Imagine Nation Brewing	1151 W Broadway St	Beer, Brewery
[Star]	Market on Front	201 E Front St	Coffee, Restaurant, Cafe, Deli, Breakfast
[Star]	Hanabi	723 California Dr	Restaurant, Ramen
[Star]	Zootown Brew	121 W Broadway St	Coffee
[Star]	Ducky's Car Wash	716 N San Mateo Dr	Car Wash
[Star]	Neo4j	111 E 5th Ave	Graph Database

Figure 8.19   A Netlify site deploy in progress

But we have a problem: the GraphQL API is pointing to http://localhost:4000, our local machine, which means anyone else loading this application won't be able to connect to the GraphQL API and view these results. We can verify this by opening the developer tools in our web browser and inspecting the network requests. We'll deploy the GraphQL API application in the next section, but let's explore a few features of Netlify first (see figure 8.20).

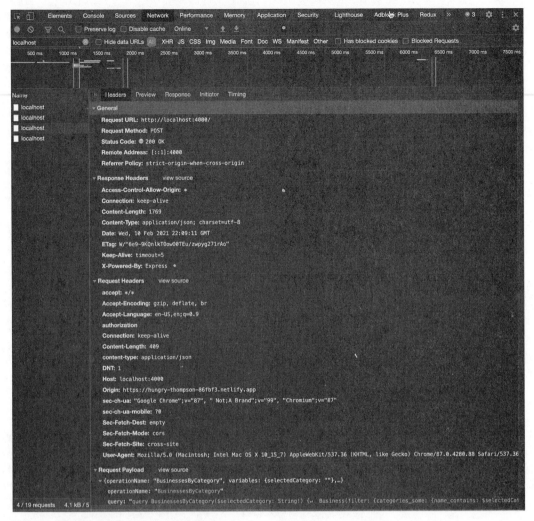

Figure 8.20   Our newly deployed application

8.3.2   *Setting environment variables for Netlify builds*

If we take a look at src/index.js, where we create the Apollo Client instance, to connect to our GraphQL API, we'll see that we've left the URI for the GraphQL API hardcoded as http://localhost:4000, as shown in the next listing.

> **Listing 8.2   src/index.js: Using an Apollo Link to connect to our GraphQL API**

```
...

const httpLink = createHttpLink({
    uri: "http://localhost:4000",
});

...
```

This is fine for local development and testing, but now we want to use the same code for local development and our deployed application. To allow for using a local GraphQL URI during development, but to connect to a deployed GraphQL API in our deployed application, we'll set an environment variable to be read at build time for the GraphQL URI. We'll determine this value depending on the environment being used—for local development, we'll leave the GraphQL URI as http://localhost:4000, but we'll configure a different value for our Netlify builds.

Let's create a .env file to store local development environment variables. One convenient feature of Create React App is that any values specified in .env will be set as environment variables, and any variables that begin with REACT_APP will be replaced in the client React application during the build. Let's set the local value we want to use for development for the GraphQL API in this .env file, as shown next.

Listing 8.3   .env: Setting environment variables for our React application

```
REACT_APP_GRAPHQL_URI=/graphql
NEO4J_URI=neo4j://localhost:7687
NEO4J_USER=neo4j
NEO4J_PASSWORD=letmein
REACT_APP_AUTH0_DOMAIN=grandstack.auth0.com
REACT_APP_AUTH0_CLIENT_ID=4xw3K3cjvw0hyT4Mjp4RuOVSxvVYcOFF
REACT_APP_AUTH0_AUDIENCE=https://reviews.grandstack.io
```

We'll update our code in the next listing to read from these environment variables when setting the URI of our GraphQL API and to specify our Auth0 domain, client ID, and audience values.

Listing 8.4   src/index.js: Using environment variables

```
...

const httpLink = createHttpLink({
    uri: process.env.REACT_APP_GRAPHQL_URI
});

...

ReactDOM.render(
  <React.StrictMode>
    <Auth0Provider
      domain={process.env.REACT_APP_AUTH0_DOMAIN}
      clientId={process.env.REACT_APP_AUTH0_CLIENT_ID}
      redirectUri={window.location.origin}
      audience={process.env.REACT_APP_AUTH0_AUDIENCE}
    >
      <AppWithApollo />
    </Auth0Provider>
  </React.StrictMode>,
  document.getElementById("root")
);
```

For local development, we want to develop using the local GraphQL API URI, but in the deployed application, we want the React application to connect to the deployed GraphQL API. To enable this, we'll now set the `REACT_APP_GRAPHQL_URI` environment variable in the Netlify building settings for our site (see figure 8.21). Choose *Site Settings* in the Netlify dashboard for our site, and then choose *Build & deploy* in the left-side navigation. We'll create a new environment variable called `REACT_APP_GRAPHQL_URI` with the value `/graphql`.

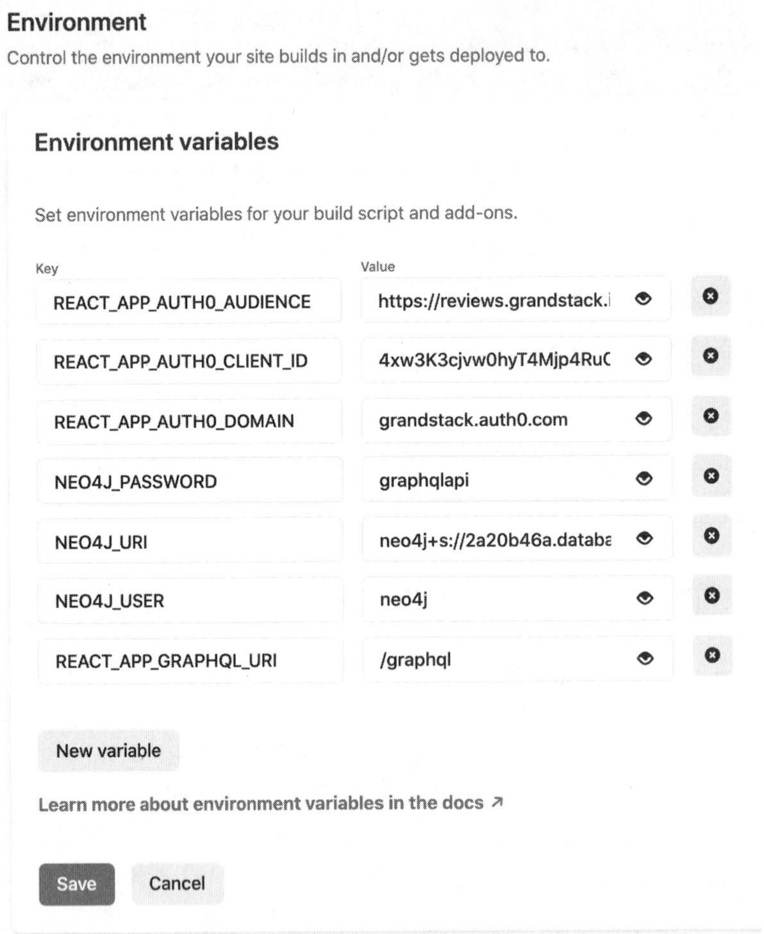

Environment

Control the environment your site builds in and/or gets deployed to.

Environment variables

Set environment variables for your build script and add-ons.

Key	Value
REACT_APP_AUTH0_AUDIENCE	https://reviews.grandstack.| ⬤ ⊗
REACT_APP_AUTH0_CLIENT_ID	4xw3K3cjvw0hyT4Mjp4RuC ⬤ ⊗
REACT_APP_AUTH0_DOMAIN	grandstack.auth0.com ⬤ ⊗
NEO4J_PASSWORD	graphqlapi ⬤ ⊗
NEO4J_URI	neo4j+s://2a20b46a.databa ⬤ ⊗
NEO4J_USER	neo4j ⬤ ⊗
REACT_APP_GRAPHQL_URI	/graphql ⬤ ⊗

New variable

Learn more about environment variables in the docs ↗

Save   Cancel

Figure 8.21   Setting Netlify environment variables

This means that our deployed application will try to connect to a GraphQL API at /graphql on the same domain. We haven't deployed the GraphQL API here yet, so our application will return an error for now until we add the GraphQL API.

8.3.3   *Netlify deploy previews*

A convenient feature of services like Netlify is the deploy preview. A *deploy preview* is a build triggered by a change to the code (often from a pull request) that is deployed to a temporary URL, different from the main application. This build has all the functionality of the main application and can be shared with teammates and other stakeholders to review before the pull request is committed and the change is reflected in the main application.

Let's see how this works by creating a pull request and deploying a preview updating our React application to read from the REACT_APP_GRAPHQL_URI environment variable. If we run the command git status, we'll see that we've made a change to src/index.js:

```
$ git status

On branch main
Your branch is up to date with 'origin/main'.

Changes not staged for commit:
  (use "git add <file>..." to update what will be committed)
  (use "git restore <file>..." to discard changes in working directory)
    modified:   index.js

no changes added to commit (use "git add" and/or "git commit -a")
```

Let's switch to a new Git branch, called env-var-graphql-uri. We'll commit our change to this new branch:

```
$ git checkout -b env-var-graphql-uri
Switched to a new branch 'env-var-graphql-uri'
```

Now, let's add our change to index.js in a commit. Since we've switched our working directory to a new Git branch, this commit will be made to the env-var-graphql-uri branch, not the main branch:

```
$ git add index.js
$ git commit -m "use environment variable to specify GraphQL URI"
[env-var-graphql-uri 92f1142] use environment variable to
specify GraphQLURI
 1 file changed, 1 insertion(+), 1 deletion(-)
```

Next, we push this new branch to GitHub. Since we're pushing a new branch to our remote repository, GitHub helpfully tells us that we can create a pull request from this new branch:

```
$ git push origin env-var-graphql-uri

Enumerating objects: 7, done.
Counting objects: 100% (7/7), done.
```

```
Delta compression using up to 16 threads
Compressing objects: 100% (4/4), done.
Writing objects: 100% (4/4), 415 bytes | 415.00 KiB/s, done.
Total 4 (delta 3), reused 0 (delta 0)
remote: Resolving deltas: 100% (3/3), completed with 3 local objects.
remote:
remote: Create a pull request for 'env var graphql-uri'on
GitHub by visiting: remote: https://github.com/johnymontana/
grandstack-business-reviews/pull/new/env-var-graphql-uri
remote:
To github.com:johnymontana/grandstack-business-reviews.git
 * [new branch]       env-var-graphql-uri -> env-var-graphql-uri
```

A pull request is a way to request a change from another branch or fork of the repository to be merged into the main branch. Let's create a pull request that requests merging the new branch, env-var-graphql-uri, into the main branch (see figure 8.22).

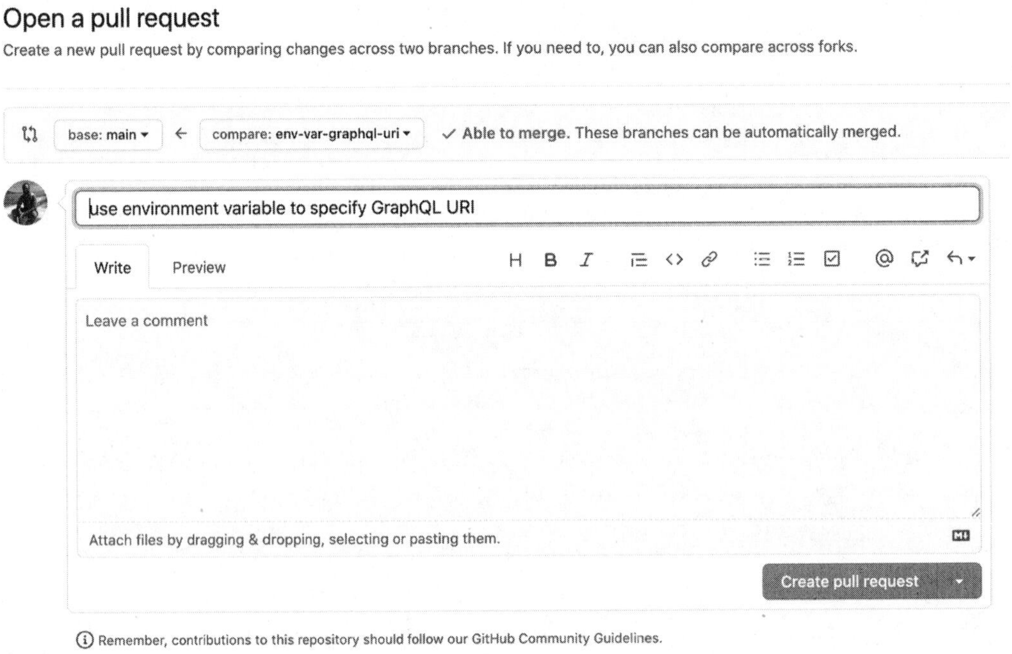

Figure 8.22   Creating a pull request in GitHub

Since we've connected Netlify to this GitHub repository, Netlify will immediately start a deploy preview build based on the changes in this pull request. We can see the status of this build in the *Checks* section of the pull request page on GitHub. Once the build is complete, we can visit this deploy preview to see the changes reflected in a live deployment (see figure 8.23). We can also share this temporary URL with others to review the changes to the site.

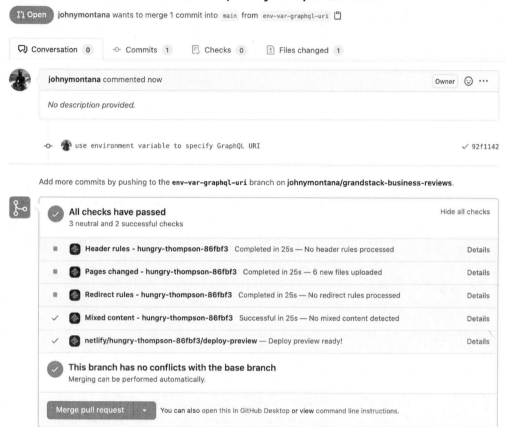

Figure 8.23 Triggering a Netlify deploy preview from a pull request

Once we're satisfied with the changes, we'll merge the pull request. We can do this on GitHub by clicking the *Merge pull request* button. This will merge the changes from the env-var-graphql-uri branch into the main branch. This merge will then trigger a build and deployment on Netify, which will then replace the main version of our application (see figure 8.24).

Now that we've deployed the React application, it's time to deploy our GraphQL API. To do this, we'll convert our GraphQL API into a serverless function so it can be deployed on the AWS Lambda service. We'll take advantage of the Netlify Functions feature to enable this for us.

Figure 8.24   Viewing the
status of our Netlify builds

8.4   Serverless GraphQL with AWS Lambda and Netlify Functions

AWS Lambda is an FaaS compute platform that allows us to run code on demand without provisioning or managing servers. Functions are invoked in response to events, such as an HTTP request. When combined with AWS's API Gateway service, Lambda functions can be used to implement API endpoints and applications, such as a GraphQL API. AWS Lambda supports Node.js, Python, Java, Go, Ruby, Swift, and C# and can include packaged dependencies. Unlike other cloud services that incur costs metered by the hour, AWS Lambda is priced based on the number of requests, and the duration of those requests is measured in increments of 1 millisecond.

The Netlify Functions service allows us to deploy Lambda functions directly from the Netlify function without the need for creating an AWS account. Netlify handles the build and deployment of Lambda functions using the same Git version control features, such as deploy previews, which means we can manage the code for our Lambda functions alongside the rest of our site. Currently, Netlify can deploy Lambda functions for Node.js and Go.

So far, we've built our GraphQL API application as a Node.js Express server using Apollo Server. In this section, we will convert our GraphQL API to a Lambda function, using a Lambda-specific version of Apollo Server, and deploy alongside our Netlify site using the Netlify Functions feature.

8.4.1   Serving a GraphQL API as a Lambda function

Since our Lambda GraphQL API will be deployed via Netlify as part of our Netlify site, we'll place the code and dependencies in our existing project. Let's install the dependencies needed:

```
npm install apollo-server-lambda @neo4j/graphql
    @neo4j/graphql-plugin-auth neo4j-driver
```

Note that we install apollo-server-lambda, a special version of Apollo Server that will allow us to structure our GraphQL API as a Lambda function. We also install the Neo4j JavaScript driver, the Neo4j GraphQL integration library, and libraries necessary for working with JWTs that we saw in the previous chapter.

Let's create a new file, src/graphql.js, in the same directory where our React application is located. Later, we'll check this file into version control and push it up to GitHub, triggering a Netlify build and deployment. We'll use apollo-server-lambda to create a simple GraphQL API with a single query field, `greetings`, that returns a greeting message, as the following listing shows.

Listing 8.5   src/graphql.js: A simple GraphQL API using AWS Lambda

```
const { ApolloServer, gql } = require("apollo-server-lambda");

const typeDefs = gql`
  type Query {
    greetings(name: String = "GRANDstack"): String
  }
`;

const resolvers = {
  Query: {
    greetings: (parent, args, context) => {
      return `Hello, ${args.name}!`;
    },
  },
};

const server = new ApolloServer({
  typeDefs,
  resolvers,
});

const serverHandler = server.createHandler();

exports.handler = (event, context, callback) => {
  return serverHandler(
    {
      ...event,
      requestContext: event.requestContext || {},
    },
    context,
    callback
  );
};
```

> Note that we are importing the apollo-server-lambda flavor of Apollo Server.

> Since we are creating an AWS Lambda function, we need to export a handler function that wraps our Apollo Server instance.

Next, we need to configure our Netlify site so it knows where we've created our new Lambda function and that we want to serve the GraphQL API at the /graphql endpoint of our site. To do this, we'll create a netlify.toml file in the root of our project, as shown in the following listing.

Listing 8.6   netlify.toml: Configuring the Netlify build

```
[build]
command = "npm run build"
functions = "src/lambda"
publish = "build"

[[redirects]]
from = "/graphql"
to = "/.netlify/functions/graphql"
status = 200
```

By default, our Netlify Functions are exposed at /.netlify/functions/, followed by the filename of the function. We create a redirect, so our GraphQL API can be accessed at /graphql.

8.4.2   *The Netlify dev CLI*

So far, we've treated Netlify as a deployment service for our React application. If we wanted to build and serve the React application locally, then when running npm run start, we used the react-scripts tool without getting Netlify involved. Now that we're adding Lambda functions, we'll need to do a bit more to test out our application locally. We'll install the Netlify command line tool to build and run our GraphQL Lambda function and React application locally using Netlify dev:

```
$ npm install netlify-cli -g
```

Now that we've installed the Netlify CLI, we can use the dev command to start our site locally. This will build and serve our React application and Lambda function locally without triggering a deployment:

```
$ netlify dev
```

After running netlify dev, we can open a web browser and navigate to http://local-host:8888/graphql. We should see Apollo Studio, where we can run a GraphQL query against our Lambda GraphQL API, as shown in the following listing.

Listing 8.7   Querying our simple GraphQL API

```
{
  greetings
}
```

The result of this query will show the greeting message we defined in the resolver:

```
{
  "data": {
    "greetings": "Hello, GRANDstack!"
  }
}
```

Of course, this is just a simple Hello World GraphQL API, so let's bring over the rest of our GraphQL API application for the business reviews application.

8.4.3 Converting our GraphQL API to a Netlify function

As shown in listing 8.8, to convert our existing GraphQL API to make use of AWS Lambda and apollo-server-lambda, we need to change a few lines. The most significant changes are the use of the apollo-server-lambda package, instead of apollo-server-express, and exporting a handler function for our AWS Lambda. Otherwise, this will look similar to the GraphQL API code we've been building up through chapter 7.

> **Listing 8.8 src/graphql.js: Converting our GraphQL API to an AWS Lambda function**

```
const { ApolloServer, gql } = require("apollo-server-lambda");          ◁──┐   Using the apollo-server-
                                                                            │   lambda flavor of Apollo
const neo4j = require("neo4j-driver");                                      │   Server, instead of
const { Neo4jGraphQL } = require("@neo4j/graphql");                        │   apollo-server
const {                                                                    │
  Neo4jGraphQLAuthJWKSPlugin,
} = require("@neo4j/graphql-plugin-auth");

const resolvers = {
  Business: {
    waitTime: (obj, args, context, info) => {
      var options = [0, 5, 10, 15, 30, 45];
      return options[Math.floor(Math.random() * options.length)];
    },
  },
};

const typeDefs = gql`
  type Query {
    fuzzyBusinessByName(searchString: String): [Business]
      @cypher(
        statement: """
        CALL
        db.index.fulltext.queryNodes('businessNameIndex',
          $searchString+'~')
        YIELD node RETURN node
        """
      )
  }

  type Business {
    businessId: ID!
    waitTime: Int! @computed
    averageStars: Float!
      @auth(rules: [{ isAuthenticated: true }])
      @cypher(
        statement: """
          MATCH (this)<-[:REVIEWS]-(r:Review) RETURN avg(r.stars)
        """
      )
```

```
    recommended(first: Int = 1): [Business!]!
      @cypher(
      statement: """
      MATCH (this)<-[:REVIEWS]-(:Review)<-[:WROTE]-(u:User)
      MATCH (u)-[:WROTE]->(:Review)-[:REVIEWS]->(rec:Business)
      WITH rec, COUNT(*) AS score
      RETURN rec ORDER BY score DESC LIMIT $first
      """
    )
  name: String!
  city: String!
  state: String!
  address: String!
  location: Point!
  reviews: [Review!]! @relationship(type: "REVIEWS", direction: IN)
  categories: [Category!]!
    @relationship(type: "IN_CATEGORY", direction: OUT)
}

type User {
  userId: ID!
  name: String!
  reviews: [Review!]! @relationship(type: "WROTE", direction: OUT)
}

extend type User
  @auth(
    rules: [
      { operations: [READ], where: { userId: "$jwt.sub" } }
      { operations: [CREATE, UPDATE, DELETE], roles: ["admin"] }
    ]
  )

type Review {
  reviewId: ID! @id
  stars: Float!
  date: Date!
  text: String
  user: User! @relationship(type: "WROTE", direction: IN)
  business: Business! @relationship(type: "REVIEWS", direction: OUT)
}

extend type Review
  @auth(
    rules: [
      {
        operations: [CREATE, UPDATE]
        bind: { user: { userId: "$jwt.sub" } }
      }
    ]
  )

type Category {
  name: String!
  businesses: [Business!]!
```

```
        @relationship(type: "IN_CATEGORY", direction: IN)
    }
`;

const driver = neo4j.driver(
    process.env.NEO4J_URI,
    neo4j.auth.basic(process.env.NEO4J_USER, process.env.NEO4J_PASSWORD)
);

const neoSchema = new Neo4jGraphQL({
    typeDefs,
    resolvers,
    driver,
    plugins: {
        auth: new Neo4jGraphQLAuthJWKSPlugin({
            jwksEndpoint: "https://grandstack.auth0.com/.well-known/jwks.json",
        }),
    },
});

const initServer = async () => {
    return await neoSchema.getSchema().then((schema) => {
        const server = new ApolloServer({
            schema,
            context: ({ event }) => ({ req: event }),   ◁
        });
        const serverHandler = server.createHandler();
        return serverHandler;
    });
};

exports.handler = async (event, context, callback) => {   ◁
    const serverHandler = await initServer();

    return serverHandler(
        {
            ...event,
            requestContext: event.requestContext || {},
        },
        context,
        callback
    );
};
```

> **We use event here because the request signature for AWS Lambda is slightly different than Express.**

> **Exporting a handler function for our AWS Lambda function**

We can now commit our changes to this file and push to GitHub to deploy. Deploying our application is almost complete. In the next section, we add a custom domain and assign it to our site in Netlify.

8.4.4 Adding a custom domain in Netlify

So far, our application has been running on the https://hungry-thompson-86fbf3 .netlify.app/ subdomain assigned by Netlify. Let's set up a custom domain that better aligns with the branding we'd like for the site. In Netlify, select *Domains* from the top navbar. From here, we can add custom domains and assign them to our sites in Netlify (see figure 8.25).

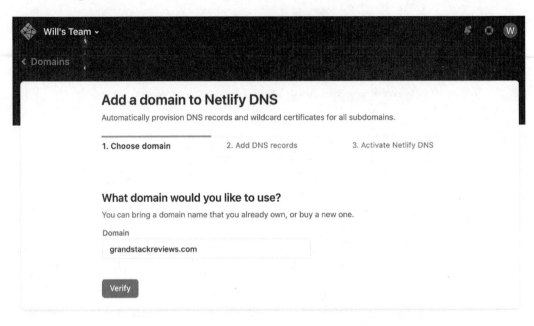

Figure 8.25   Adding a custom domain to Netlify

We can purchase domain names directly from Netlify or add domains purchased through other registrars. In this case, I want to add a domain I've purchased elsewhere, so I'll point the domain at Netlify's nameservers, allowing Netlify to manage the domain and DNS records for the domain (see figure 8.26).

Figure 8.26   Pointing our domain at the Netlify nameservers

Finally, we'll need to update the Auth0 application settings so the authentication functionality provided by Auth0 works, using the new domain. We'll update the *Allow Callback URLs* and *Allowed Logout URLs* in Auth0, adding the default localhost URLs as well as our Netlify site URL and our custom domain (see figure 8.27).

Allowed Callback URLs	http://localhost:3000, http://localhost:8888, https://hungry-thompson-86fbf3.netlify.app/, https://grandstackreviews.com

After the user authenticates we will only call back to any of these URLs. You can specify multiple valid URLs by comma-separating them (typically to handle different environments like QA or testing). Make sure to specify the protocol (`https://`) otherwise the callback may fail in some cases. With the exception of custom URI schemes for native clients, all callbacks should use protocol `https://` .

Allowed Logout URLs	http://localhost:3000, http://localhost:8888, https://hungry-thompson-86fbf3.netlify.app/, https://grandstackreviews.com

A set of URLs that are valid to redirect to after logout from Auth0. After a user logs out from Auth0 you can redirect them with the `returnTo` query parameter. The URL that you use in `returnTo` must be listed here. You can specify multiple valid URLs by comma-separating them. You can use the star symbol as a wildcard for subdomains (`*.google.com`). Query strings and hash information are not taken into account when validating these URLs. Read more about this at https://auth0.com/docs/logout

Figure 8.27 Updating the allowed callback URLs in Auth0

And with that, our application is now deployed and ready to use on our custom domain (see figure 8.28).

Business Search application:

Business Search

Select Business Category: [All ▾] [Submit]

Results

Star	Name	Address	Category	Average Stars
Star	Missoula Public Library	301 E Main St	Library	3
Star	Ninja Mike's	200 W Pine St	Restaurant, Breakfast	4.5
Star	KettleHouse Brewing Co.	313 N 1st St W	Beer, Brewery	4.5
Star	Imagine Nation Brewing	1151 W Broadway St	Beer, Brewery	3.5
Star	Market on Front	201 E Front St	Coffee, Restaurant, Cafe, Deli, Breakfast	4
Star	Hanabi	723 California Dr	Restaurant, Ramen	5
Star	Zootown Brew	121 W Broadway St	Coffee	5
Star	**Ducky's Car Wash**	716 N San Mateo Dr	Car Wash	5
Star	**Neo4j**	111 E 5th Ave	Graph Database	5

Figure 8.28 Our deployed full stack GraphQL application after signing in

8.5   *Our deployment approach*

In this chapter, we explored an approach to deploying our full stack GraphQL application that embraced taking advantage of managed services, specifically Neo4j Aura, Netlify, and AWS Lambda (see figure 8.29). At the beginning of this chapter, we discussed some of the advantages and disadvantages of managed services in general. Let's review the services from the developer's perspective.

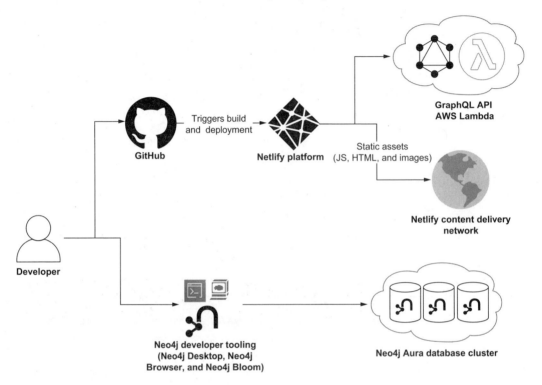

Figure 8.29   A full stack GraphQL deployment, from the developer's perspective

Netlify allows for automated builds and deployment of our React application to the Netlify global content delivery network, ensuring our frontend application is accessible to anyone in the world without unnecessary network latency. Converting our GraphQL API to an AWS Lambda function and leveraging Netlify Functions means we can integrate the API application into the same application codebase. By integrating with GitHub, our workflow for development and deployment is improved, allowing us to create preview deployments from pull requests.

With the Neo4j Aura database as a service, we are able to take advantage of developer tooling like Neo4j Desktop and Neo4j Browser for development and not have to concern ourselves with maintaining and operating a Neo4j cluster in the cloud. Now that our application has been deployed, in the next chapter, we move away from our business reviews application and focus on more-advanced GraphQL features, such as abstract types, cursor-based pagination and the Relay connection model, and working with relationship properties in the graph.

8.6 Exercises

1 Use Neo4j Bloom to find the user who has reviewed businesses belonging to the greatest number of categories. What are the categories of the businesses this user has reviewed? Hint: creating a Neo4j Bloom search phrase might be helpful with this exercise. Consult the documentation at http://mng.bz/XZR6.

2 Create a new pull request that updates the business review application to always order the results by business name. Use Netlify's deploy feature to review this update before merging the pull request and updating the application.

3 Create a new Netlify Function that uses the Neo4j JavaScript driver to query our Neo4j Aura cluster and return a list of the most recent reviews. Run it locally using the `netlify dev` command before deploying. Use the netlify.toml configuration to redirect /reviews to this function.

Summary

- Leveraging managed cloud services can smooth the developer experience for deploying and maintaining web applications and address scale, operations, and pricing that can be appealing for full stack developers who may be responsible for all components of the application.

- Neo4j Aura is a managed cloud database service that provides Neo4j clusters that can be provisioned with a single click. These database instances can be scaled up and down as needed and remove the need for maintenance or operations of Neo4j.

- The Netlify platform and CDN can be used to automate building and deploying web applications, taking advantage of GitHub integration and deploy previews that make it easier to review changes to an application before it is shipped.

- GraphQL APIs can be deployed as an AWS Lambda function, taking advantage of the stateless scale and demand-based pricing that make AWS Lambda appealing. Netlify Functions can be used to provision AWS Lambda functions as part of a Netlify site, removing the need for a separate code base or deployment process.

Advanced GraphQL
considerations

This chapter covers

- Using abstract types of unions and interfaces for their benefits
- Paginating query results, using offsets and cursors
- Working with relationship properties, using Relay connection types

So far, we haven't leveraged one of the most powerful and important features of GraphQL's type system—*abstract types*—which allow us to represent multiple concrete types in a single GraphQL field. Similarly, we also haven't really made use of an important feature of the property graph model—*relationship properties*—which allow us to associate attributes with the relationships that connect nodes rather than just nodes themselves. In this chapter, we will see how to leverage the abstract union and interface types supported by GraphQL. We will also make use of relationship properties and, along the way, introduce GraphQL Connection objects and pagination methods. We will move away from our business review application and simplify our data model, focusing instead on an API for a simple online store that sells two types of products: books and videos.

9.1 GraphQL abstract types

GraphQL supports two abstract types: *interfaces* and *unions*. Abstract types allow us to represent multiple concrete types (or arrays of multiple types) in a single field. Interfaces are used when one or more fields are shared across concrete types and they declare the shared fields that must be implemented in the concrete type. In this way, an interface can be thought of as a contract that specifies the minimal set of fields that a type must have to implement the interface. Unions do not need to share fields across concrete types and do not share this idea of a contract. Unions are, therefore, simply a grouping of concrete types.

9.1.1 Interface types

Interface types are used to represent multiple object types that are conceptually similar and share at least one common field. For example, our store API may have the concept of a *person*. Each person could be either a customer or an employee. Every person would have fields such as first name, last name, and username. However, only a customer would have a shipping address, and only an employee would have a hire date. In GraphQL type definitions, we can represent this concept, as shown in the next listing.

Listing 9.1   Defining an interface in GraphQL type definitions

```
interface Person {
  firstName: String!
  lastName: String!
  username: String!
}

type Customer implements Person {
  firstName: String!
  lastName: String!
  username: String!
  shippingAddress: String
}

type Employee implements Person {
  firstName: String!
  lastName: String!
  username: String!
  hireDate: DateTime!
}

type Query {
  people: [Person]
}
```

The implementing (or concrete) type must implement all the fields declared in the interface and can then define other fields associated with the type. Here, `Customer` and `Employee` both implement the `Person` interface and, therefore, must include the firstName, lastName, and username fields. Customer adds a shippingAddress field, and Employee adds a hireDate field.

Querying the people Query field would return an array of objects, where each object could be either an Employee or a Customer object. We use an *inline fragment* in the GraphQL query to specify the selection set and fields to be returned for each type, as shown in the following listing. Inline fragments allow us to request fields on the concrete type and include a type condition.

Listing 9.2   Querying an interface using inline fragments

```
{
  people {
    __typename
    firstName
    lastName
    username
    ... on Customer {
      shippingAddress
    }
    ... on Employee {
      hireDate
    }
  }
}
```

We also include the __typename meta field that tells us the concrete type of each object in the people array.

9.1.2   Union types

Unions are similar to interfaces in that they are abstract types that can be used to represent multiple concrete types; however, the concrete types composed in a union do not need to have any common fields. A common use case for unions is to represent a search result. For example, our store API may support a product search feature that allows a user to search for items that may be either books or videos. To enable this, we create a Product union that contains both Book and Video types and a Query field search that returns an array of Product objects, as shown in the next listing.

Listing 9.3   Defining a union in GraphQL type definitions

```
type Video {
  name: String!
  sku: String!
}

type Book {
  title: String!
  isbn: String!
}
```

```
union Product = Video | Book

type Query {
  search(term: String!): [Product!]!
}
```

Similar to how we query fields of the concrete type of an interface using an inline fragment, we use an inline fragment when querying unions. However, since a union type
itself does not contain any fields, we can only ask for the __typename meta field when
querying a union without using an inline fragment, as shown in the following listing.

Listing 9.4 Querying a union

```
{
  search(term: "GraphQL") {
    __typename
    ... on Book {
      title
      isbn
    }
    ... on Video {
      name
      sku
    }
  }
}
```

9.1.3 *Using abstract types with the Neo4j GraphQL library*

Now that we've explored interfaces and unions a bit, let's see how we can make use of
abstract types in a GraphQL API using the Neo4j GraphQL Library. Let's leave behind
our business reviews application and start a new application for our imagined book
and video store. In a new directory, run the following command to create a new
Node.js project:

```
npm init -y
```

Next, we'll install the dependencies for our new Node.js GraphQL API application,
which should be familiar by now:

```
npm install @neo4j/graphql graphql apollo-server neo4j-driver dotenv
```

If you'd like to keep working with the business reviews application from previous
chapters, you can create a new Neo4j database in Neo4j Aura or locally, using Neo4j
Desktop. Alternatively, you can keep using the same database and run the following
Cypher statement to delete the business review data:

```
MATCH (a) DETACH DELETE a
```

Create a new file .env to define the environment variables that specify the connection credentials for your Neo4j database, setting values for the environment variables NEO4J_USER, NEO4J_URI, and NEO4J_PASSWORD, as shown in the following listing.

> **Listing 9.5   .env: Be sure to replace the values with your Aura connection credentials**

```
NEO4J_URI=neo4j+s://932a071e.databases.neo4j.io
NEO4J_USER=neo4j
NEO4J_PASSWORD=wH4-tvNOxzKlDZwIEqgNPm-8iS-tJ9gOgr1ScSq9yiM
```

Now that we have a new Node.js project and either a new or an empty Neo4j database, let's start by defining the GraphQL type definitions for our API and see how abstract types can help simplify our API schema.

MODELING AN ONLINE BOOK AND VIDEO STORE API

Let's start our new API by going to the (virtual) whiteboard: https://arrows.app. Following the graph data modeling process we identified in chapter 3, we will identify the entities (nodes) in our application, how they are connected (relationships), and their attributes (node properties). Let's keep things simple and focus on users who will place orders and orders that will contain books and/or videos. Creating the property graph model to handle these requirements, we end up with a fairly straightforward graph model (see figure 9.1).

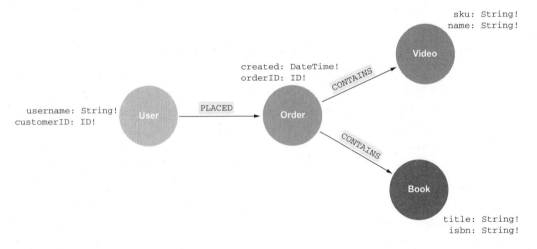

Figure 9.1   Graph data model for an online store that sells books and videos

As we saw in chapter 4, we can use this property graph model diagram to translate GraphQL type definitions that map to this property graph model, using the @relationship GraphQL schema directive to capture the direction and type of our relationships, as the next listing shows.

Listing 9.6 **GraphQL type definitions for our online store data model**

```
type User {
  username: String
  orders: [Order!]! @relationship(type: "PLACED", direction: OUT)
}

type Order {
  orderId: ID! @id
  created: DateTime! @timestamp(operations: [CREATE])
  customer: User! @relationship(type: "PLACED", direction: IN)
  books: [Book!]! @relationship(type: "CONTAINS", direction: OUT)
  videos: [Video!]! @relationship(type: "CONTAINS", direction: OUT)
}

type Video {
  name: String
  sku: String
}

type Book {
  title: String
  isbn: String
}
```

Note that we're making use of the `@id` and `@timestamp` directives to autogenerate these values, so the client won't need to pass them to the API. Our client shouldn't be concerned with generating a random unique ID for orders or passing the time that the order was created, as doing this would also open up security implications.

But take a look at the `Order.books` and `Order.videos` fields. To see what products are contained in the order, our client will need to request both of those fields—one of which may be an empty array. This is a bit awkward for the client; let's see how we can improve this with the use of abstract types, specifically with the use of a union type, since our `Video` and `Book` type do not share any common fields. Instead of the `Order.books` and `Order.videos` fields, let's define a new union type `Product` in the next listing and add an `Order.products` field, which will allow us to work with products connected to the order (whether they be books or videos) in a single field.

Listing 9.7 **GraphQL type definitions for our online store data model using a union type**

```
type User {
  username: String
  orders: [Order!]! @relationship(type: "PLACED", direction: OUT)
}

union Product = Video | Book     ◁──  Defining a union type named Product, which
                                       can be of type either Video or Book
type Order {
  orderId: ID! @id
  created: DateTime! @timestamp(operations: [CREATE])
  customer: User! @relationship(type: "PLACED", direction: IN)
```

```
  products: [Product!]! @relationship(type: "CONTAINS", direction: OUT)    ◄
}
```
                                                    **Using our new Product type
                                                    in a relationship field on the
                                                                     Order type**

```
type Video {
  name: String
  sku: String
}


type Book {
  title: String
  isbn: String
}
```

CREATING THE GRAPHQL SERVER

Now that we've finalized our GraphQL type definitions, let's use them to create a
GraphQL API using the Neo4j GraphQL Library. Let's create a new index.js with
these new type definitions and the code necessary to create a GraphQL API using
Apollo Server and the Neo4j GraphQL Library, as shown next.

Listing 9.8   index.js: GraphQL API for our online store

```
const { gql, ApolloServer } = require("apollo-server");
const { Neo4jGraphQL } = require("@neo4j/graphql");
const neo4j = require("neo4j-driver");
require("dotenv").config();

const typeDefs = gql`
  type User {
    username: String
    orders: [Order!]! @relationship(type: "PLACED", direction: OUT)
  }

  union Product = Video | Book

  type Order {
    orderId: ID! @id
    created: DateTime! @timestamp(operations: [CREATE])
    customer: User! @relationship(type: "PLACED", direction: IN)
    products: [Product!]!
      @relationship(
        type: "CONTAINS"
        direction: OUT
      )
  }

  type Video {
    name: String
    sku: String
  }

  type Book {
    title: String
    isbn: String
  }
```

```
  }
`;

const driver = neo4j.driver(
  process.env.NEO4J_URI,
  neo4j.auth.basic(process.env.NEO4J_USER, process.env.NEO4J_PASSWORD)
);

const neoSchema = new Neo4jGraphQL({ typeDefs, driver });

neoSchema.getSchema().then((schema) => {
  const server = new ApolloServer({
    schema,
  });
  server.listen().then(({ url }) => {
    console.log(`GraphQL server ready on ${url}`);
  });
});
```

The structure of this file should be familiar from past chapters in which we defined GraphQL type definitions, created a Neo4j driver instance, and generated a GraphQL schema using the Neo4j GraphQL Library to be served by Apollo Server. Now let's start our GraphQL server:

```
node index.js
GraphQL server ready on http://localhost:4000/
```

USING ABSTRACT TYPES IN GRAPHQL MUTATIONS

Next, let's open our web browser and navigate to http://localhost:4000, where we will use Apollo Studio and start creating some data in the database, using the GraphQL mutations generated by the Neo4j GraphQL Library in our schema. First, let's create two users, using the generated `createUsers` GraphQL mutation, as shown next.

Listing 9.9 GraphQL mutation: Creating users

```
mutation {
  createUsers(
    input: [{ username: "bobbytables" }, { username: "graphlover123" }]
  ) {
    users {
      username
    }
  }
}
```

In the response to this GraphQL operation, we should see the user objects with the usernames we passed in the mutation operation:

```
{
  "data": {
    "createUsers": {
```

```
      "users": [
        {
          "username": "bobbytables"
        },
        {
          "username": "graphlover123"
        }
      ]
    }
  }
}
```

In the next listing, let's create some products for our store, which we said sells books and videos. To do this, we'll use both the `createBooks` and `createVideos` mutations.

Listing 9.10   GraphQL mutation: Creating products

```
mutation {
  createBooks(
    input: [
      { title: "Full Stack GraphQL", isbn: "9781617297038" }
      { title: "Graph Algorithms", isbn: "9781492047681" }
      { title: "Graph-Powered Machine Learning", isbn: "9781617295645" }
    ]
  ) {
    books {
      title
      isbn
    }
  }

  createVideos(
    input: [
      { name: "Intro To Neo4j 4.x", sku: "v001" }
      { name: "Building GraphQL APIs", sku: "v002" }
    ]
  ) {
    videos {
      sku
      name
    }
  }
}
```

And in the response, we will have arrays with the book and video objects we just created:

```
{
  "data": {
    "createBooks": {
      "books": [
        {
          "title": "Full Stack GraphQL",
```

```
        "isbn": "9781617297038"
      },
      {
        "title": "Graph Algorithms",
        "isbn": "9781492047681"
      },
      {
        "title": "Graph-Powered Machine Learning",
        "isbn": "9781617295645"
      }
    ]
  },
  "createVideos": {
    "videos": [
      {
        "sku": "v001",
        "name": "Intro To Neo4j 4.x"
      },
      {
        "sku": "v002",
        "name": "Building GraphQL APIs"
      }
    ]
  }
 }
}
```

Now we're ready to create some orders. There are a few different ways we could go about this—for example, by using the `updateUsers` mutation—but let's use the `createOrders` mutation, as shown in the next listing. Since the values for the `created` and `orderId` fields are being autogenerated for us, we don't need to specify those values in the mutation.

Listing 9.11   GraphQL mutation: Creating a single order

```
mutation {
  createOrders(
    input: {
      customer: {
        connect: { where: { node: { username: "graphlover123" } } }
      }
      products: {
        Book: {
          connect: [
            { where: { node: { title: "Graph Algorithms" } } }
            { where: { node: { title: "Full Stack GraphQL" } } }
          ]
        }
        Video: {
          connect: { where: { node: { name: "Building GraphQL APIs" } } }
        }
      }
    }
```

```
) {
  orders {
    orderId
    created
    customer {
      username
    }
    products {
      __typename
      ... on Book {
        title
        isbn
      }
      ... on Video {
        name
        sku
      }
    }
  }
}
```

Notice the use of inline fragments in the products selection. We know that this field returns an array of Product objects, which is a union type, and each object could resolve to be either a Book or Video. We can add the __typename field to the selection, which will tell us the concrete type of each object, but to return the actual fields of the concrete type (Book or Video), we need to use an inline fragment to specify the fields to be returned when the concrete type of the object being resolved matches the type specified in the inline fragment:

```
products {
  __typename
  ... on Book {
    title
    isbn
  }
  ... on Video {
    name
    sku
  }
}
```

In the response object, we will see that our order objects have been assigned random ID values as well as timestamps. Notice that our products array is a mix of Book and Video objects:

```
{
  "data": {
    "createOrders": {
      "orders": [
        {
          "orderId": "dfdebf08-3ce5-494e-9843-d5286f4dc8f4",
```

```
              "created": "2021-08-15T13:43:15.117Z",
              "customer": {
                "username": "graphlover123"
              },
              "products": [
                {
                  "__typename": "Video",
                  "name": "Building GraphQL APIs",
                  "sku": "v002"
                },
                {
                  "__typename": "Book",
                  "title": "Graph Algorithms",
                  "isbn": "9781492047681"
                },
                {
                  "__typename": "Book",
                  "title": "Full Stack GraphQL",
                  "isbn": "9781617297038"
                }
              ]
            }
          ]
        }
      }
    }
```

If we use Neo4j Browser to inspect the data we've created in the database via our GraphQL API so far, we can see the graph representation of our order, users, and products and how they are connected (see figure 9.2).

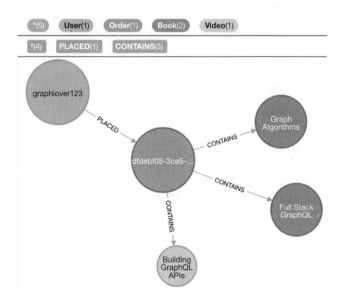

Figure 9.2   An order containing two books and a video

In the next listing, let's create a few more orders using another GraphQL mutation.

Listing 9.12   GraphQL mutation: Creating multiple orders

```
mutation {
  createOrders(
    input: [
      {
        customer: {
          connect: { where: { node: { username: "bobbytables" } } }
        }
        products: {
          Book: {
            connect: { where: { node: { isbn: "9781617297038" } } }
          }
        }
      }
      {
        customer: {
          connect: { where: { node: { username: "graphlover123" } } }
        }
        products: {
          Book: {
            connect: { where: { node: { isbn: "9781492047681" } } }
          }
        }
      }
      {
        customer: {
          connect: { where: { node: { username: "graphlover123" } } }
        }
        products: {
          Book: {
            connect: [{ where: { node: { isbn: "9781617295645" } } }]
          }
          Video: { connect: { where: { node: { sku: "v001" } } } }
        }
      }
    ]
  ) {
    orders {
      orderId
      created
      customer {
        username
      }
      products {
        __typename
        ... on Book {
          title
          isbn
        }
        ... on Video {
          name
          sku
```

```
            }
          }
        }
      }
    }
  }
}
```

Notice that we can pass an array of input objects to create several orders in a single GraphQL mutation:

```
{
  "data": {
    "createOrders": {
      "orders": [
        {
          "orderId": "38cfd8e4-f866-4c8a-ae97-e9e7c9e72b0b",
          "created": "2021-08-16T13:33:08.288Z",
          "customer": {
            "username": "bobbytables"
          },
          "products": [
            {
              "__typename": "Book",
              "title": "Full Stack GraphQL",
              "isbn": "9781617297038"
            }
          ]
        },
        {
          "orderId": "597ba737-de86-4772-b541-6a0bf4a25817",
          "created": "2021-08-16T13:33:08.288Z",
          "customer": {
            "username": "graphlover123"
          },
          "products": [
            {
              "__typename": "Book",
              "title": "Graph Algorithms",
              "isbn": "9781492047681"
            }
          ]
        },
        {
          "orderId": "dfc08de3-68f9-407c-8c72-1b02eb7a9b4e",
          "created": "2021-08-16T13:33:08.288Z",
          "customer": {
            "username": "graphlover123"
          },
          "products": [
            {
              "__typename": "Video",
              "name": "Intro To Neo4j 4.x",
              "sku": "v001"
            },
            {
```

```
                "__typename": "Book",
                "title": "Graph-Powered Machine Learning",
                "isbn": "9781617295645"
              }
            ]
          }
        ]
      }
    }
}
```

Now that we've created several orders and their associated books and videos, let's explore how we can paginate data results in GraphQL.

9.2   Pagination with GraphQL

Many applications display data in tables or lists. When populating these list views, it may make sense for the application to only request a subset of the total result set from the server—often, only the data needed to render the current view. For example, in the context of our online store, we may want to show a list of all orders sorted in chronological order or allow a specific user to view all their orders. However, there may be thousands, or even millions, of orders; we don't want to fetch all of these orders from the server (that would be a lot of data to send over the network).

Instead, we would *paginate* the order data by requesting certain chunks (or pages), as they are to be rendered in the application. For example, we may initially request the first 20 orders, sorted by date of creation. Then, when the user scrolls to the end of the first 20, the next page of results is requested from the server. GraphQL offers two types of pagination: *offset* and *cursor*.

9.2.1   Offset pagination

Offset pagination uses two field arguments, commonly called `limit` and `offset`, to chunk the results of an array field into pages. We typically use a third argument, `sort`, to specify the sort order for the array. The `limit` argument specifies the number of results to be included, and `offset` is the number of objects to skip before returning values and is incremented by the value used for `limit` to fetch the next page. For example, if we wanted to chunk our results into pages of size 10, then the first page would use an offset value of 0 and a limit value of 10, the second page would use an offset value of 10 and a limit value of 10, and so on.

Let's imagine our store application has a *View Orders* view, in which all orders are displayed in a table, initially sorted by date of order creation. Our GraphQL query to load *all* that data might look something like the following.

> **Listing 9.13   Querying for all orders sorted by date created**

```
query {
  orders(options: { sort: { created: DESC } }) {
    orderId
```

```
      created
    }
  }
}
```

This query is returning *all* orders. What if we have millions of orders? We would be sending too much data over the network, and our user would be waiting a long time for the page to load and show the orders! Our application is only capable of displaying so many orders at a time, anyway, so we end up not making use of most of the data. Instead, we want to *slice* our order results and only return a subset that is relevant for display in the application. We'll paginate our orders into pages of size 2, requesting the first page, as the next listing shows.

Listing 9.14   Querying for orders using offset pagination

```
query {
  orders(options: { limit: 2, offset: 0, sort: { created: DESC } }) {
    orderId
    created
  }
}
```

GRAPHQL COUNT QUERIES FOR PAGINATION

We then increment the `offset` value to give us the next page. But how do we know how many pages to request? We typically want to be able to display the total number of pages in the application so the user knows how much data they are dealing with. To facilitate this, we can make use of the *count queries*. The Neo4j GraphQL Library generates a count query field for each type that returns the number of nodes of that type in the database, as shown in the next listing. The client application can then use this number to compute the total number of pages.

Listing 9.15   Offset pagination, including the `ordersCount` field

```
query {
  ordersCount
  orders(options: { limit: 2, offset: 0, sort: { created: DESC } }) {
    orderId
    created
  }
}
```

If we are using a filter, such as filtering for orders placed after a certain date, we can pass the same filter argument to the count query to determine the total number of results and calculate the number of pages to be displayed on the client.

9.2.2   Cursor pagination

Cursor pagination is another commonly used model. Instead of using a numeric offset to slice the results into pages, we use a cursor, which is an opaque string value that identifies the last object in a page of results. To see cursor pagination in action, let's imagine our application has a view of orders for a particular user; for example, a user may wish to view all orders they have placed, sorted by the date the order was created.

To use cursor pagination with the Neo4j GraphQL Library, we start by requesting the `ordersConnection` field, instead of the `orders` field. The `ordersConnection` field is what is known as a Relay connection object. Let's first see how these Relay connections are used and then explore the Relay connection model.

Listing 9.16   Using the `ordersConnection` Relay connection type

```
query {
  users(where: { username: "graphlover123" }) {
    username
    ordersConnection(sort: { node: { created: ASC } }) {
      edges {
        node {
          created
          orderId
        }
      }
    }
  }
}
```

Notice that our selection set for the `ordersConnection` field now includes nested `edges` and `node` fields. What's going on there?

THE RELAY CONNECTION MODEL

These *connection* fields are generated by the Neo4j GraphQL Library for each relationship field and conform to the "Relay Cursor Connections Specification" (https://relay .dev/graphql/connections.htm), commonly referred to as the *Relay specification* or *Relay connections*. *Relay* is a GraphQL client that includes many features beyond the scope of this book; however, this Relay specification has become a common blueprint for implementing cursor pagination in GraphQL and introduces the concept of a connection type.

These connection types provide a standard method for cursor pagination in two ways. First, common field arguments `first` and `after` are used for slicing and paginating results. Second, connections enable a standard method of paginating results, providing cursors and other meta information about the result set, such as whether any more results are available for the client to fetch in the paginated results.

According to the Relay specification, each connection object must contain an `edges` array field and a `pageInfo` object field. The `edges` field is a list of *edge types*, defined by the Relay specification, that wrap the relationships, connecting nodes in our graph. The `pageInfo` field contains metadata about the page, such as `hasNextPage` and `hasPreviousPage`, as well as the cursors used for requesting the next and previous pages: `startCursor` and `endCursor`. Additionally, the Neo4j GraphQL Library adds a `totalCount` field that tells us the total number of edges.

Let's see this in action in the next listing. We will add the `first: 2` field argument to our previous query to paginate orders in pages of size 2. We'll also request the `pageInfo` object and the `totalCount` field.

> **Listing 9.17   Using the `pageInfo` object to retrieve metadata**

```
query {
  users(where: { username: "graphlover123" }) {
    username
    ordersConnection(first: 2, sort: { node: { created: ASC } }) {
      totalCount
      pageInfo {
        endCursor
        hasNextPage
        hasPreviousPage
      }
      edges {
        node {
          created
          orderId
        }
      }
    }
  }
}
```

Now our results include the first two orders, wrapped in the `edges` array, as well as the `pageInfo` metadata object that includes a cursor, `endCursor`, that we can use to fetch the next page of results:

```
{
  "data": {
    "users": [
      {
        "username": "graphlover123",
        "ordersConnection": {
          "totalCount": 3,
          "pageInfo": {
            "endCursor": "YXJJyYXljb25uZWN0aW9uOjE=",
            "hasNextPage": true,
            "hasPreviousPage": false
          },
          "edges": [
            {
              "node": {
                "created": "2021-08-15T13:43:15.117Z",
                "orderId": "dfdebf08-3ce5-494e-9843-d5286f4dc8f4"
              }
            },
            {
              "node": {
                "created": "2021-08-16T13:33:08.288Z",
                "orderId": "dfc08de3-68f9-407c-8c72-1b02eb7a9b4e"
```

```
                }
              }
            ]
          }
        }
      ]
    }
}
```

To request the next page of results, we include the value of the endCursor as the value of the after field argument for the ordersConnection field, as shown next.

Listing 9.18   Using cursor pagination to retrieve the next page of orders

```
query {
  users(where: { username: "graphlover123" }) {
    username
    ordersConnection(
      first: 2
      after: "YXJJyYXljb25uZWN0aW9uOjE="
      sort: { node: { created: ASC } }
    ) {
      totalCount
      pageInfo {
        endCursor
        hasNextPage
        hasPreviousPage
      }
      edges {
        node {
          created
          orderId
        }
      }
    }
  }
}
```

This time, we will see in our results that hasNextPage is false, which tells us there are no more paginated results for the client to fetch:

```
{
  "data": {
    "users": [
      {
        "username": "graphlover123",
        "ordersConnection": {
          "totalCount": 3,
          "pageInfo": {
            "endCursor": "YXJJyYXljb25uZWN0aW9uOjI=",
            "hasNextPage": false,
            "hasPreviousPage": true
          },
```

```
        "edges": [
          {
            "node": {
              "created": "2021-08-16T13:33:08.288Z",
              "orderId": "597ba737-de86-4772-b541-6a0bf4a25817"
            }
          }
        ]
      }
    }
  ]
}
}
```

The Relay connection model provides a useful standard for cursor pagination. The edge types defined by the Relay specification also introduce a way of representing a powerful feature of the property graph model that we have yet to work with: relationship properties.

9.3   *Relationship properties*

In the property graph model, *relationship properties* are attributes stored on the relationship and are used to represent values that have meaning in the context of both end nodes connected by the relationship. For example, in our store data model, how would we represent the quantity of a specific item added to an order? The best way to represent this concept of quantity is by storing a property on the CONTAINS relationship that represents the quantity of that item (book or video) added to the order.

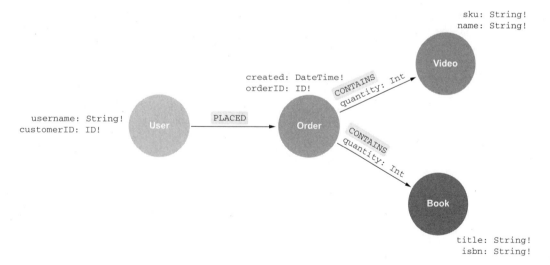

Figure 9.3   Updating the online store data model to include relationship properties

In figure 9.3, we've added a quantity integer property to the CONTAINS relationship. Now, if, for example, we want to purchase two copies of the *Full Stack GraphQL* book when placing an order, we can set a value, 2, for this property. But how do we represent this in our GraphQL API?

9.3.1 Interfaces and the @relationship GraphQL schema directive

We've used the `@relationship` directive with the Neo4j GraphQL Library to specify the property graph relationship type and direction, using the `type` and `direction` arguments. The `@relationship` directive also takes an optional argument, `properties`, that can be used to specify relationship properties. The `properties` argument takes the name of an interface type that defines the GraphQL fields to map to the relationship properties.

To represent the fields for our relationship properties, we first define an interface type that includes our relationship property fields. Since we only want to add a single relationship property field, `quantity`, on the CONTAINS relationship, we will create a `Contains` interface with a single field. Next, in the `@relationship` directive used on the `Order.products` field, we add `properties: "Contains"` to indicate we want to use the `Contains` interface to represent the relationship properties for the CONTAINS relationship. Our updated GraphQL type definitions are shown in the following listing; let's go ahead and update these in index.js.

> **Listing 9.19 Using an interface to represent relationship properties in GraphQL**

```
interface Contains {
  quantity: Int
}

type User {
  username: String
  orders: [Order!]! @relationship(type: "PLACED", direction: OUT)
}

type Order {
  orderId: ID! @id
  created: DateTime! @timestamp(operations: [CREATE])
  customer: User! @relationship(type: "PLACED", direction: IN)
  products: [Product!]!
    @relationship(type: "CONTAINS", direction: OUT, properties: "Contains")
}

type Video {
  title: String
  sku: String
}

type Book {
  title: String
  isbn: String
}

union Product = Video | Book
```

Note that since `Product` is a union type representing both the `Video` and `Book` type, we have captured defining the `quantity` relationship property for both videos and books—a great example of the power of abstract types! After updating the GraphQL type definitions in index.js, we'll need to restart our GraphQL Node.js application.

9.3.2 Creating relationship properties

Now that we have updated our GraphQL type definitions to include the `quantity` relationship property, let's see how we can make use of this new relationship property. First, we'll create a new order, but this time, we'll place an order for 10 copies of the *Full Stack GraphQL* book. To do this, we'll include `edge: { quantity: 10}` in the `connect` object for the input object when using the `createOrders` mutation, as shown next.

> **Listing 9.20 Using relationship properties in a GraphQL mutation**

```
mutation {
  createOrders(
    input: {
      customer: {
        connect: { where: { node: { username: "graphlover123" } } }
      }
      products: {
        Book: {
          connect: {
            edge: { quantity: 10 }
            where: { node: { title: "Full Stack GraphQL" } }
          }
        }
      }
    }
  ) {
    orders {
      created
      orderId
      productsConnection {
        edges {
          quantity
          node {
            ... on Book {
              title
            }
          }
        }
      }
    }
  }
}
```

To retrieve the quantity value, we now have a field `quantity` on the edge type objects in the `productsConnection` field that indicates this order contains 10 units of the book, as seen in the query results:

```
{
  "data": {
    "createOrders": {
      "orders": [
        {
          "created": "2021-08-18T22:17:28.285Z",
          "orderId": "48faa3f4-553b-42ed-a08f-e7781aed3c17",
          "productsConnection": {
            "edges": [
              {
                "quantity": 10,
                "node": {
                  "title": "Full Stack GraphQL"
                }
              }
            ]
          }
        }
      ]
    }
  }
}
```

Thanks to the power of the Relay connection specification, we can now represent and work with relationship properties in GraphQL!

9.4   *Wrapping up Full Stack GraphQL*

We've now learned how to leverage the power of GraphQL, graph databases, React, and cloud services to build and secure full stack web applications. The goal of this book was largely to show how the pieces of Full Stack GraphQL fit together. Let's review what we've covered in the book and outline some paths for further learning resources.

In part 1, we introduced graph thinking, GraphQL, and the Neo4j graph database. We learned the benefits of GraphQL, how to write GraphQL queries, and the basic approach to building GraphQL servers. Our graph thinking expanded to cover graph databases, and we introduced Neo4j and the Cypher query language. In part 2, we covered the React JavaScript framework for building user interfaces and using Apollo Client for GraphQL data fetching with our React application. Finally, in part 3, we tackled authentication and authorization in our GraphQL API and React application and deployment, using managed cloud services, like Auth0, Neo4j AuraDB, Netlify, and serverless functions.

The Neo4j GraphQL Library is a core component of *Full Stack GraphQL*, providing the ability to create powerful GraphQL APIs backed by Neo4j without writing boilerplate code; however, there are many features of the library we didn't have a chance to cover in this book. As you continue your journey building applications with GraphQL, I encourage you to learn more about some of these features, such as working with aggregations and more of the schema directives, like @cypher and @auth, that allow us to enrich our GraphQL APIs. A resource for further learning around the Neo4j GraphQL Library is the documentation at neo4j.com/docs/graphql-manual/current.

Another topic I would have liked to include in the book is working with React frameworks and tooling to improve the developer experience of building frontend applications with React. Next.js is one such framework that builds upon React and bundles many common features that are absent from React itself. With its API Routes feature, Next.js even includes the ability to build GraphQL APIs, an interesting approach to colocating backend logic. The Next.js Getting Started tutorial included in the Next.js documentation is an excellent hands-on introduction: nextjs.org/docs/getting-started.

To continue your graph journey with graph databases and Neo4j, the free online trainings at Neo4j's GraphAcademy are an excellent resource and cover many topics, including those not covered in this book, such as graph data science and building applications using different languages and frameworks. You can get started with GraphAcademy at graphacademy.neo4j.com.

Finally, I publish a blog and newsletter that dive into many of these topics. You can find it online at lyonwj.com.

9.5   Exercises

1   The price a customer pays for an item can vary. For example, the price may change or be temporarily reduced as part of a promotion. Add a relationship property to store the price for each item paid in an order.

2   Write a @cypher directive field to compute the order subtotal. Be sure to take into account the quantity of each item included in the order.

3   Write a GraphQL query to paginate the items included in an order, first using offset pagination and then using cursor-based pagination. Can you navigate from the last page to the first page as well?

Summary

- GraphQL supports two abstract types that can be used to represent multiple concrete types: unions and interfaces.
- Interfaces are used when the concrete types share common fields and can be thought of as a contract that defines the requirements for implementing the interface.
- Unions do not share this idea of a contract and can be used when the concrete types do not share common fields.
- Two common approaches to pagination with GraphQL include using offsets and cursors. Offset pagination uses numeric offsets to chunk results into pages, while cursor pagination uses an opaque cursor.
- The Relay specification defines a common connection type that can be used to enable cursor-based pagination with GraphQL.
- These Relay connection types can also be used to model relationship properties with GraphQL.

index

RELATED MANNING TITLES

GraphQL in Action
by Samer Buna

ISBN 9781617295683
384 pages, $49.99
February 2021

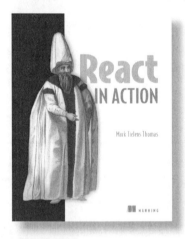

React in Action
by Mark Tielens Thomas

ISBN 9781617293856
360 pages, $44.99
May 2018

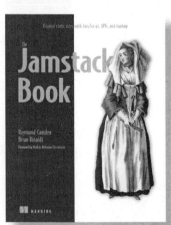

The Jamstack Book
by Raymond Camden and Brian Rinaldi
Foreword by Mathias Biilmann Christensen

ISBN 9781617298882
280 pages, $49.99
April 2022

For ordering information go to www.manning.com